THE GLOBALIZATION
OF CAPITALISM IN
THIRD WORLD
COUNTRIES

THE GLOBALIZATION
OF CAPITALISM IN
THIRD WORLD
COUNTRIES

Priyatosh Maitra

PRAEGER

Westport, Connecticut
London

Library of Congress Cataloging-in-Publication Data

Maitra, Priyatosh.
 The globalization of capitalism in Third World countries / Priyatosh Maitra.
  p. cm.
 Includes bibliographical references and index.
 ISBN 0–275–95159–6 (alk. paper)
  1. Capitalism—Developing countries—Case studies. 2. Capitalism—
India—Case studies. 3. India—Economic policy—1980—Case
studies. 4. India—Economic conditions—1947—Case studies.
 I. Title.
HC59.72.C3M355 1996
330.12′2′091724—dc20   95–7549

British Library Cataloguing in Publication Data is available.

Library of Congress Catalog Card Number: 95–7549
ISBN: 0–275–95159–6

First published in 1996

Praeger Publishers, 88 Post Road West, Westport, CT 06881
An imprint of Greenwood Publishing Group, Inc.

Printed in the United States of America

The paper used in this book complies with the
Permanent Paper Standard issued by the National
Information Standards Organization (Z39.48–1984).

10 9 8 7 6 5 4 3 2 1

Copyright Acknowledgments

The author and publisher gratefully acknowledge permission for use of the following material:

Dynamic Forces in Capitalist Development by Angus Maddison. 1991. London: Oxford University Press. Used by permission of Oxford University Press.

"The Demographic Effects of Technological Change and Capitalist Transformation—UK and India" by Priyatosh Maitra. 1992. *Arthavijnana*, 34 (June), no. 2: 125–54. Copyright © 1992 by Indian Council of Social Science Research, New Delhi.

Contents

Tables and Figures   vii

1   Historical Perspective on Capitalist Transformation   1

2   Industrial Growth   33

3   Economic Structural Change and Capitalist Transformation   61

4   The Internationalization of Capitalism   85

5   The Indian Economy   131

6   The Demographic Transition, Technological Change, and   175
    Capitalist Transformation

7   The Development of Education, Technological Change, and   201
    Capitalist Transformation

8   Conclusion   223

References   227

Index   239

Tables and Figures

TABLES

1.1	Population, 1500–1989	4
1.2	Levels of GDP per Head of Population, 1820–1989	5
1.3	Population Growth Rates per Annum, 1500–1975	24
3.1	Five Countries' Agricultural Employment as a Proportion of Total Employment	64
3.2	Changes in Manufacturing and Nonmanufacturing Employment in the United Kingdom, 1950–1978	69
3.3	Composition of Japan's Working Population by Industry	77
4.1	British Foreign Investment, 1865–1914	86
4.2	Shares of Primary Products and Manufactures in Total Trade of Each Region, 1876–1913	87
4.3	Trade in Manufactures: Regional Shares, 1876–1913	87
4.4	Trade in Primary Products: Regional Shares, 1876–1913	91
4.5	Stock of Outward Foreign Direct Investment of Selected Countries Compared to GDP, 1967 and 1988	92
4.6	FDI in Developing Regions and Countries, 1980–1989	93
4.7	Real Growth of U.S. FDI and GNP, 1950–1985	94
4.8	U.S. FDI by Area	95
4.9	U.S. FDI in Manufacturing by Area	96

4.10	Private U.S. Investment Abroad, Assets Held at Year End, 1950–1987	98
4.11	International Investment Position, 1976 and 1987	100
4.12	Geographical Distribution of International Production in Manufacturing by Source Country, 1982	101
4.13	Geographical Distribution of International Production and Indigenous Firm Exports in Manufacturing Combined, by Source Country, 1982	102
4.14	National Firms' Shares of International Production by Manufacturing Sector, 1982	103
4.15	National Firms' Shares of Exports by Manufacturing Sector, 1974	104
4.16	National Shares of Exports by Manufacturing Sector, 1974	105
4.17	National Shares of Exports by Manufacturing Sector, 1982	106
4.18	Sales of U.S. Manufacturing Affiliates in Europe, 1957–1975	107
4.19	Comparison of the Ten Largest Multinational Corporations and Selected Countries According to Size of Annual Gross Domestic Product, 1990	110
4.20	The Rise of Multinationals in Continental Europe, Outward FDI from the European Community, the United States and Japan, 1980–1989	112
4.21	Foreign Aid Allocations and the Poor	113
4.22	Unemployment in OECD Countries, 1985	114
4.23	Unemployment in OECD Countries, 1992	120
5.1	Population of Undivided India, 1600–1800	134
5.2	Population Growth Rates in European Countries	135
5.3	Social Structure of the Mughal Empire	142
5.4	Social Structure at the End of British Rule	156
5.5	Wealth in the Private Sector between 1956 and 1964	157
5.6	Wealth in Crores of Rupees, 1964–1980	159
5.7	Growth of Wealth in the Private Sector, 1969–1980	160
5.8	Public and Private Sector Investment in the First, Second, and Third Plans	162
5.9	Allocation of Public Sector Plan Outlays, 1974–1979	163
5.10	Foreign Aid Utilized in the Periods 1951–1956, 1956–1961, and 1961–1966	166
5.11	Import Availability Ratios by Industry Groups	166
5.12	Sales of Top 20 Industrial Houses	167
5.13	Annual Rate of Growth of Capital Formation in India's Public Sector	168
5.14	Savings and Investment Ratios	169

6.1   Distribution of Workers in India, 1981   182

6.2   Population Change in India and the United Kingdom: Crude   191
      Birthrate and Crude Death Rate

6.3   Population of Undivided India   195

6.4   Broad Occupational Distribution of the Labor Force: United   196
      Kingdom

7.1   Japan: Numbers of Students in Universities and Institutes of   218
      Higher Learning

7.2   Educational Advancement in the Developed Countries and the   219
      Third World, 1950 and 1981

7.3   Share of the Third World in Enrollment in Higher Education,   220
      1950 and 1981

7.4   Number of Educated Unemployed in India   220

7.5   Changes in the Rate of Illiteracy, Selected Asian Countries   220

7.6   Percentage of the Male Working Population Occupied in the   221
      Manufacturing Industry

FIGURES

4.1   World Trade in Manufactures, 1913–1937   88

4.2   Distribution of Foreign Investment, 1914   90

6.1   Birth-rate in Several European Countries in the Nineteenth   179
      Century

6.2   Death-rate in Several European Countries in the Nineteenth   180
      Century

6.3   The Demographic Transition Model Reinterpreted   198

THE GLOBALIZATION
OF CAPITALISM IN
THIRD WORLD
COUNTRIES

1

HISTORICAL PERSPECTIVE ON CAPITALIST TRANSFORMATION

CAPITALISM, CAPITALIST TRANSFORMATION, AND TECHNOLOGICAL CHANGE

The main focus of attention of classical political economy is the development of capitalism in Britain and, by implication, in Western Europe. Industrial capitalism emerged first in history in England and was transmitted to Western Europe (see Henderson 1954; Maitra 1980, 1986). However, later neoclassicists and Keynesian schools included countries presently known as the Third World in their scheme of capitalist development. The classicists, however, could not ignore the Third World. They discussed these economies as far as the interests of Western capitalism needing them. Marx, in his model of capitalist development, used Europe as its main initiating center; eventually, he predicted, by the inherent need of capitalism to increase the rate of accumulation, that it would reach every corner of the earth. Capitalism has reached that stage today (see Chapter 4). Marx saw the rise of capitalism in Europe in terms of a twofold process—the accumulation of money capital along with its investment in the means of industrial production and the emergence of a free (from feudal bondage) proletariat that is dispossessed of the means of production and forced to work for the owners of capital in return for wages. This process is discussed in detail in the following two sections.

Economic development implies the transformation of a feudal, agrarian economy into an industrial, capitalist economy and society. In industrial capitalism, capital accumulation results from the more productive use of the labor force. Generating an increasing rate of capital accumulation requires economic structural change. It means reallocating labor from overcrowded, less-productive types of agriculture to capitalist agriculture, as well as the production of industrial capital (the latter to supply the former with capital equipment). A third need is a service sector, which acts as the source of inputs of technology, communication, knowledge, and information in order to make the former two sectors more productive. These changes take place automatically, due to the inherent dynamic force generated by technological progress and capital accumulation (see Chapter 3). Thus, the capitalist transformation of an economy is briefly defined as the economic structural change caused by a dynamic change in the sectoral distribution of the labor force. This is accompanied by a consequent, and inevitable, demographic transition and by changes in economic organization from family, labor-based cottage and small-scale industry to large-scale, wage-based manufacturing. The factor-pricing system in an economy undergoing capitalist transformation from the feudal economy is characterized by payment in terms of the marginal contribution of the factor to the output replacing the average contributions of an unorganized sector (e.g., household industry, artisans workshops, etc.).

The most remarkable contributions of capitalism are:

1. a sustained upward thrust in productivity and real income per head;
2. the transformation of a feudal, stagnant, and nature-worshipping social mind into an active, humane, scientific, and reason-based social consciousness (which Marxists consider ultimately prepares society for socialism, whereas the non-Marxist takes the capitalist transformation as the ultimate end).

The first contribution will invariably follow whenever capitalism has penetrated the production system, but whether it will bring about a capitalist transformation of the system and create conditions for the development of the social consciousness of a precapitalist society depends on the nature and source of technological change. We will examine this in Chapter 5, using India as a case study. India has, in recent times, recorded a tremendous growth in industrial capitalism, which began in the late nineteenth century. Hence, it has proved a most appropriate case for such a study.

The economists classify capitalist countries mainly into two groups. The first and original industrial capitalist country was the United Kingdom, which later, in the nineteenth century, transmitted industrial capitalism to the Western European economies and their offshoots (United States, Canada, New Zealand, and Australia). The only Asian country that entered into this orbit of the original Western capitalist system was Japan, having been fortified with Western technology, capital, skills, and knowledge (see Henderson 1954, Maitra 1981).

The other group consists of all twentieth-century latecomers in Asia, Africa, Latin America, and the South Pacific Island economies. These latest additions result from the penetration of capitalist production from the original capitalist countries, which seek markets for their products. By this process, world capitalism, originating in the United Kingdom, has been penetrating all corners of the earth. A discussion follows of the process of the internationalization of capitalism and its implications for India's capitalist development in Chapter 5.

These latter groups differ from the original group of latecomers in respect to the basic nature of capitalism namely, the twentieth-century latecomers have achieved tremendous growth in productivity as a result of the penetration of capitalist production into their feudal or tribal economies but have failed to bring about a capitalist transformation of their economies (see Chapters 3 and 5). Because of this failure on the part of introduced capitalist economies, social consciousness has remained feudal, dominated by religious or sectarian blind faith. The existence in India of growing communalism, casteism, and religious fundamentalism side by side with rapid industrial growth is a case in point.

With this introduction of capitalism's dual role (one in Western Europe and the other in Third World countries), I will briefly discuss here some other economic aspects of capitalist development that are relevant to the present work. Since 1800, with the rise of industrial capitalist production (although it arose earlier by at least half a century, because of the need for reliable data, 1800 is used as the starting point), the total product of the original capitalist group has increased by a factor of 70; population, by nearly a factor of 5; and per capita product, by a factor of 14 (Maddison 1971, 7–9). Annual working hours, shown in Tables 1.1 and 1.2, have been halved since the late nineteenth century. On that count, there is a strong case today for reducing the workday by half, as there has been a second technological revolution accompanied by remarkable growth in high-level human capital since the 1950s. However, today, at its internationalization of production phase, capitalism, cannot afford it; moreover, at this phase, employment in the organized sector has fallen sharply and will keep on falling, to be gradually replaced by the spread of self-employment. The length of a workday has little relevance to low-income self-employment and low-wage occupations.

The interpretation of capitalism has been confined in this book to two groups—bourgeois, or non-Marxist, economists and Marxist economists. Bourgeois economists include those who believe in a free market system, in one form or another, as the dominant force that brings about dynamism in economic activities and regard it as the ultimate system. To these economists, capitalism began with the free play of domestic market forces and their development and culminated in the growth of money, money capital, and industrial capitalism (see Chapter 2). In the process, it eliminated any vestiges of a precapitalist society and penetrated into the international market, first through the internationalization of goods and commodity capital, through investment, and finally through the internationalization of capitalist production of the present day. At present, the

TABLE 1.1   Population, 1500–1989

	1500	1700	1820	1989	Coefficient of multiplication, 1820–1989
Australia	0	0	33	16,807	509
Austria	1,420	2,100	3,189	7,618	2
Belgium	1,400	2,000	3,397	9,938	3
Canada	0	15	640	26,248	41
Denmark	600	700	1,097	5,132	5
Finland	300	400	1,169	4,962	4
France	16,400	21120	30,698	56,160	2
Germany	12,000	15,000	24,905	61,990	2
Italy	10,000	13,200	19,000	57,525	
Japan	12,000	30,000	31,000	123,116	4
Netherlands	950	1,900	2,355	14,850	6
Norway	300	500	970	4,228	4
Sweden	550	1,260	2,574	8,439	3
Switzerland	650	1,200	1,829	6,723	4
UK	4,440	8,400	21,240	57,202	3
USA	0	251	9,618	248,777	26
Total	60,970	98,046	152,714	709,715	5

Source: A. Madison (1991) *Dynamic Forces in Capitalist Development*. London: Oxford University Press, 6. Used by permission of Oxford University Press.

Note: 1500–1820 figures for Australia, Canada, and the US exclude indigenous populations.

domestic market or domestic demand as determined by the high wage of a fully employed workforce has lost its importance, as discussed in Chapter 4.

Both non-Marxist and Marxist economists consider that the market and capitalism (including the state capitalism or state welfarism of the 1950s and 1960s) have brought about an unprecedented and unlimited capacity to produce, improve, and diversity output, along with unprecedented affluence involving full employment and consumerism, to vast masses of population in the original or advanced capitalist countries of the West. The quest for increasing profit and capital accumulation under capitalism has, in the late twentieth century, not only brought about the internationalization of production but also dynamic economic structural change. This change evolved from the domination of agriculture at the early stage of industrial capitalism to the present day, as led by the service sector

TABLE 1.2 Levels of GDP per Head of Population, 1820–1989 (in 1985 $US)

	1820	1870	1913	1950	1793	1989	Coefficient of multiplication 1820-1989
Australia	1,242	3,123	4,523	5,931	10,331	13,584	11
Austria	1,041	1,433	2,667	2,852	8,644	12,858	12
Belgium	1,024	2,087	3,266	4,228	9,416	12,876	13
Canada	n.a.	1,347	3,560	6,113	11,866	17,576	n.a.
Denmark	988	1,555	3,037	5,224	10,527	13,514	14
Finland	639	933	1,727	3,480	9,072	13,934	22
France	1,052	1,571	2,734	4,149	10,323	13,837	13
Germany	937	1,300	2,606	3,339	10,110	13,989	15
Italy	(960)	1,210	2,087	2,819	8,568	12,955	13
Japan	(588)	(618)	1,114	1,563	9,237	15,101	26
Netherlands	1,307	2,064	3,178	4,706	10,267	12,737	10
Norway	(856)	1,190	2,079	4,541	9,346	16,500	19
Sweden	947	1,316	2,450	5,331	11,292	14,912	16
Switzerland	n.a.	1,848	3,086	6,556	13,167	15,406	n.a.
UK	1,405	2,610	4,024	5,651	10,063	13,468	8
USA	1,048	2,247	4,854	8,611	14,103	18,317	17
Arithmetic average	1,002	1,653	2,937	4,693	10,396	14,456	14

Sources: A. Maddison (1991). *Dynamic Forces in Capitalist Development*. London: Oxford University Press, 6. Used by permission of Oxford University Press.

Note: figures are adjusted for differences in the purchasing power of currencies. They refer to GDP per capita within the geographic boundaries of the years cited. Per capita consumption was probably around 85 percent of GDP per capita in 1820 and averaged 58 percent in 1989. Figures in brackets are rough estimates made by extrapolation of inference rather than hard evidence. For Italy, GDP per capita was assumed to move at the same rate from 1820 to 1861 as it did from 1861 to 1890. For Norway, it was assumed that the 1820-1870 movement was the same proportionately as in Sweden.

via the phase of domination of the industrial sector from the mid-nineteenth century to the early part of the twentieth century (see Chapter 3). According to these economists, however, it has simultaneously prepared its own grave. Marxist economists consider capitalist development as an essential condition for unleashing the forces of production, on one hand, and for creating and organizing socialist social consciousness, on the other. Capitalism is a necessary evil for the rise of socialism as the halfway house to communism, the ultimate goal. However, socialism is not a stagnant state; it constantly undergoes dynamic changes as nature and humanity interact and thereby enrich each other without being constrained by the superstructure of class systems that characterized the human society of the past. The interaction between humanity and nature will ultimately result in a naturalization of human beings and a humanization of nature.

I will first discuss the views of bourgeois economists as they originated with the rise of industrial capitalism, concentrating on the founders of classical capitalist theories, Adam Smith, Thomas Malthus, and David Ricardo. J. Schumpeter, the Neoclassicists, and Keynesian versions of capitalist economy will also be discussed as offshoots of classical studies. Marxian groups will include neo-Marxians.

Adam Smith (1723–1790) published the *Wealth of Nations* in 1776, when industrial capitalism was just raising its head in the preindustrial British economy. Angus Maddison (1991) described this preindustrial stage as Proto-Capitalist, referring to a stage dominated by merchant capital and mercantile trade in combination with cottage and small-scale industry organized mainly as household industries. Malthus's (1766–1834) famous essay *Essays on the Theory of Population*, was published in 1798, while Ricardo's work, *Principles of Population*, was published in 1818, when the Industrial Revolution was in full swing in England. Latecomers in Western Europe, which had a huge accumulation of merchant capital and mature prototechnology, were marking time as they lagged behind in the supply of sufficient surplus labor. Adam Smith did not make any distinction between the benefits occurring from technological progress and those from economics of scale. Malthus too, shows no consideration of the possibility of technological change offsetting the tendency of diminishing returns as a result of population pressure on agriculture. The reasons for ignoring both technological progress and economies of scales may be explained by the fact that capital at that stage is essentially working capital, generated by the organization of production based on prototechnology (see Hobsbawm 1969; Lilley 1976).

Gradually evolving along with this process was an extensive phase of technological change. The institution of large-scale organization, using more extensively the process of division of labor in the place of the household and the artisan's workshop, made possible a more productive use of labor (hitherto a large part of which was disguised as the employed) and raised output and the rate of capital accumulation. The technological change in this situation may be considered to have been embodied in the organizational change that facilitated an increased division of labor, leading to a more productive use of the surplus, or disguised unemployed, labor of household industries. The concept of technological change in the sense in which it is understood today—of using science in production—did not arise at that early stage of industrial capitalism. Adam Smith over emphasized the natural harmony of interests, which are essential, according to him, for the expansion of trade in manufactured goods worldwide, thereby helping attain a higher rate of capital accumulation and offsetting the tendency toward the law of diminishing returns to arise in the industrial sector. It is true that in a capitalist system, an expanding market is considered one of the basic conditions for introducing technological change. The need for technological change at this stage did not occur to Adam Smith. Karl Marx was the first economist of the period to deal with the question of technological change as a way out of the problem of diminishing returns. The extensive phase of technological change brought about economic structural change, with an increasing proportion of the labor force being pulled away from agriculture to industry. When the science-based, intensive phase of technological change began in the 1860s, the movement of the labor force away from agriculture to industry began to be accompanied by a higher rate of shifting of labor from the industrial sector to the service sector. This latter trend has continued since then, culminating in the postindustrial stage of capitalist development since the 1950s. Adam Smith gave more importance to the opportunities arising from removing backwardness than those arising from new technology (Maddison 1991, 16). By injecting industrial goods, commodity capital, and knowledge through trade, industrial countries stimulate backward nations to higher aspirations of material life and increased levels of economic activities.

Maddison pointed out that Adam Smith treats capital mainly as a stock that can be increased in per capita terms to make it possible to use more complex methods of production rather than new techniques (1991, 16). Maddison ignored the basic underlying factor. That is, the stock of capital was, in those days, mainly working capital plus labor-intensive simple tools and equipment. The existence of fixed capital as a proportion of total capital was negligible or nil. With the growth of a stock of capital, a capital-widening process instead of a capital-deepening one comes into play. Therefore, Adam Smith defined capital as consisting of working capital; namely, the cost of the workers' subsistence wage and provisions for raw materials, simple tools, and equipment. Thus, the circulating capital was much bigger than the amount of fixed capital (see also Mantoux 1928). Adam Smith's famous example of the pin-making industry illustrates the process of division of labor and the potential gain from exploiting complex processes. Obviously, relative to the prototechnology used in a household, an artisan's workshop reflects the early period of the extensive phase of technological change. At that stage, the question of economics of scale and technological change as the means to offset diminishing returns caused by the growth of capital stock did not occur to economists of the day. According to Adam Smith and, later, David Ricardo, the expansion of trade beyond the domestic market is considered to be the solution. The supply of surplus labor was not exhausted and the population growth rate was high, as was the supply of labor, which included child labor. Adam Smith, therefore, stressed the natural harmony of interests of individuals (i.e., factors of production, meaning the allocation of resources, etc.) and of nations (meaning free trade between nations), which were the basis of his arguments for laissez-faire policies of nonintervention.

The Malthusian scheme was essentially a product of a dying feudal economy, which is why, in his scheme, man-made capital was not included as a factor of production. According to him, there were only two factors of production—natural resources and labor. The technological change and capital formation aspects of development were completely ignored. Therefore, it is not surprising to see the position he took regarding the effect of population growth on food supply. Malthus took the position that believes population grows faster than food production and creates pressure on limited supply of law, making aspiration of law in diminishing return inevitable. Therefore, famine, malnutrition, and epidemics become frequent. To avoid these calamities, Malthus suggests that a society should give priority to population control.

Clearly, preindustrial capitalist economics based on prototechnology were not completely technologically stagnant, although the term *technological change* in the sense we use it was not applicable in those days for obvious reasons, including the absence of an industrial capitalist class, competition, and modern, science-based technology. Medieval innovations were not seen as a way out of operation of the law of diminishing returns or as a means of having economics of scale or being competitive. To increase output, simple and piecemeal technological innovations in the form of windmills, horseshoes, horse harnesses, (at the time when enclosure resulted in individual, large-scale farms), heavy ploughs, the haystack, the scythe replacing the sickle, fertilization, and three-field rotation took place. Innovation was much slower during this period than it is now because the main center of activities was confined to the agricultural sector, including artisan workshops, and the markets were confined to local or, at the most, adjacent areas. For urban handicrafts, guild restrictions also limited the possibilities for change. Entry to skilled occupations was carefully controlled, and technological knowledge was regarded as a mystery (Maddison, 1991, 14). However, after the introduction of printing around 1500, the diffusion of knowledge was speeded up and written communication took place in the vernacular rather than in Latin (Maddison, 1991, 15). However, these developments did not help these merchant capital–dominated, small-scale, manufacturing rural economies to graduate to industrial capitalism.

Ricardo clearly recognized the augmentation in productive power that machinery could bring and the perspectives it offered for substantial growth in the nonagricultural sector. According to him, productivity growth was likely to be much slower in agriculture than in industry; because the supply of land was fixed, a fast-growing population resulted in increased demand for food, which was met by using less fertile land. Consequently, industrial costs would rise with the rise in food prices. This would squeeze profit, and the economy would face the prospect of stagnation. It may also be looked at from another angle, namely, with population growth, the pressure of the population on land that is fixed in supply would result in a situation of factor disproportion and, consequently, in diminishing returns. International trade in manufacturing in return for the importation of food would ease the situation, according to Ricardo. Thus originated international division of labor theory of trade.

There are three faults in Ricardo's arguments. First, nonagricultural productivity in those days could not increase if there was not a substantial improvement in agricultural productivity. Land reforms policy (e.g., enclosure) and the development of agricultural tools (see Jones 1967) brought about initial growth in agricultural productivity and supplied agricultural surpluses for the industrial sector. With the development of the industrial sector, agriculture benefited from the supply of more productive inputs (machinery, fertilizer, etc.) from an industrial sector, which began to absorb increasing numbers of rural workers. The growth of productivity in agriculture meant better and a greater variety of food products and raw materials but rapidly decreasing numbers of workers. Today, most developed economies are not only self-sufficient in food but also enjoy a surplus, using a tiny proportion of the labor force (i.e., varying between 2 and 7 percent). The problem Ricardo pointed out may be applicable to the Third World, where the industrial sector has not evolved from agricultural development but rather has been transplanted from overseas, creating the food problems currently facing the Third World.

Second, he did not visualize the possibility of technological change, based on science, which would offset the tendency to the law of diminishing returns in both the agricultural and industrial sectors. Third, without population growth, the large-scale industrial capitalist sector could not have emerged. The labor shortage in those days would have kept workers in agriculture and small-scale cottage industries, as in the sixteenth and seventeenth centuries (see Chapter 2). The consequent high wage cost would have acted as a great hindrance to the investment in large-scale industrial activities. This had been the case in England, in the sixteenth century, and Holland, in the seventeenth and eighteenth centuries (see Dobb 1947). An increased supply of surplus labor was made possible with land reforms (i.e., enclosures in the United Kingdom), which led to better food and living conditions and decreasing death rates, thereby, increasing population growth. According to an important study, average life expectancy at birth rose from about 32.4 to 38.7 years between the 1680s and 1820s (Hudson 1992, 56). Besides, protoindustrialization, which involved the growth of mercantile capitalism, affected fertility. The age of marriage tended to decline because protoindustry gave a source of independent income early in life; new households could be established without having to await the inheritance of land, and marriage rates also tended to be higher because they were unconstrained by the availability of inheritable land (Hudson 1992, 34–35).

To Adam Smith, the productive and accumulative character of capitalism is a solution to the profound historical crisis of feudal society. The crisis in feudalism, he said, arose because any surplus created by the society was squandered by unproductive workers and the aristocracy, which brought the society and its economy to a halt. He was also critical of the mercantilist concept of wealth in terms of gold and silver, which can be accumulated without creating or resulting in any increase in productivity of resources, such as labor. This explains why he criticizes the Physiocrats' ideas that industrial labor is unproductive. He was an original advocate of a free and unrestricted market, which he considered crucial to the accumulation of capital and profit and, thereby, constantly rising productivity. Thus, as M. Dobb (1947) said, Adam Smith's doctrine can be understood only as a reflection of a period of transition, when problems essentially consisted of clearing the ground for industrial investment and expansion, which he identified with the sweeping away of obstructive and sectionally protective regulation. Adam Smith defined development as the extension of the division of labor and the application of machinery to the production process so that the productivity of labor could be enhanced. The fulfillment of this condition requires an unrestricted market. Capitalism has become worldwide today through riding on the market's back (see Chapter 4).

According to Smith, development is promoted only when an increasing proportion of the workforce becomes engaged in productive work, as opposed to what happened in a feudal economy. To this concept of Smith's, we can trace the origin of the idea about the role of economic structural change in an economy. Workers engaged in agriculture begin to be shifted away to the industrial sector, initially with an enhancement of productivity of the workforce. Agriculture does not need the labor of an overwhelming proportion of the workforce with low productivity, which was hitherto dependant on a limited land supply. He also stresses the need for an extensive division of labor as a source of increased productivity which, in a capitalist system, is achieved through the expansion of the market and international trade. That is how capitalist accumulation, the division of labor process, the market, and international trade are functionally related to economic structural change.

Following Adam Smith's definition, higher productivity results from an increased division of labor, which involves the apportionment of labor in the production of food and raw materials, on the one hand, and on the other, in the production of machinery and equipment to produce both capital goods and consumption goods. These activities belong to productive sectors, which are then coordinated by service sectors as a source of inputs, communication, infrastructure, and so forth. According to Ricardo, the greater part of the capital is directed to agriculture because it mobilizes a greater proportion of productive labor. It is true that the initial stage of economic development resulting from the Industrial Revolution is different from the industrialization process in latecomer countries in the nineteenth and twentieth centuries. These economies would require a greater provision of capital to be invested in agriculture, as a great majority of the labor force is dependent on agriculture. With increased worker productivity, agriculture begins to release labor, surplus food, and raw materials for industrial growth. Agriculture, therefore, needs in due course a greater supply of physical capital to replace labor in this sector. This has been happening ever since the Industrial Revolution and may be interpreted as a part of the process of capitalist transformation of the economy. In the latecomer countries, the greater part of capital is invested in the industrial sector, which is based on borrowed technology, capital, and skills, originating from the United Kingdom, in the case of the nineteenth-century latecomers, from the West in general, and from Japan, in the case of the Third World. The proportion of capital invested in agriculture in Japan was negligible compared to what was invested in the nonagricultural sector, including infrastructure, manufacturing, and service activities.

Technological change as a way out of the law of diminishing returns does not have any place in Adam Smith's schema, or that of Ricardo, for that matter. It is, however, not expected in the sense that the condition needed for science-based technological change did not arise at that time. However, organizational changes, as a means to offset the tendency toward the diminishing returns resulting from the disproportionate use of factors in relation to the growth in population, play a role. This happens in the development of small household industries into large-scale manufactories and, thus, the more productive use of a labor force that was hitherto underemployed; in addition, the potential of prototechnology becomes available.

In Ricardo's schema, population growth results in the cultivation of progressively less fertile land, with diminishing returns, while it pushes up rents, raises the price of food, and thereby raises wages, which affects the profitability of investments. However, the law of diminishing returns has become a thing of the past today with the development of modern, science-based production technology and management and organizational changes in both agriculture and industry.

According to Ricardo, a limited supply of land hinders the self-sustained accumulation of capital and growth, and thereby, development. This reflects Adam Smith's neglect of the role of technological change, which was not expected because science-based technology had not emerged at that time. However, the role of organizational change in offsetting this tendency toward the law of diminishing return was ignored by Smith (1976, 462–463, 483). However, Ricardo wrote: "Let these be supplied from abroad in exchange for manufactured goods, and it is difficult to say where the limit is at which you cease to accumulate wealth and to derive profit from its employment" (Ricardo, 1951). Schumpeter criticized Smith's views as pessimistic, stagnationistic, and revealing of a complete lack of imagination. Ricardo's views of importing food as a means to counterbalance diminishing returns in agriculture are also devoid of any concept of the possible role of science in counterbalancing natural limitations of the supply of factors. Today, science-based technological change has helped the capitalist system achieve unlimited capacity to produce, diversify, and improve output—capitalism today can produce whatever is desired. Adam Smith spoke vehemently against the monopolistic control of colonial trade which, according to him, "depresses the industry of all other countries, but chiefly that of the colonies, without in the least increasing, but on the contrary diminishing, that of the country in whose favour it is established" (Smith [1863] 1976, 275).

In this respect, Adam Smith was an economist of the era of rising industrial capitalism, the continuous prosperity of which depends on the free movement and exchange of goods, facilitated by unrestricted trade and market forces. Smith wrote, "We must carefully distinguish between the effects of the colony trade and those of monopoly of that trade" (1976, 273). The former is always and necessarily beneficial because it encourages the international division of labor, thus offering larger markets for products at decreasing cost. However, the basic problem of capitalism is that the more it advances and brings the world economy into its orbit, the more it loses its capacity to consume the unlimited output. We will reach that state of condition in the near future (see Chapter 4).

Marx put it thus: "The Classics, like Adam Smith and Ricardo, represent a bourgeoisie which, while struggling with the relics of feudal society, works only to purge economic relations of feudal traits, to increase the productive forces and to give a new upsurge to industry and commerce" (1976, 115).

Even as early as Adam Smith's time, the question of whether to give priority to agriculture or industry troubled economists. Obviously, the question arose only in the case of latecomer nations, whether of the nineteenth or mid-twentieth century. However, it should be noted that during the nineteenth century, the transfer of capital and technology to build industrial capital in Western Europe (Germany, France, etc.) brought about an integrated development of agriculture and industry in a very short time, although initially it generated a dualistic structure (Hohenberg 1972; Landes 1969; Maitra 1980). Adam Smith advocated the policy of giving priority to manufacturers and trade. Capitalist accumulation based on the development of manufacturers requires an expanding market; hence the need for trade. Smith wrote: "As the political economy of the nations of modern Europe has been more favourable to manufacturers and trade, the industry of the towns than to agriculture, the industry of the country, so that of other nations has followed a different plan, and has been more favourable to agriculture than to manufactures and trade" (Smith [1863] 1976, 307). The consequence of this is backwardness. The free movement of trade through the absence of any restrictions against foreign manufacturing was the most effective expedient for supplying the backward and poor people in due time with all the artisans, manufacturers, and merchants they wanted at home (Smith [1863] 1976). Smith regarded the British empire as a vast commercial enterprise to which both Great Britain and the British colonies should contribute and that would benefit both on equal terms. Thus, Smith represented the views and interest of rising British industrial capitalism, as opposed to merchant capitalism, as represented by the East India

Company in the colonies. In India the Charter Acts of the nineteenth century gradually ended the stranglehold of the East India Company over mercantile trade and political matters (Maitra, 1956).

Adam Smith, who was born during the rise of industrial capitalism in England, denounced the mercantilist policies of the European nations toward the Third World (as it is now called), which they exploited for the importation of gold and silver. However, that was an essential condition for capitalist production. An increased supply of real output must be accompanied by a proportionate increase in the money supply. In a market capitalist economy, the exchange of goods and services and pricing of the factors of production (as means of accumulating capital) requires money as a medium of exchange. Therefore, the interrelationship between the money market, product market, and factor market constitutes the foundation of all growth models, including those of the classicists, Marxists, and Keynesians.

In those days of simple production dominated by working capital, money supply measures represented the value of goods and services sold in the market. Capitalist producers owned the money and, using it as means, they also owned labor and productivity. In the ultimate analysis, however, productivity and products belonged to the workers, ownership of which was lost to the owners of money with the workers' rise in a society.

Marx is, perhaps, the most cited and discussed analyst of capitalism and capitalist production. However, the following interpretation by Marx of capitalist production is rarely cited in economics text books or research papers, and therefore, I quote it at length:

In the ancient conception, man always appears (in however narrowly national, religious or political a definition) as the aim of production. It seems very much more exalted than the modern world, in which production is the aim of man and wealth the aim of production.

In fact, however, when the narrow bourgeois form has been peeled away, what is wealth, if not the universality of needs, capacities, enjoyments, productive powers etc of individuals, produced in universal exchange? What if not the full development of human control over the forces of nature—those of his own nature as well as those of so-called nature? What, if not the absolute elaboration of his creative dispositions, without any preconditions other than antecedent historical evolution which makes the totality of evolution—i.e. the evolution of all human powers as such, unmeasured by any previously established yardstick—an end itself? . . . The ancient provide a narrow satisfaction, whereas the modern world leaves us unsatisfied, or, where it appears to be satisfied with itself, is vulgar and mean.

The First objective condition of labour appears as nature, earth as an inorganic body. The condition is not something he has produced, but something he finds to hand; Something existing in nature and which he presupposes.

The original conditions of production can not initially be themselves produced—they are not the results of production. (1964c, 84)

Marx also wrote:

> The way in which men produce their means of subsistence depends first of all on the nature of the actual means they find in existence and have to reproduce. This mode of production must not be considered simply as being the reproduction of the physical existence of the individuals. Rather it is a definite form of expressing their life, a definite mode of life on their part. As individuals express their life, so they are. What they are, coincides with their production, both with what they produce, and with how they produce. The nature of individuals thus depends on the material conditions determining their production.
>
> This production only makes its appearance with the increase of population. In its turn this presupposes the intercourse of individuals with one another. The form of this intercourse is again determined by production. (1964a, 121)

TRANSFORMATION OF HOUSEHOLD PRODUCTION INTO LARGE-SCALE INDUSTRIAL PRODUCTION

The Process of Change from Household Industry to the Manufactory

This section briefly presents the process of development of household industry into manufacturing industry via the manufactory. The importance of this discussion is immense to a study on India, which had a developed household industry that had begun to evolve into a manufactory industry in preindustrial days. However, because of the transplantation of British manufacture, India's own household and manufactory industry could not graduate to machinofacture, as it did in England in the eighteenth century (see Chapter 5). The historical course of India's industrial development was thus aborted.

The Process of Change from Household Industry to the Manufactory—The Process of Growth of Industrial Capitalism

This section deals with the process of change from the domestic or household industry of the feudal and mercantile period to the manufactory and is essentially based on John Hobson's classical work, *The Evolution of Modern Capitalism* ([1894] 1926). It also discusses briefly the findings of M. Dobb (e.g., 1947) and E. Mandel (e.g., 1968) in this respect, which largely support Hobson. Economic historians in general are in agreement with these studies on the rise of industrial capitalism.

The first thing that characterized the preindustrial economic organization in England was the lack of division of labor even in the broadest sense of the term (see also Dobb 1947, 149–50). Different types of employment and occupations were not clearly separated from one another. Agriculture and manufacture not only operated in the same locality but were run by the same people. Obviously, this was due to a self-sufficient household economy, which attempted to supply all the basic needs of its members and was operated by the members of the family. Hobson referred to the case of the textile industries, which were largely combined with agriculture. However, these operations had some division of labor for the sake of convenience rather than for any economic gains; for example: "The women and children spun while the men attended to their work in field" (Defoe 1720, 37, cited in Hobson 1926, 52). Every woman and every child above the age of five found full employment in the spinning and weaving trades of Somerset and the West Riding. This example illustrates the condition of shortage of labor discussed. Another simple kind of division of labor practiced in those days was influenced by the seasons. Weaving furnished a winter occupation to villagers, who devoted the bulk of their summer time to agriculture. In tropical countries, there is little division of labor in this sense. Defoe (1720, 78) described the condition of the rural part of England: "The land divided into small enclosures from two acres to six or seven scores each, seldom more; every three or four pieces of land had a house standing out of speaking distance from another—at every house a tenter, and on almost every tenter a piece of cloth or kersie or shallon—every other keeps a horse—so every one generally keeps a cow or two for his family" (1720, 78). We should note here that later enclosures resulted in much larger plots of land and thereby made possible its more economical use, as well as saving time, which enabled agricultural labor to help develop more productive tools and fertilizers (Jones 1967). This obviously led to the absorption of labor in agriculture initially but also to the development of agricultural equipment (i.e., capital accumulation in physical terms).

Thus, not only were agriculture and many forms of the manufacturing process jointly operated. The division of labor and differentiation of process within several industries were not very far advanced, specialization of land for pasture or for particular grain crops did not come into vogue until the early eighteenth century, and each little hamlet was engaged in meeting the inhabitants' basic needs through different kinds of crops, milk, bread, and nonagricultural products. This was a self-subsisting community until, with the advancement of the century, which was marked by a sustained growth of population together with the last stage of enclosures of the commons, resulting in an increase of large farms, and the availability of a large supply of labor. In due course, the application of new science, new forms of organization of production in the form of domestic industries, and new types of simple capital equipment led to a differentiation in the use of land for agricultural purposes.

In the earlier part of the eighteenth century, there was little specialization of land or division of labor before agricultural pursuits, and cottage industry hardly existed. Hobson summed up this condition: "A typical but simplest form of 'manufacturing' business was one in which an industrial family, growing or bringing the materials and tools and working with the power of their own bodies (i.e., labour) in their own home under the direction of their head of the household, produce commodities partly for their own consumption, partly for a small local market" (Hobson 1926, 55). This pattern still operates in India and many other Third World countries.

"The workshop of the weaver was a rural cottage, from which, when he was tired of sedentary labour, he could sally forth into his little garden and with his spade or hoe tend its culinary productions. The cotton wool which was to form his weft was picked clean by the fingers of his younger children, carded and spun by the elder girls, assisted by his wife and the yarn was woven by himself assisted by his sons" (this passage is from a study by Ure, 224, cited in Hobson 1926, 56). This kind of household operations characterized precapitalist production. The element of labor operated as a member of the family and not as a factor of production and, therefore, shared the total output with other members and did not get paid a wage for the contribution.

Because of lack of money capital and the nonexistent division of labor between production and selling one's own products, artisans' production was limited to use for self-consumption and as a means of barter to meet other needs. The trouble of finding a market and the uncertainty associated with it, kept this kind of activity initially to self-consumption (Hobson 1926, 51–55). One important reason was that with low productivity in such an economy, to produce any surplus for the market over that needed for self-consumption was a real problem. With the rise of the merchants, their money capital entered into the arena of the self-employing artisan's manufactures and thereby solved the latter's problem of finding markets for products. In the name of covering the trouble, delay, and risk of finding consumers, the merchants added money value to the product over and above the paltry sum paid to the artisans. They did so without increasing the use value of the product and took advantage of the demand of other persons with purchasing power. In the process, however, the real producer's labor was divorced of the value of its product. This implies two important developments.

1. surplus-producing income was created
2. the consequent extention of the division of labor to marketing products resulted in a higher income over cost (i.e., profit became a reality).

This is when money capital began to enter into production for earning surplus value or profits, that is, the nascent form of industrial capitalism was emerging. The process began to evolve further as from the practice of selling a product to professional middle men, it was a small step to start receiving orders from them. The extension of division of labor meant, at that stage, that products, instead of themselves trying to produce or supply the required materials, began to buy them from the same merchant who bought the products from the producers. In those days, it was as difficult for producers to buy raw materials as to sell them, as the market system was not developed. Hobson wrote: "So the ownership of the raw materials often passes from the 'independent' small workman into the hands of the organising merchant who as early as the seventeenth century in the clothing trade is found usurping the title 'manufacturer' " (1926, 56).

As the market for cotton goods expanded and the pressure of work made itself felt, the practice grew of receiving not only linen wrap but cotton weft from the merchant or middleman. Thus, the ownership of the raw material passed out of the hands of the weavers, who previously had supplied themselves, using, for example, the yarn span by their own families or purchased in the neighborhood. The weavers, however, continued to ply their domestic craft as before. To avoid wasting of time and the difficulty of obtaining a steady, adequate supply to meet the growing market, this division of labor became inevitable. Although it resulted in a reduction in the cost of production per unit of output, it also led the weavers into a transition from independent to dependent (Hobson 1926, 57). The actual producers lose ownership of the product to the owner of their labor, that is, to the owner of money capital.

This had become the normal condition of trade by the mid-eighteenth century. Soon, the stocking trade began to show a further extension of the division of labor and the encroachment of the capitalist system on the domestic industry in that the merchants not only supplied materials but also the frames used for weaving, which they owned and rented to the weavers, who continued to work in their own homes. This development of business organization whereby the material is provided and the product taken by an outsider (a merchant or customer) was by no means confined to the country weaver but rather spread to other important activities in the country.

The Transition to the Factory and Manufacture

The most important capitalist development in the transition from the domestic to the manufactory system was the gradual removal of workers from their homes to factories and workplaces owned by the capitalists. The motive was to economize time, labor, and resources and thereby reduce the cost of production. More important, it gave direct control over the workers and facilitated the cooperation of the different processes of production. This reduced the labor cost of production per unit of output and also helped the workers to learn the trade and develop their skills. All these developments resulted in an increasing accumulation of surplus in the hands of owners of capital and, needless to say, not in the hands of the actual producers. According to bourgeoisie economists, growth of this kind of inequality is essential for economic growth. This transition process took time and, even up to the close of the eighteenth century, the large, organized business—half factory, half domestic—continued to prevail in the important western region of England (Hobson 1926, 59).

Defoe's accounts show that the weaving industry had, by the late eighteenth century, become highly concentrated, with rich employers owing considerable numbers of looms. Some of this work was contracted out by master manufacturers, but other work was done in large sheds or other premises owned by the master. However, the process began to be a complex one as a result of increasing accumulation of surplus and its concentration in the hands of owners of capital. The most significant conclusion that may be drawn was that craftsmen and cottagers began to lose the ownership, not only of the products of their labor, but of their labor itself (see also Dobb 1947, Mandel 1968). When receiving orders and materials from merchants or consumers, although they were producing exchange value by adding labor or skill to the materials, it was at the cost of their ownership of the product less the money value of their labor power. This was the beginning of the breakdown of these independent businesses.

Proportions of Capital and Labor in Production

Although in the process of loss of ownership, the penetration of money or mercantile capital into production began to take place, the distinctive characteristic of the premachinery age of capitalism was that capital comprised a small proportion compared to labor in the industrial unit. It implies that the mechanical techniques were still labor-oriented, tools were simple, and the proportion of fixed capital to the business was small or negligible and fell within the means of the artisans who operated their crafts at home. However, when production began to be organized in a manufactory on a large-scale basis using an extensive division of labor, which brought about greater productivity than the previous, domestic industry, economies of time and other resources and a gradual dependence on the owners of capital began. The household industry gradually lost ground and the labor of independent artisans and cottagers became the commodity labor.

This development implied that the demand for labor was growing as manufactory production began to spread. The demographic effect was to stimulate and maintain the high birthrate of the past together with a slowly declining death rate due to better living conditions, beginning with land reforms, a relative certainty of livelihood, and a better supply of food following the development of production and transport communications. The result was a high population growth rate. This supply of, and demand for, labor helped keep wage rates low compared to productivity. As the production mode was simple and required almost no prior skill or education, children as young as 7 and women joined the workforce. The age at which children started work was now at its lowest. In the late nineteenth century, when science began to be used in production, the age was 16 to 18, the age at which a child graduated from school. Today it takes 23 to 25 years to prepare for the highly technical production process.

With the high population growth and higher income, markets for products began to expand at a faster rate and competition among capitalists extended beyond local borders to an increasingly national market. This required rapid improvement in the process of manufacture, machines, communication, and transport, which together created a tremendous demand for labor. The extensive phase of technological change can be seen in terms of labor absorption and the more productive use of labor via large-scale organization and the division of labor. The consequent development of relatively large-scale manufacturing became evident. With the increased demand for labor, increasing and widening competition made the use of science and mechanical power in production imperative, indicating the need for a new phase of intensive technology, which has since occured.

The most important lesson is that with the growth of money capital and its subsequent penetration into production dawned a period of dynamic and fundamental change in economic organization (from domestic to factory organization). The dominance of agriculture in production and consumption gave way to non-agricultural production and particularly, industrial production first and, subsequently, to dynamic economic structural change. There was a change from production for self-consumption to production for markets, first local and then beyond, and an evolution from simple competition for finished consumer goods to complex competition for the means of production as well. This development of capitalism also created the indispensable condition for turning quantity labor to quality labor and, in the process, automatically produced an environment that was conducive to population control. This indicated the end of the first phase of the capitalist transformation of an economy, the main example of which was the United Kingdom, followed by Western Europe and, later, Japan. The second phase of capitalist transformation resulted from the emergence of an intensive phase of technological change when the increasing demand for labor in excess of its supply began to cause a rise in wages and hurt entrepreneurs. This critical situation was solved by introducing science into production to make the factor of labor more productive and, thereby, reduce the need for quantity labor. These changes in technology were to have profound effects on demographic transition and the development of education (see Chapters 6 and 7 for a detailed analysis).

The increased supply of labor resulting from the land reforms and sustained high rate of population growth in an economy that had already accumulated sufficient amount of merchant capital gave rise to industrial capitalism only in cases where the following conditions were met:

a. When the prototechnology of the pre-industrial merchant capital period reached an advanced stage and the accumulation of merchant capital became sufficient and organized under larger-scale manufactory (i.e., larger than the cottage industry). At this stage of merchant capitalism, the breakdown of urban localism and formation of monopolies by the craft guilds became inevitable.

b. The nascent industrial capital itself had to be freed from the restrictive monopolies in the sphere of trade in which merchant capital had already penetrated. Otherwise, any extension of the field of industrial investment would remain limited and gains and profit from industrial investment and the consequent accumulation of capital would be modest compared to the fortunes yielded by the monopoly export trade. Without this condition, the incentive to invest in industrial production would be thwarted and would in turn halt the development of industrial capitalism. However, the dynamism of the penetration of merchant capital in industrial production would, by legal coercion, establish this emancipation of the nascent industrial capital.

c. The most important condition in the development of industrial capital is that of retarding the investment of capital in agriculture in the sense of developing capitalist farming to generate surpluses including, most important, a labor surplus, or *primitive accumulation*, for further investment in agriculture and industry.

Not only does such employment generally play an important role in increasing the rural proletariat, it is also a crucial factor in creating an internal market for the products of manufacture. This is a factor that was absent over most of France in the eighteenth and early part of the nineteenth centuries on account of feudal demands on agriculture and local trade restrictions. This condition of lack of investment of primitive accumulation or surplus labor in agriculture in the Third World explains the underdevelopment of these economies. There has been, of late, considerable investment of modern resources and capital from outside which, as expected by critics, has failed to use this surplus to generate capital. In Third World countries, agriculture has always been neglected and industrial development has been based on borrowed capital and technology. Therefore, surplus labor or primitive accumulation has not been productively employed. On one hand, there is disguised unemployment in land and cottage industries and, on the other, money capital has been engaged either in the petty export-import business and not in industrial development or in shares of industries based on borrowed capital and technology, with little employment effects (see Chapter 5).

Agricultural Surplus and the Development of Industrial Capitalism

I have drawn substantially from E. R. Mandel's 1968 study. The agricultural surplus has been considered by economists as the main ingredient in the development of industrial capitalism. Mandel wrote: "Agricultural surplus is the basis of all surplus product and thereby of all civilisation. If society had to devote all its working time to producing the means of subsistence, no other specialised activity, whether craft, industrial, scientific or artistic should be possible" (1967, 95). In the primitive days, when population was small, the whole tribe was engaged from morning to evening collecting food from an unknown environment just for survival. With the growth of population, as the need and ability to produce more settled agriculture evolved after a long period of "slash and grow" methods of producing food, the population was still small relative to the vast area of land. The period of settled agriculture began with the growth of population when the need and ability to produce more food began to be felt (see also Boserup 1965). The settled agriculture needed sufficient savings of surplus food to keep the farmers fed between the sowing and reaping of food, plus seed. Tools were, at the outset, of a simple nature and made by the cultivators themselves from available resources.

The four hypotheses of Simon Kuznets (1964) relating to the contribution of agriculture in economic development deal with:

1. product contributions
2. factor contributions (i.e., capital labor)
3. market contributions, which include the fourth hypothesis, a foreign exchange contribution

Most Third World economies, having been drawn in to the orbit of world capitalism through trade, are making all these contributions today except that of labor, as indicated by the large agricultural population and large volume of rural immigrants to towns of these economies. Later I will discuss why these economies are failing to make labor contributions to industrial and service sector development, unlike those in the developed capitalist economies.

Agricultural surplus labor is the source of capital. When the supply of this surplus labor is available in sufficient quantity, the condition for transforming money capital into industrial capital is met. The rise of industrial capitalism has been facilitated by surplus agricultural product, which appears in three forms:

a. in the form of work, that is, labor surplus
b. in the form of products, namely, use values to be consumed by peasants
c. later, in the form of money, that is, through the sale of surplus output in the market by the owners of surplus

Agriculture, and in particular food production, was the main occupation of the workers who made up the bulk of the population. Surplus labor product in kind implies that trade or exchange of goods and the use of money and capital exist only superficially within the boundary of a natural economy. The bulk of the producers were left with no surplus to bring to the market. They consumed or bartered to meet their needs, as they continued to do after the appropriation of the landlord's lion's share.

However, with the rise of the system of payment of rent in money in the place of rent in kind, peasants were now obliged to sell their products in the market themselves in order to pay their rent. The introduction of this system of payment of rent in money and the consequent practice of selling and buying against money in the market brought about an unprecedented dynamism in the previously calm, quiet, and unchanging natural economy.

The peasants left the condition of a natural economy and entered the money economy, which was previously limited to a handful of rich landowners and merchants. Thus, markets for various products began to expand, as did the quantity and variety of products, although they were still of simple quality. This heralded the dawn of money capital and its subsequent introduction into production, giving birth to industrial capitalism (Mandel 1968, 78).

The concentration of money in the hands of the new wealthy or bourgeois classes signaled a new social and economic environment. The original wealthy classes accumulated wealth and money, as in use values or means of acquiring them, whereas in the hands of the new possessing classes, the accumulation of money was done in the form of money capital, with the sole object of increasing its accumulation.

However, the accumulation of money capital does not guarantee its development into industrial capital. True, money is accumulated to bring in surplus value. The surplus value thus accumulated after payment of the minimum necessary for subsistence is, in its turn, capitalized, mainly by lending against a return in money or in possessions, so as to earn further surplus value. Such an accumulation of wealth that increases in new value is, in the long run, impossible to continue by mere periodical transfers of wealth from one country to another or from one class to another because there is a limit to the supply of such wealth. Either the accumulation of capital kept within the limits of such a transfer will cease because its sources inevitably must dry up or else it will find a new way forward through its introduction into production. In other words, merchant capital through the process of its accumulation over time exhausts its source by a "beggaring thy neighbor" process. Any further accumulation is possible only if it could be used to increase the supply of goods which, at that point, must be transformed into industrial capital. Merchant capital needs to be combined with surplus labor to produce industrial capital (see Chapter 1). It was done at that stage via organizational change and an increased division of labor, so as to use the growing surplus of workers and thereby increase production.

Here, too, labor is necessary for the subsistence of workers and surplus labor becomes profit for the owners of money capital. Money capital was used to hire labor and buy raw materials and the ultimate stage of development of capital into industrial capital emerged as the penetration of capital into the sphere of production created the conditions for an unlimited advance of productive forces via economic structural change. On the other hand, the growth of production in a class-based society gradually stimulated an increasing diversity in production and consumption which, in turn, created further opportunity for using surplus labor toward capital accumulation, and so on. "This penetration of capital into the sphere of production creates the conditions for an unlimited advance of the productive forces" (Mandel 1968, 100). It works through technological change, from the extensive phase of using quantity labor more productively to the intensive phase which, in turn, transforms quantity labor into quality labor (see Chapters 6 and 7). No longer do the limited consumer needs of the possessing classes restrict the productive forces in the need to increase the value that accrues to capital, instead, the abolition of every restriction on their development is made possible. However, over the course of time, the desire of the possessing classes to increase the rate of capital accumulation ultimately restricts their ability to do so, even when they are capable of creating unlimited productive capacity and diversifying output through technological change (see Chapter 4 on the internationalization of production). The rise of industrial capital in the West has been explained by Marx.

Because of the comparatively hard life caused by the harsh weather and lack of sufficient vegetation in the medieval West, bare subsistence living required greater efforts and better organization of production to organize and generate resources than in the East, and the period of primitive agriculture ended much earlier. The development of industrial capital from accumulated commercial capital in England required land reforms to release labor for the industrial sector, which proved insufficient in the case of Britain, as seen from Dobb's (1947) account. Britain's high population growth compared to that of other European countries, in addition to the land reforms introduced earlier, made possible the development of commercial capital into industrial capital. In France, Germany, and Holland, the bourgeoisie class that emerged with commercial capital solved the problem of insufficient surplus labor by importing capital from England (Henderson 1954, chs. 1, 2). It saved them the resources that would have been used in developing technology through trial and error, which Britain had to undertake. True, these countries also were at a comparable stage of prototechnology, which made it possible for them to adopt the British technology without creating a dualistic structure for long periods (see Maitra 1980, for a detailed discussion).

According to Mandel (1968), it was the superior fertility of their soil and the greater growth of their population that doomed these civilizations of the East to stop midway in their development. However, the population growth rate was not greater than in Europe, particularly when one considers lush vegetation, clement weather, and superior fertility of the soil in the East, which required fewer resources (i.e., labor) in eking out a subsistence living for the masses. The need for bringing about land reforms was not felt intensely, and neither was there any interest on the part of mercantile capitalists or owners of wealth to enter into industrial production. India lent millions of rupees to the East India Company to help in commercial pursuits there (see Table 1.3). The much more primitive agriculture of medieval Europe could not carry the weight of a density of population

TABLE 1.3 Population Growth Rates per Annum, 1500-1975 (in Percentages)

Region	1500-1750	1750-1900	1900-1975
China	0.2	0.6	0.6
Indian Subcontinent	0.1	0.3	2.2
Europe	0.4	1.3	1.9
Japan	0.1	0.3	1.9

Source: Based on Boserup (1981), 10.

comparable to that of China or Egypt (i.e., the Nile valley in the prosperous periods). Marx wrote:

> It is not true that the most fruitful soil is the most fitted for the growth of the earliest mode of production. This mode is based on the dominion of man over nature. Where nature is too lavish, she keeps him in hand like a child in leading strings. She does not impose on him any necessity to develop himself. It is not the tropics with their luxuriant vegetation, but the temperate zone that is the mother country of capital. It is not mere fertility of the soil, but the differentiation of the soil, the variety of its natural products, the changes of the season which form the physical basis for the social division of labour and the multiplication of his wants, his capabilities, his means and modes of labour. It is the necessity of bringing a natural force under the control of society, of economising, of appropriating or subsidising it on a large scale by the work of man's hand that first plays the decisive part in the history of industry. (Marx 1861, 1: 563–69)

Table 1.3 shows that between 1500 and 1750, population growth in China and India was much smaller than in Europe. In the later period, when these economies came into contact with industrial Europe, population growth became much higher for reasons that are already well known; P. E. Ehrlich and A. H. Ehrlich (although I do not agree with their main thesis about population growth) wrote that population growth in Asia between 1750 and 1850 was slower than that in Europe, amounting to an increase of about 50 percent in 100 years, when a population boom was taking place in England (Ehrlich and Ehrlich 1970, 16; see also Maitra 1986, 24–26).

An analysis of the growth of capital shows the revolutionary role that the rise of industrial capitalism played in bringing about economic structural change and the development of social consciousness from a feudal one of blind faith and religion into the Age of Reason, from helpless dependence on the mercy of nature to science and reason-based efforts to unveil the mystery of nature for the development of humanity, as well as the consequent period of humanity and social consciousness. This analysis also will preface:

1. The effects of such revolutionary change on demographic transition, technological change, and the development of human resources into human capital (Chapters 6 and 7).

2. Lack of these effects in the Third World, where capitalism has been introduced by way of the transfer of industrial goods, capital, and technology rather than evolving by use of the indigenous resources and, thus, bringing about revolutionary changes in feudal production relationships and economic structure. I will show that a simple transfer of highly productive capital, technology, and knowledge does not bring about capitalist transformation.

3. The spread of world capitalism from its center in the West to the furthest corner of the earth has taken place since the late nineteenth century, via (a) trade in goods and commodity capital; (b) transfer of investment resources in loans, credits, and foreign investment, particularly since the 1950s, and (c) direct transfer of capitalist production under the multinational corporations of the West

A brief review of enclosures, labor supply, and the growth of industrial capital in England will be useful to understand the issue.

Enclosures, Labor Supply, and the Growth of Industrial Capital (a Brief Review)

First, the key factor that set England apart from much of the rest of Europe in the early modern period and that uniquely underpinned its early industrialization was the absence of a significant peasant class in the countryside and the associated growth of large-scale capitalist agriculture. In England, the mass of the peasantry never gained firm freehold rights and was more easily shifted, dispossessed, and proletarianized in the process of enclosure, engrossment, and the commercialization of farming (Brenner 1976). The commercialization of farming was able to proceed in a relatively unhindered fashion, allowing national agriculture to support a growing nonagrarian sector; the conservatism inherent in peasant culture had less effect on attitudes toward leisure, work, and consumption than it had in France; and, finally, the push factors created by the development of agrarian capitalism ensured a ready supply of cheap landless, and potentially mobile labor for nonagricultural pursuits. However, this did not happen until after completion of the enclosures.

Second, using trends in urbanization and population growth as a guide, Wrigley calculated that each worker in agriculture was producing food for 1.5 nonagricultural workers in 1650, 2.5 by 1800, and 6.0 by 1911. His estimates show that labor productivity rates in England and France in 1500 and 1600 were similar but that output per worker in English agriculture rose by between 60 and

100 percent over the period 1600–1800 (compared with less than 20 percent in France) and continued to grow by about 1 percent per annum in the period 1811–1851. By 1800, labor productivity in France was only 69 percent of the English level. As output per acre was similar in England and France, England's higher labor productivity is shown to arise from lower employment per acre (Wrigley 1988; Hudson 1992, 67–68).

In the century or so after 1750, virtually all the remaining open field areas were enclosed. Village rules and regulations governing crops, livestock, and farm techniques were abolished in favor of the management of farms by individual farmers or landlords. Rights of ownership were now recognized through Parliament as exclusive rights to use, so that common lands and common usage declined dramatically (Dahlaman 1980). Thus, although the relationship between enclosure in itself and increased labor productivity is debatable, enclosure appears to have been accompanied by an increasing turnover in the land market and a rationalization of tenancies at the poorer end of the scale. Life on the land was made considerably more difficult for smallholders, cottagers, and squatters. In addition, the loss of common land took away much employment (such as pig and poultry keeping, grazing cows, and gleaning) that was specifically considered women's work or that of juveniles and children. Hence, an important pillar of family earnings was removed, making families less secure and creating pools of underemployed female and juvenile workers. These were often the first to be soaked up by manufacturing, by employment, or by intermittent laboring or service trades in nearby urban centers. With such points from recent research in mind, it is perhaps not surprising that enclosure is again receiving the attention of historians as a major factor in the industrialization process (Snell 1985, ch. 4).

In most textbook analyses following the classicists and neoclassicists, the supplying of capital and technology along with a policy of population control to negate diminishing returns and raise growth per capita have been advocated, with markets of developed countries as the target. In India, these policies have been followed since it started planning its economic development. There has been tremendous growth and diversity in industrial production, rapid introduction of modern consumption (though confined to a tiny proportion of the population), and sophisticated energy use patterns, with, paradoxically a stagnating economic structure bearing the burden of over 70 percent of population in agriculture. Just by analyzing the role of capital and technology, we cannot resolve the paradox. We need to know the process of capital accumulation and its overall effects on economic structural change, technological change, and human resource and energy use. Even when the annual rate of capital accumulation as a proportion of gross national product (GNP) is high, capitalist transformation of the economy remains negligible in terms of sectoral distribution of the labor force, demographic transition effects of rising income, and the elimination of feudal social consciousness (India and most Third World countries, including the Middle East, supply ample proof).

The development of capital as the means of production today needs to be discussed historically; otherwise, we will not realize the social and economic implications of the growth of capital and of capitalism, which has been dominating the world economy for over 200 years. Today, all developing countries are being showered with unlimited quantities of physical and financial capital from rich and developed capitalist economies. The rate of capital formation to gross domestic product (GDP) has increased remarkably in recent years, from nearly 5 percent in the 1950s to 22 percent, which is a much higher rate than it was in the West at the comparable stage. This is happening with little economic structural change effects, again unlike the case of developed capitalist economics (see Tables in Chapters 6 and 7). Therefore, we need to understand the role of the growth of capital in economic structural change, the development of social consciousness, and economic development. The growth of capital and capital accumulation in latecomer countries like India has produced only the effects of augmenting, diversifying, and bringing about qualitative improvements of products, with little effect in terms of demographic transition, economic structural change, or the development of the feudal social mind into a rational and science-based social consciousness. However, when capitalism has evolved indigenously, as has been the case with the Industrial Revolution in the United Kingdom, followed by the growth of industrial capitalism in the other West European countries, like France, Germany, and Holland, which use their own human resources in production, these effects *have* emerged.

This explains the need to study the factor that led to the development of capital, from surplus labor in the form of ground or labor rent to rent in kind and, later, money rent, and then to mercantile capitalism, which evolved into industrial capitalism. This last phase brought about a capitalist transformation of the economy and the development of rational social consciousness. Obviously, agricultural economy has played the key role in this process. In the present-day development approach, whether in a capitalist or in the hitherto socialist systems, priority has always been given to the development of industry and industrial capital, neglecting agriculture. This has been possible because of the availability of unlimited supplies of capital and technology from the West. Hence, the role of agriculture has been neglected. Thus, we are missing the basic factors that operate behind the rise and accumulation of money capital and its transformation into industrial capital (see Chapter 5).

The four features of capitalism are: commodity production, wage labor, accumulation of capital, and rational organization. The commodity production as a system emerges in a society when the economic activities undertaken by independent or free agents are coordinated by market exchange. This is a system whereby a worker's labor becomes a commodity, the price of which is determined by the market. This is the most distinctive feature of capitalism. In the ultimate analysis, labor is the only factor of production—and the origin of all other factors—capital, land or other natural resources (as productive resources), and the organization of production depend on labor.

In precapitalist economies, commercial activities existed, but only as peripheral activities generally involving trading activities rather than production. At this stage, the workers still sold the products of their labor and not their labor as a commodity. Mainly urban activities in agricultural economies may be cited as examples. Their importance in economic life develops with the decline of economic relations based upon personal relations, such as serfdom, or family relationships, as in all peasant economics of traditional societies. This decline directly follows the rise of capitalism. In such societies, labor remuneration of a family member takes the form of a share in the total output of the family enterprise, irrespective of one's contribution. The wages or remunerations of all family members are equal to their subsistence wage which, in sum, is equal to total earnings or their products. Capitalist enterprise employs labor on the wage equal to the worker's marginal product. Lewis's model of the development of labor surplus economies of the Third World has shown this very clearly (Lewis 1954). His study is applicable to the preindustrial economies of Western Europe in the nineteenth century.

The dominance of markets as the mechanism of economic coordination (i.e., pricing of factors of production and their products) does not, in itself, characterize capitalism. The more basic conditions that characterize complete capitalism are those that turn human labor into a commodity. In the Lewis model (1954), which is based on classical theory, the precapitalist system of factor pricing has been distinguished from the capitalist pricing system, as exists under the capitalist mode of production.

The one important characteristic of Marx's concept of capitalism is its productive and accumulative character, which is designed to raise the rate of accumulation (i.e., profit), which in turn results in dynamic growth in productivity. Capitalists are motivated by expansion via growth in the production of value rather than by the accumulation of specific forms of wealth like land or precious metals, merchant capital, or objects of conspicuous consumption, as under the feudal, landowner, or mercantilist systems.

Thus, use value must never be looked upon as the real aim of the capitalist, for whom the expansion of value becomes the subjective aim (Marx 1970, 152). The extension of the money relationship was designed to promote the rational acquisition of wealth via raising the productivity of human labor in combination with natural resources. This injected the vital element of dynamism. In those days, with social consciousness at a low level and the working population completely unorganized due to a lack of communication and division of labor and to an unorganized production process, competition among the owners of money capital provided another rationale for the drive toward the accumulation and expansion of value of resources, (that is, human labor), which resulted in increased and diversified output and capital accumulation.

Competition at the early stage of capitalism motivated the system to make more productive use of labor through the introduction of large-scale organization based on division of labor, to replace the small and unorganized units of household production of the preindustrial days. By bringing the entire process of production under one roof and by introducing, to some degree, the extension of the division of labor and a more productive use of resources, it became possible to raise the rate of capital accumulation that had been previously derived from household production. In this process, the labor of a family became a commodity, which is the basic criterion of capitalism, and when labor as a commodity is used in industrial production as a factor of production, industrial capitalism emerges.

This social and economic relationship of capitalism brings out the inherent laws of capitalist production. The competition for markets by each capitalist so as to raise the rate of capital accumulation brings about technological progress from its early extensive phase. At this phase, a sufficient quantity of labor is available at a low wage to be organized for large-scale production using prototechnology to use labor more intensively and, thus, prepare the condition for the rise of quality labor (see Chapter 7).

Capitalist motivation to raise the rate of accumulation induces each capitalist to constantly extend his or her capital with the help of increasing technological progress into the capitalist production. In the ultimate analysis, technological change is essentially the result of the development of human resources brought about, first, by the organizational change from the family artisans' workshop through the large-scale manufactory process and to machinofacture. Technological progress thus takes the form, first, of an extensive phase of using labor more productively through organizational change and, then, of using it more intensively through the use of science. Thus, human resources become human capital. This brings about economic structural change, from agriculture through industry to service. The striving to raise capital accumulation is the force behind this dynamic change.

According to Adam Smith, the productive and accumulative character of capitalism provided the solution to the profound historical crisis of feudalism. Smith condemned the mercantilist practice of the accumulation of wealth in precious metals. He was also a critic of the Physiocrats' view of industrial labor as unproductive. He was an advocate of free trade as an engine of world capitalism, which has helped it today to reach every nook and corner of the earth in the quest of raising the rate of capital accumulation. However, in that process it has blocked the independent development of capitalism elsewhere. Ricardo, too, opposed protectionism and strongly advocated free trade, as it was crucial for capitalist profits and their progressive acquisition as capital to be maintained. In other words, first, the expansion of the domestic markets, with increasing employment of the formerly rural disguised unemployed population, followed by an expansion of unrestricted trade, was considered the main force behind the expansion of capitalism. The emphasis on free trade, however, changed with the times (see Chapter 4). Dobb commented that Adam Smith's doctrine could be properly understood only as a reflection of a period of transition (from the feudal-mercantilist period to Industrial capitalism), whose problems essentially consisted in clearing the ground for industrial investment and expansion, which he identified with the sweeping away of obstructive and seasonally protective regulation (Dobb 1947, 6).

In Adam Smith's analysis, development meant the extension of the division of labor and the application of the machinery to the productive process so that an increase in labor productivity could be achieved. The extension of the division of labor in the manufactory production process, which replaced self-sufficient, simple, family labor–based agriculture and rural industries, played a dynamic role in generating further economic surplus and capital accumulation using surplus labor that hitherto had been unproductively engaged. Adam Smith defined economic activity in terms of the physical production of material goods. For Smith, productive work is only that which allows the accumulation of material wealth, and material wealth has value only insofar as it embodies human labor. In other words, in the period of industrial capitalism, "labour is the source of wealth." Thus, the labor of manufacturers (e.g., workers engaged in manufacturing production) adds generally to the value of the materials on which they work, of their own maintenance, and of their master's profits. "The labour of a menial servant, on the contrary, adds to the value of nothing" (Smith [1863] 1976, 9). During the preindustrial period, a large part of labor was as Smith described. Productive labor in this sense, fixes and realizes itself in some particular subject or vendible commodity, part of which is meant for consumption and the other part for use as stock to be employed for further production in the future. This includes both agricultural products and manufactured goods (i.e., capital and consumer goods). In Adam Smith's view, economic development involves the employment of an increasing proportion of the workforce in productive work, which is precisely the reverse of the situation in feudalism.

However, the development of industrial capitalism, although it initially creates an increasing demand for labor in more productive activities, later creates a condition for employing the labor force at a decreasing wage rate compared to their contribution to output. The difference accrues as "profit." Initially, the availability of increasing surplus labor through land reforms and a sustained high rate of population growth made possible the accumulation of profit. According to Smith, the key to an increase in productivity was the division of labor achieved through the expansion of the market and international trade. David Ricardo later observed that the value of a commodity is the result of the amount of labor incorporated into it, as measured by the time taken to produce it. Thus, in his view, profits, wages, and rent, the rewards of the main three classes of society, could only come out of the fixed magnitude of the value produced by the available labor force, whatever the pattern of distribution.

For Ricardo, development was a process of the self-sustained accumulation of capital and growth, which could be arrested only by the limitations of land. In other words, he did not visualize the growth and role of technological change as a force in offsetting the effects of a shortage of resources, including labor. That is why he advocated the case for the free import of corn as the essential counteracting force to diminishing returns in agriculture. However, a more plausible reason was that the import of corn, and later wheat and meat, helped enormously the British expansion of industrial capitalism and capital accumulation, as it helped increase the supply of cheaper labor in the more productive industrial production sector instead of engaging a large part of it in agricultural production. Otherwise, the consequent high demand for labor at that stage of labor supply would have drastically raised wages and, thereby, costs. This had helped keep wages under control. He therefore stressed the importance of importing food and raw materials in exchange for manufactured goods as the basis for his international division of labor theory of trade. This was to be a condition to offset the tendency toward diminishing returns in manufacture. He advocated for free trade in corn on the ground that, so long as trade is free and corn is cheap, profits will not fall, however, great the accumulation of capital. Thus Smith and Ricardo advocated the use of international trade as a weapon to fight against a possible stationary society. International trade, as history shows, led to the revolutionary development of technological change, which acted as a weapon in the hands of world capitalism to keep the economy dynamic. Simultaneously, it has created a severe crisis of market and employment in the long run (see Chapter 4).

Side by side with this analysis, let us take a brief look at what Marx wrote about capital, capitalism, and the division of labor and see how these three economists looked at the role of capitalism in bringing about the capitalist transformation of an economy via change in economic structure. The previous discussion covered the concept of division of labor as Adam Smith and David Ricardo—the two founders of modern bourgeois economies—defined it. Marx looked at it as the most important indicator of the development of a nation's productive forces. In an underdeveloped feudal economy, the division of labor did not, and could not operate, because of a lack of sufficient population, the limited needs of the masses, and a low level of production technology. Self-sufficiency in simple needs characterized the social life. "Each new productive force, in so far as it is not merely a quantitative extension of productive forces already known (for instance the bringing into cultivation of fresh land), brings about a further development of the division of labor" (Marx 1964c, 121–22).

We should include a more important factor in defining this concept of the quantitative extension of productive forces, which is an increase in the quantity of labor, with technology and the organization of production remaining constant. The increased number of hands, which was due to a rising population growth and a supply of labor that was released by land reforms was organized in large-scale production, which at first led to a rise in capital accumulation. However, with technology and the organization of production remaining constant, a rise in population, supplying cheaper labor, would result in diminishing returns. With the division of labor, the seed of economic structural change is sown. That the division of labor is the key to raising the rate of capital accumulation is an accepted view by both non-Marxists and Marxists. Marx also regarded the division of labor as the key to the accumulation of capital, but he presented it in a different way. He wrote:

> The division of labour inside a nation leads at first to the separation of industrial and commercial from agricultural labour and to the separation of town and country and a clash of interests between them. Its further development leads to the separation of commercial from industrial labour. At the same time, through the division of labour, there develops further, inside these various branches, various division among the individuals cooperating in definite kinds of labour. The relative position of these individual groups is determined by the methods employed in agriculture, industry and commerce (1964c, 22).

Manufactory, or bringing artisans under one roof to engage in production as their full-time occupation, did not materialize because of the labor shortage in preindustrial days. They were working in their off period from cultivation—they could not spend the whole time away from their plots of land.

The division of labor as the basic force to increase output and capital accumulation has been advocated by classical economists and by Marx. The need to raise the rate of capital accumulation is met by surplus labor resulting from the increased pressure of population on a limited supply of land, which is then shifted to the production of industrial capital (A discussion of this process occurs in Chapter 3).

2

INDUSTRIAL GROWTH

MERCHANT CAPITALISM AND INDUSTRIAL GROWTH

Industrial capitalism emerged from the internal process of the dissolution and change of the feudal mode of production. It happened thus: during this period, merchant capital operated to move goods produced by the guilds or peasants but remained external to the specific mode of production. This was the period of the putting-out system, under which merchants appropriate the surplus generated by exchange in faraway markets. Later, in late sixteenth-century England, merchant capital that was thus accumulated began to fasten upon the mode of production to organize it more effectively so that more surplus or profit could be earned. This occurred in two ways: first, a portion of the producers themselves accumulated capital, took to trade, and began to organize production on a capitalist basis; thus landowners became industrialists; and second, a section of the existing merchant class moved into the control and organization of production. Usually, the process begins with merchants first gaining control over small producers (Dobb 1947, 123). According to Marx and Dobb, the first method was revolutionary. However, Dobb mentioned in his study that because of the labor shortage, manufacturing could not graduate into industrial capitalism (see "Labor Shortages—Preindustrial Period," in this chapter).

Sweezy, Dobb, and Takahshi (1976, 72) criticized Dobb on the grounds that Dobb ignored the fact that feudalism was a system of production for known community needs, namely, it is a system in which *use value* rather than *exchange value* (to use two familiar Marxist terms) predominates. In other words, it was a natural economy; no compulsion existed from the nature of production itself to extend surplus labor or transform working methods. However, Sweezy did not take into consideration the relevance of the matter of ownership of land, which was not natural and, rather, a matter of compulsion. In a natural economy, land belongs to everybody, and when the land and its fruits are appropriated by feudal landowners without them making any contribution to it, the element of compulsion becomes evident. According to Sweezy, techniques and forms of organization form an established pattern and the whole life of society tends to be oriented to custom and tradition.

However, according to Sweezy, the crucial question of change from a feudal or natural economy revolves around the process by which money, trade, and exchange gave rise to a system of production for the market and the impact of this system on the preexistent feudal system of production for local use. Urban centers based on long-distance exchange became generators of commodity production (i.e., goods produced for sale), in that they had to be provisioned from the countryside and produced manufactures (handicrafts) that the rural population could purchase with the proceeds from food sales. The introduction of money in this process helped generating surplus output in the sense that producers produced goods, not only for use, but also for earning money to pay rent or buy land and other products. This practice was soon accompanied by the sale of labor on the part of producers in the place of the sale of goods produced by their labor. The process of commodity production, with its tremendous impact on capitalist production of the future thus began to emerge. In the sixteenth century, this development was confined to manufacturing production in England and some other countries of Europe and, due to the labor shortage, it could not develop into industrial capitalism.

However, in terms of Sweezy's explanation, these urban-oriented islands of production for exchange interacted with the surrounding areas of production for use, making the inefficiency of the manorial form of organization clearly apparent, transforming attitudes toward the pursuits of wealth, spreading the desire for new articles of consumption, and opening to the peasant population of the countryside the prospect of a freer and latter life. According to Sweezy, this development had the effect of creating areas of capitalist production in and around the trading towns, while areas distant from them the peasants remained at the mercy of the landed aristocracy. He defined this situation as the dualistic one, with a capitalist center and a feudal periphery (Sweezy 1976, 49). Sweezy's explanation is applicable to the cases of latecomers in industrialization, both of the nineteenth and the twentieth centuries, and surely not to the case of the Industrial Revolution (Maitra 1980). Sweezy described the condition of feudalism as moribund before capitalism was born, and the period in between was neither feudal nor capitalist but one of precapitalist commodity production. In this period, merchant capitalists who had accumulated large blocks of capital from trade financed manufacturing production, launching full-fledged enterprises.

Sweezy emphasized the point that feudalism broke down due to its inability to accommodate external forces of market exchange, which stimulated merchant capitalists to grow into industrial capitalists. According to Dobb, the primary force that brought down feudalism was the internal contradictions that developed within the feudal natural economy along with the growth of money and exchange economy. The latter introduced dynamism in the static feudal economy by creating opportunities for expanding the market. The expansion of the market and trade accentuated the internal conflicts within the old mode of production. The development provided peasants and cottage workers the scope for a better utilization of their labor and their products. The history of the period, which included a labor shortage problem in the sixteenth and earlier centuries, acted as a serious hindrance to the development of small producers of the precapitalist days into the full-fledged, capitalist, large-scale, industrial enterprise (Dobb 1947; Sweezy, Dobb, and Takahshi 1976; see also "Labor Shortages—Preindustrial Period," in this chapter). Land reforms in the form of last enclosure movement in the late eighteenth century led to the creation of surplus labor but proved insufficient to induce large-scale manufactories. High and sustained population growth, resulting partly from the better living conditions and food supply effects of land reforms in the later part of the eighteenth century, created tremendous pressure on the static feudal-merchant capitalist economy and served as a source of cheap surplus labor for initiating large-scale industrial enterprises based on a relatively extensive division of labor (see Wrigley 1988). Chapter 1 discussed the process of growth of protoindustries into large-scale manufactories. According to the model of the first bourgeoisie economist, Adam Smith, the development of markets, trade, and the division of labor brought about the development of industrial capitalism. The development of trade helped in accumulating surplus and developing economics of scale of production and, thereby, increased profits and the accumulation of capital. Adam Smith's concept of development is basically related to capital-created productivity which is a function of the division of labor, that is, specialization. The latter is achieved through the separation of agriculture and manufacture, and the degree of specialization depends on the degree of the development of trade. Therefore, according to Smith, the division of labor is limited by the extent of the market. He therefore advocated increasing trade with the British colonies which, according to him, would offset the tendency toward the operation of the law of diminishing returns.

In a more recent work Brenner (1977, 47), pointed out that the mere rise of trade cannot, in and of itself, determine the processes of dissolution of the feudal relations of production. The important factors were the contradictory character of precapitalist production and exchange and the social relations that emerge with money capital and exchange within the economy, together with the growth in the primitive accumulation system, resulting from land reforms, operation of merchant capital in the putting-out system, and, more importantly, the sustained growth of population as the major source of surplus in those days.

Capitalism thrives on continually generating surplus, which is achieved initially through a more productive use of surplus labor via organizational change and, later, by making labor more productive (i.e., through the development of capital-intensive technological change). These changes over time are evident in the capitalist system in its development of education and population growth, and energy use patterns—the three basic sources of increased productivity and technological change under capitalism that increase capital accumulation (see Chapters 6 and 7).

Marx saw the rise of capitalism in Europe in terms of a twofold process: the accumulation of capital in the hands of a bourgeoisie and its investment in the means of industrial production and the emergence of a free proletariat that was dispossessed of means of production and forced to work for the bourgeoisie in return for wages. Bourgeois economists consider the rise of capitalism as the result of savings generated by economic inequality and the rise of income from the expansion of free market opportunities (i.e., the rise of industrial capitalism) as a simple offshoot of the maturity of commerce and commercial capital. The commercial bourgeoisie turned into the industrial bourgeoisie only when the two factors, the accumulation of money capital and the supply of a sufficient amount of surplus labour (that is the proletariat class) had appeared in the society. These are the two essential ingredients in initiating industrial capitalism, and once it comes about, the economy and society cannot remain the same.

Marx himself noted the dynamic possibilities inherent in the feudal mode, not only in an extensive territorial sense, but in terms of its struggle for a share of the surplus product. It was this that determined the limits of the seignorial demesne economy and, hence, the alternative outcome of the fourteenth-century crisis, the victory of the peasant commodity production system with the emergence of a class of peasant farmers—yeomen or laborers—in the West.

The dynamics of feudal society can be found, first, in the antagonism between landowners and peasants in the act of the appropriation of the unretained portion or surplus of peasant production. They are found, second, in the geographic distance between family-based peasant and artisan production and the feudal and merchant capitalist appropriators, which constituted an inescapable weakness for the appropriators. This weakness led to the suppression of the fact that in the complex conjuncture of social, demographic, and political difficulties of the late Middle Ages, petty commodity production in agriculture and artisan production were able to thrive, generate a social differential, and lay the basis for the transformation of the character of capitalism (Hilton 1979, 18–19).

Dobb mentioned the difficulties in manufacturing of that era that hindered its ability to evolve into capitalist industrial manufacturing, mainly because of the labor shortage, which caused high wages and inflation and hindered the development of industrial capitalism. The completion of enclosures helped mobilize surplus labor in rural manufactories and, combined with a sustained rise in population, helped provide surplus labor at a cheaper price to aid in the rise of capitalist, large-scale manufactories, followed by power-operated factories. Sustained population growth at a relatively high rate was the key to the supply of surplus labor, in addition to that which resulted from the enclosure land reforms. Growing population pressure on the peasants' agriculture and artisans' production meant, in modern economic terms, a disproportionate factor supply condition resulting in diminishing returns (i.e., the creation of surplus labor, the main ingredient in the initiation of large-scale manufactories). Brenner mentioned that under capitalism, surplus in labor productivity (e.g., producing values with the same amount of labor as previously), making it possible for society to reproduce itself with less labor in the same amount of time, produce a larger surplus, and plough this back into further innovations in the process of production. Brenner was right but failed to show the operation of the process. He did not take into account the effects of population growth, which resulted in an increase in cheap surplus labor supply that, in turn, helped extend the division of labor, increase productivity, and expand markets and innovations.

Only under capitalism was labor separated from its independent means of production and itself turned into the means of production of capital (in modern textbook terms, the major factor of production existed side by side with factor capital). The transition from feudalism to capitalism is explained in terms of a transition of ownership and the use of wealth from the situation under feudalism; landowners extracted a heavy surplus, most of which was spent on military expeditions and conspicuous consumption. Therefore, little surplus was left for investment in the development of productive forces. Moreover, the motivation to develop productive forces was lacking because of the fact that landowners were assured of a lion's share of the output from their land without having to make any contribution and because, due to low population growth, a shortage of factor labor acted as a primary constraint on technological change. Whenever landlords needed increased income, it was obtained, not by increasing productivity, but by a ruthless extraction of the already poor peasants, who thereby lost their ability and incentive to improve the plough or animals, which were a source of manure, thus leading to deterioration of the soil. This eventually resulted in a demographic crisis in the preindustrial period of the fourteenth to, largely, the sixteenth centuries.

On the other hand, with the emergence of capitalism from the ashes of the feudal and mercantile system of property ownership, there also arose a system of surplus extraction through which the extractors—the capitalist owners—were obliged to increase their surplus, corresponding to an unprecedented, though enormously imperfect, degree to the needs of productive forces (Brenner 1976, 68). Under the mercantile capitalist system, surplus that accumulated in the hands of merchants did not result from the extraction of increased productivity but from the exploitation of the poverty of the artisans and the advantage of the market. Under capitalism, however, capital accumulation resulted from the extraction or exploitation of surplus labor, however, the latter was the consequence of increased labor productivity. Labor was denied of the benefits of its productivity. In the later period of commercial capitalism, the putting-out system may be called the poor beginning of the system of capitalist accumulation.

The differences in the nature of exploitation under feudalism and mercantile capitalism have been briefly depicted by Gruevich thus:

> Wealth for the feudal lord was the weapon with which he maintained his social influence and confirmed his honour. Wealth of itself did not command respect—on the contrary in medieval society the merchant who horded stores of goods and who used his money only for profit in commerce or money lending, inspired many negative feelings: envy, hate, contempt, and fear, but never respect. On the other hand, the lord who spent without counting the cost, even when he did not live within his means but who arranged feasts and gave away gifts, earned respect and fame among his peers and even among bourgeois and peasants. From a noble's point of view the mass of the people needed nothing. Wealth was seen as a means to ends which far surpassed the merely economic. Wealth was a witness to valour, generosity and the largesse of the lord. Thus the peak point of the enjoyment of wealth was to disburse it in the presence of the greatest number of people who received their share of the lord's generosity. Here, wealth was a way of affirming the personality which had not yet learned to turn in on itself but which remained turned outwards to the group, the corporation and the audience. (1977, 17; cited in Peet 1980, 68–69)

The growth of autonomous towns and the rise of commerce in Europe did not evolve into capitalist industrialization in the eighteenth and nineteenth centuries. Medieval England had the least independent towns, yet England was the first European nation to bring about the Industrial Revolution, that is, industrial capitalism. On the other hand, medieval Germany had some of the most powerful autonomous towns in Europe, yet Germany was the nineteenth-century latecomer in industrialization. This is equally true of Italy, which experienced urban progress in the Middle Ages followed by relative industrial backwardness. In some cases, the success in commerce and ownership of tremendous accumulation of money capital in a nation did not result in rapid industrialization; Holland is a good example.

The commercial bourgeoisie did not show any enthusiasm in modern industrial development without government encouragement and support; the cases of France, Germany, and even Japan may be cited as examples. It is important to note that these are all cases of latecomers with low population growth (Maitra 1980).

Absolute surplus value is defined as an increase in surplus value resulting from prolonging the working day or engaging increased numbers of workers when they are available cheaply due to an increased supply of labor from population growth. The production of absolute surplus value forms the general groundwork of the capitalist system and the starting point for the production of relative surplus value. The production of absolute surplus value depends exclusively on the length of the work day and the availability of cheaper labor. The production of relative surplus value revolutionizes the technical process of labor. Mechanization cheapens commodity and by shortening the labor time necessary for production, lengthens the portion for the production of relative surplus value. The intensification of labor is possible by raising the quality of labor into human capital via education. This is realized when the rate of capital accumulation is accompanied by the dynamism of capitalist transformation. The intensification of labor (the condensation of a greater amount of labor into a given time period) counts as a greater quantity of labor and increases the relative yield of relative surplus value.

In most latecomers of the nineteenth century, industrial investment was forthcoming only after vigorous efforts were made by the government to prove its potential and profitability and to eliminate risk. This was not so the case, and could not be the case, with the Industrial Revolution in England. The U.S. bourgeoisie invested in railway development only when it was encouraged by large state subsidies in the form of land giveaways. It appears that Japan's bourgeois sector would have remained commercially oriented in the absence of direct government intervention and would have doomed the nation to industrial backwardness. States in Europe in the nineteenth century were engaged in policies that promoted commerce and industry by providing subsidies to industry and unifying tolls and tariffs.

There is a functional relationship between capitalism and industrial growth. Industrial capitalism is essentially a matter of rising productivity, which generates economic surplus (that is, labor surplus), which is used for further production as the market expands with productivity. Thus, it is different from the previous system of feudal or mercantile capitalism. In a feudal system, economic surplus is created by bringing more resources (land, for example) in production or by legal coercion, which is used for further production as the market expands through productivity, and not as a result of increased productivity of the labor force.

This is also true of the mercantile system, where the accumulation of money capital results from the exchange of goods (i.e., by the transfer of surplus from one individual to the other, indicating no increase in output nationally or globally). On the contrary, in the case of industrial capitalism, the creation of economic surplus is it's life's blood, and is only made possible by raising the productivity of the labor force. It results in an increase in output nationally and globally. True, the system of exploitation of the producers of capital by the owners of capital results in its accumulation in the hands of limited group of owners; nonetheless, it invariably adds to the total output when nationally or globally accounted. The following section shows this process historically.

Collective labor becomes rich in productive power because of the division of labor, which generates capital, while in this process an individual worker uses his or her ability to produce a complete commodity and takes pride in it. According to Marx, in order to make the collective laborer and, through him, capital rich in productive power, each laborer must be made poor in individual productive power. That is how production becomes social production, and naturally, its distribution should also be social. However, in a capitalist ownership system, although production remains social, its distribution is class based. It is also historically true that because of the class ownership of land, the growth of population pressure on the limited supply of land gradually results in the rise of landless peasants or a disguised unemployed sector and becomes a source of cheap surplus labor. This was used by the growing merchant capital in its putting-out system and subsequently by the owners of industrial capital.

Briefly, mercantile trade and the accumulation of money capital were facilitated by the rise of landless peasants or disguised unemployed in the sense that the families of the artisans cum cultivators (working with little division of labor in a family labor–based production system) now can give more time to meet the needs of the putting-out stage of merchant capitalism. With the expansion of the mercantilist putting-out system, which was based on the part-time occupation of family labor in artisanal work and agricultural products, which were scattered all over the villages and towns, the organizing and collection of the final products depended on an uncertainty in supply of definite quantities at a specific time and therefore began to prove expensive. To eliminate this uncertainty and the unnecessary expenses connected with organizing the supply, it was felt to be more convenient and much less expensive to bring the artisans together under one roof. However, in this way, a process began of artisans losing their ownership of the products of their labor and themselves (i.e., their labor becoming commodity eventuated). This is the beginning of the penetration of money capital into production, which becomes completely possible only when, on one hand, there has accumulated a sufficient amount of money capital and, on the other—and more important at that—there is available sufficient labor at a subsistence wage.

The expansion of commerce and rise of a world market in the sixteenth century, and continuing partly in the seventeenth century, brought about the fall of the feudal or precapitalist mode of production and prepared the ground for the emergence of industrial capitalism. Sufficient accumulation of merchant or money capital in this period and the expansion of world market required the abolition of the feudal restriction of factor movements and, thereby, the supply of sufficient surplus labor. Because of the development of merchant capital into the putting-out system, in order to meet its expanding market demand, the general economic quality of life improved, with the effect of causing a decline in the death rate, leading to increased population (i.e., surplus labor). In the United Kingdom, this period was also marked by the enclosures movement (i.e., land reforms), which also pushed up the fertility rate and reduced the mortality rate (see Hudson 1992, 133–35).

However, there is a limit to the expansion of commerce and merchant capitalism, as it is nothing but a "beggar thy neighbor policy." Therefore, owners of money capital transformed the putting-out system by introducing capital in production, that is, by bringing about large-scale production under one roof and turning labor itself into a commodity. The manufactory and the early stage of the extensive phase of organizing labor into large-scale production based on the division of labor emerged.

Knowels (1930, 26), Habbakkuk (1962, 1–10), and others have tried to point out that the world market forms the basis for the capitalist mode of production. This may be true for latecomer countries in the nineteenth and twentieth centuries, but it is in no way true of the country where the Industrial Revolution heralded the rise in industrial capitalism. True, the market played the dominant force in the emergence of industrial capitalism, but this market that stimulated capital accumulation was the latter's own creation, a by-product, which at first is limited to the locality of its origin. This market resulted from the increased output of an increasing amount of labor that was available to be engaged in more productive activities. This created employment and income opportunities for the hitherto disguised unemployed at the subsistence level and the expansion of other industrial and nonindustrial activities. These changes brought about a high population growth rate and thereby, a high labor supply, which helped in the further expansion of the market. Obviously, the availability of cheaper labor and expanding incomes, economic activities, and markets increased the rate of capital accumulation.

However at a later stage (i.e., after about 50 years), the Continental European economies and Britain's vast colonies provided the market that helped with the rapid transition from the extensive phase into the intensive phase of technological change. Modern science began to be used in production, and unlimited possibilities of capitalist production were opened up starting in the late nineteenth century. In the case of the latecomers of the nineteenth century, the world market and the expansion of local markets together were responsible for the introduction of industrial capitalism, although most of these countries were as rich as, if not richer than, England in the possession of merchant capital. In the case of the Third World, the world market has been the only force in the introduction of capitalism, which has remained important in transforming these economies into a full-fledged capitalist systems. An examination of economic structural change will illustrate this. This book uses India as a case study (see Chapter 5).

As soon as manufacture gains sufficient strength (particularly, large-scale industry), it creates, in its turn, a market for itself, which it captures through its commodities (Marx 1967, 3:336). However, Marx did not take note of the fact that the expansion of manufacturing, in those days, created employment for an increasing number of the population and, thus, the market for its products. The expansion of employment in the industrial and service sectors absorbed less productive labor from agriculture, together with a growing urban population (including migrants from Ireland, etc.). The economic history of Britain has plenty of statistics showing this expanding nonagricultural sector (see Table 6.2). At this point, commerce becomes the servant of industrial production, for which continued expansion of the market becomes a vital necessity. This also shows the growth of commercial activities, the development of communications, and government's law and order operations. All these expansions create a market via employment opportunities. "Ever more extended mass production floods the existing market and thereby works continually for a still greater expansion of this market, for breaking out of its limits. What restricts this mass production is not commerce (in so far as it expresses the existing demand), but the magnitude of the productivity of labour" (Marx 1967, 3:336). As long as the production is dependant on the amount of labor (i.e., quantity labor), the magnitude of capital accumulation is expected to be very moderate. (In the United Kingdom, capital formation has constituted only 3 percent of total GNP, even in the later half of the nineteenth century, when its manufacturing products entered into the international market.) Therefore, to raise the rate of capital accumulation (i.e., the profit rate), the productivity of labor needed to be increased and, thus, modern science–based technology gradually replaced the quantity labor–based technology of the extensive phase. The extensive phase of technological change at its initial stage helped bring about a more productive use of labor surplus and prototechnology by bringing them under large-scale production (i.e., the labor that was previously engaged in small-scale household production with little division of labor). Wages were higher than what workers had received as shares of output of the household industry but less than their productivity as workers in an organized large-scale manufactory.

This contention needs explanation. It is true that the introduction of machines does, in the long run, create more opportunities, but this does not occur in cases where technology has become capital intensive and the capital has reached its mature phase. In the nineteenth century, machines were introduced in Western Europe that had been borrowed from England, and after a short while, the introduced machineries created employment opportunities and the integrated development of capitalist and traditional sectors emerged. That was also the basis of the Lewis model (1954). In the case of the United Kingdom, machines were the products of the country's own industrial revolution and, therefore, created simultaneously employment opportunities, as apparent from the tremendous demand for labor during the Industrial Revolution. The rapid economic structural change in the British economy of this period can only be explained by the fact of capitalism's indigenous origin (see Maitra 1986). Hicks wrote: "The English handloom weavers, who were displaced by textile machinery, could find re-employment in England; but what of the Indian weavers who were displaced by the same improvement" (first by the introduction of mill-made textile goods and then by the textile machineries to produce them)? According to Hicks (1969), there is no particular reason why it should be in India. This chapter has briefly discussed the two phases of technological change that came about with the progress of capitalism (change initially confined to local market and then penetrating the world market), which will explain the differing employment effects of introduced technology.

According to Adam Smith (1976), the increase in the productivity of labor is mainly due to the division of labor. One of the factors that raises per capita production is the invention of a great number of machines which facilitate and abridge labour, and enable one man to do the work of many. The invention of machines seems to have been originally owing to the division of labor. Many machines are developed by common workers, whereas numerous other improvements in machines are brought about not by their users but by the ingenuity of the makers of the machine. Adam Smith argued in favor of the free exchange of capital goods and the knowledge embodies in them with the motto, "consumption is the sole purpose of production." Technical progress for Smith is not an extraneous circumstance affecting economic growth but integral to his theory of development.

Ricardo puts the invention of machines on a par with the expansion of international trade and division of labor on the grounds that all three increase the amount of goods and contribute very much to an increase in human happiness. His concern for the common good is again evident in his argument against Malthus: advocacy of the restriction of grain imports because of possible losses of investment in agriculture, when he says that, by the same token, it is wrong to introduce the steam engine and improve the Arkwrights spinning frame on the grounds that the value of the old, clumsy machinery would be lost to us. Malthus (1952) likens land to machinery. Land is a set of machines that is steadily improved but whose productivity falls behind that of industry as the latter is mechanized whereas these machines are merely "gifts of nature." Labor as the main source of development of the machine is ignored. According to Malthus, even the most fertile land can not keep up with the effective demand of an increasing population. This is perfectly true, but what is wrong with the statement is the fact that increased productivity of the labor force and better technology can make a limited land supply increasingly productive. Malthus and Ricardo could not foresee the development of high technology.

The development of capitalism through the main phases into which its history falls has been essentially associated with technical change affecting the character of production, and for this reason, the capitalists associated with each new phase have tended to be, initially at least, a different from the capitalists who had sunk their capital in the older type of production. This was markedly the case in the Industrial Revolution.

With the Industrial Revolution, the change in the structure of industry affected the social relations within the capitalist mode of production: it radically influenced the division of labor; thinned the ranks of the small contracting worker-power type of artisans, the intermediates between the capitalists and the wage earner; and transformed the relation of the workers to the productive process itself (Dobb 1947, 22). We noted this change earlier, with evidence from Hobson's *The Evolution of Modern Capitalism* (1926). This kind of change has serious implications for the future capitalist transformation of an economy.

A capitalist class arose as the creation, not of theft and abstinence, as economists have traditionally depicted it, but of the dispossession of others by dint of economic or political advantage with the sole object of raising the rate of capital accumulation. For capitalism as a system of production to mature, said Marx:

> two very different kinds of commodity possessor must come face to face and into contact; on the one hand, the owners of money, means of production, means of subsistence, who are eager to increase the sum of values they possess by buying other people's labour—power; on the other hand, free labourers, the sellers of their own labour power. With this polarisation of the market for commodities, the fundamental conditions of entry of money capital into production emerge. The capitalist system presupposes the complete separation of the labourers from all property in the means by which they can realise their labour. The so-called primitive accumulation, therefore, is nothing else than the historical process of divorcing the producer from the means of production. The expropriation of the agricultural producer, of the peasant, from the soil is the basis of whole process. (Marx 1961, 737–39)

Primitive accumulation may be defined as the accumulation of surplus labor, along with agricultural surplus and money capital. The Lewis model (A. Lewis 1954, 139–91) of development is based on this concept of using primitive accumulation but lacks in fundamental aspects. In the model, the capitalist sector is transplanted, in the growth of which agriculture makes no contribution and consequently, the mobility of capital to agriculture and of labor from agriculture hardly ever takes place, as the stagnant economic structure of most Third World countries would show even after their rapid and substantial development of capitalist industries (India, for example). So long as capitalism in agriculture itself is undeveloped and agriculture remains primarily peasant agriculture, its exploitation in favor of industry is capable of widening the scope of profitable investment for capital. According to Dobb, in England, however, capitalism in agriculture developed appreciably in the late seventeenth century with the introduction of money capital and later enclosures, which were used to develop industrial capitalism (1947, 95).

Foreign Trade, Money Capital, and Industrial Growth

A striking example of how the fortunes of the foreign trade and foreign loan business during the later period of merchant capitalism rival the growth of industry is afforded by the Netherlands:

Despite the growth of merchant capitalism in this early stronghold of cloth industry, which was at its proto-technology stage, industrial investment in latter centuries
was to mark time; and in the eighteenth century, Holland was to be entirely
eclipsed by England in the progress of capitalist production. The fortunes made
from dealing in foreign stocks seem to have attracted capital and enterprise from
industry. British securities become the chief object of speculation on the Amsterdam Bourse, ousting from this position over Dutch East India companies securities;
and the Dutch capitalist could, merely by making contact with an attorney in London, collect his 5 percent on investments in English funds or by speculation in normal times win up to 20 or 30 percent. (Wilson 1947, 62)

Import and export merchants, whose interests lay in keeping open the door to
foreign products, were powerful enough to prevent the protective tariff policy for
which industry was clamouring (Dobb 1947, 195). It is also noted that the scarcity of labor expressed itself in a relatively high cost of labor, which acted as a
brake on industrial investment.

Wilson wrote: "So far from stimulating Dutch industrial development, Holland's eighteenth century loans almost certainly obstructed and postponed it, directly and indirectly. The attitude of the staplers and their allies the bankers . . .
interfered with the free flow of internal capital, prevented . . . the fertilisation of
industry by Commercial Capital. Dutch economic development was postponed
by a leakage of capital into international finance" (Wilson 1947, 61). Scarcity of
labor in the United Kingdom in the sixteenth and seventeenth centuries, making
it costly, prevented the small-scale factories based on prototechnology from developing into large-scale factories and industrial capitalism. As Dobb concluded,
"the launching of a country on the first stages of road towards capitalism is no
guarantee that it will complete the journey" (Dobb 1947, 195).

In the early days of manufacturing, investment in new industries or the extension of existing industries was evidently hampered by the prevailing notion that
the market for commodities was limited and that new enterprise only stood any
chance of success if either a new market was simultaneously opened abroad or
some political privilege was accorded to enable it to elbow its way successfully
into existing markets at the expense of rivals. For that mood of optimism to be
born that was so essential an ingredient of the pioneering activities of the industrial revolution, the notion of a rigid "vent" for the products of industry and the
commercial timidity essentially connected with it had first to be banished and, to
provide room for the immense growth in the productive powers of industry that
the industrial revolution occasioned, it was essential that an expansion of the
market, larger in dimensions than anything witnessed during the earlier period of
handicraft, should occur. However, until the vast potential of new mechanical age
and of the new division of labor introduced by machinery had become apparent,
it was understandable that even the most enterprising of the bourgeoisie should
look to trade regulation and political privilege for the assurance that the enterprise would prove profitable (Dobb 1947).

The very growth of industrial capitalism develops its own market in two ways:

a. by the investment of profits, it yields to gain further accumulation of capital

b. by creating employment opportunities, as the technological change at that stage involved organizational change to make a more productive use of resources (i.e., surplus labor)

These two developments together result in breaking down the self-sufficiency of natural economics and, thereby, bringing about increasingly a larger number of the population and their wants within the orbit of commodity exchange, capitalist production, and the capitalist production relation. The introduction of capitalism in the Third World today by transplanting investment and production from the center would not have the same effect. Transplanted industrial capitalism does not penetrate into the fabric of society; it remains isolated and the society remains essentially feudal in outlook. India supplies plenty of examples of such a feudal mind today.

The history of industrial growth in the latecomer countries of the twentieth century has, basically, little similarity with the late nineteenth century and early twentieth century latecomers, in the sense that the so-called industrial capital in these economies has trade and the external market as the target, at the cost of local markets. Primitive accumulation of capital combined with highly productive technology from overseas form the basis of industrial growth. Government monetary policy and foreign loans and investment supplied these economies with sufficient money capital which was used to buy real capital or inputs from overseas to produce goods but created little demand for labor. The main target of this kind of industrial growth was an international market designed to increase capital accumulation. Therefore, industrial capitalism in these economies remained very limited and did not create effects of economic structural change or, in other words, capitalist transformation of the economy. Thus, this kind of growth has fundamentally retained its character of commercial capitalism. India is an example (see Chapter 5).

Adam Smith and the others of the classical school regarded the expansion of market as the precondition for the growth of production and investment. They believed that markets grow *pari passu*, with growth of the progress of industry and of division of labor (in other words, expansion of the domestic market) initially. This was the precondition to the growth of industrial capital. Later, however, to earn and maintain the higher rate of accumulation of capital, foreign trade (i.e., the external market) becomes the sole engine of growth of capital. In this process, capitalism, which initially evolved in Britain and later spread to Western Europe, began to penetrate the world market. This necessity led to revolutionary improvements in transport and communication (see Chapter 4).

Capitalism presupposes the existence of landless peasants (i.e., a proletariat). However, the presence of such a class is contingent on a particular set of historical circumstances of the putting-out system under merchant capitalism, land reforms, and population growth. Britain, by the late eighteenth century, did not have any peasant class.

In Britain, the enclosures movement (land reform policy) preceded the industrial revolution and the development of industrial capitalism, whereas in India, land reform policy was introduced long after the penetration of industrial capitalism from abroad. Obviously, the two scenarios have completely different effects and roles to play in subsequent development.

Primitive Accumulation and the Rise of Industrial Capitalism

The concentration of ownership of both money capital and labor, that is, so-called primitive accumulation, inevitably enters into industrial production and industrial capitalism develops over time. Monetary policy and the growth of centralized banking led to the concentration of sources of money capital, while appropriate land reforms and high population growth together became the source of surplus labor. The operation of the putting-out system and waves of enclosures in England resulted in the improvement of living conditions, causing a decline in the death rate. Later, with the expansion of industrial capitalism, came an increased demand for labor which helped maintain a high birth rate. Thus, an increasing supply of cheap surplus labor became available. That is why agricultural surplus as unpaid work or labor services is considered the basis of Industrial capitalism. The former reaches this stage via the rise of the system of payment of rent in money (from rent in kind of the natural economy) to money capital of the mercantile period. However, the ultimate transformation into the industrial capital needs the fulfillment of one vital condition (i.e., a sufficient supply of surplus labor).

The increased supply of precious metals since the sixteenth century supplied "an essential factor in the development of capitalist production and hence, the need for quantity of money sufficient for the circulation and the corresponding formation of a hoard and . . . this must not be interpreted in the sense that a sufficient hoard must first be formed before capitalist production can be high. It rather developes simultaneously" (Marx 1933, 2:396). Lewis (1954), in his model, laid emphasis on credit creation to monetize economic activities so that the mobilization and transformation of resources into capital formation can materialize.

Dobb made an important point here. The appearance of a reserve army of labour as a source of the rise of capitalist system was a simple product of growing population, which created more hands than could be given employment in existing occupations, and more mouths than could be fed from the then cultivated soil. Therefore, the historic function of capital was to endow this army of re-dundant hands with the benefit of employment (Dobb 1947, 150–55).

Capital in production evolves from labor rent (it is an appropriation of labor through institutional coercion) through rent in kind (which is contractual), to money rent (the coercion is exercised through legal and merchant price relations), characterizing feudal production relation. At this stage, money capital emerges with the rise of merchant capitalism, which culminates into reproducible capital with the rise of industrial capitalism. One basic condition needed to be fulfilled for the rise of industrial capitalism, that is, of sufficient supply and growth of surplus labor. With the progress of industrial capitalism (i.e., with the progress of the production of reproducible capital), the economy undergoes rapid capitalist transformation.

I will discuss briefly the process of penetration of money capital into production, which gives rise to industrial capitalism. Money capital or merchant capital, even when there is a huge accumulation, cannot automatically be transformed into industrial capital. It has been noted by economic historians that the feudal constitution and the guild organization prevented the development of money capital formed by means of usury and commerce (i.e., mercantile capital) into industrial capital. This eventually happened when the economic conditions for this transformation matured in the economy, that is, only when a sufficient accumulation of money capital is accompanied by the growth of surplus labor adequate enough for the penetration of money capital in production. The preconditions appeared to be indispensable in this development.

1. Land reforms to do away with restrictive feudal regulations (for the development of industrial capital, so that surplus labor could be made available). In England, enclosures played this role.

2. Land reforms must be accompanied by a sustained and high rate of growth of population. Again, in England at the time, population was growing at a rate unprecedented in history. The development of the putting-out system and prototechnology absorbing surplus labor, as well as the land reforms (enclosures), had favorable effects on fertility, raising its rate, and negative effects on mortality, reducing its rate due to the availability of better food and so forth.

In my view, a slowly growing population for some time weakened the feudal system and helped the rise and expansion of mercantile capitalism with small-scale cottage industries, which, together with the progress of enclosures, began to improve living conditions and thus stimulated a sustained population growth. This latest development signaled the transformation.

It is also claimed in textbook economics that capital results from savings, that is, from surplus over consumption. This is a non-Marxist definition. Obviously, in this definition, the existence of income inequality or class distinction is as-sumed, in the sense that the upper-income group has income in excess of its con-sumption and a higher propensity and ability to save. Poorer people seldom have income in excess over subsistence in the preindustrial phase. When this surplus over consumption is used (i.e., invested for raising production and productivity of the factors of production), it is turned into physical capital. In this process of turning surplus into physical capital, money capital plays the role of a catalyst in a free market, laissez-faire system. Money is the medium of exchange of prod-ucts of different factors. Labor is paid wage in money for the labor it sells to cap-ital owners, who earn profit for the sacrifice of immediate consumption.

During the period of mercantile capitalism, the merchant owns the surplus that results from the exchange of goods and not from an increase in productivity of the factor of labor. Merchant capital at this early stage had a purely external rela-tionship to the mode of production, which remained independent of, and un-touched by, capital, the merchant being merely the person who "removes" the goods produced by the guilds or the "peasants," in order to gain from price dif-ferences between different productive areas. This is the way the actual producers (i.e., artisans and peasants) were deprived of their surplus. At this stage, however, workers sell the products of their labor, while at the capitalist stage, they sell their labor and thus labor becomes the commodity. The market determines its price. Merchant capitalism, pure and simple, emerges only when merchant be-gins to fasten upon the mode of production, partly in order to exploit the latter more effectively, to impoverish the condition of the direct producers and thereby appropriate their surplus labor on the basis of the old mode of production. That is merchant capitalism, true and simple. However, in the course of time and in the interests of greater profit, its transformation process in this old system followed two main roads:

1. A section of the producers themselves accumulated capital, took to trade, and in course of time, began to organize production on a capitalist basis, free from the guild's restrictions on handicrafts.
2. A section of the existing merchant class began to take over direct control of production and thereby serving historically as a mode of production but eventually becoming a hindrance to a real capitalist mode of production and declining with the development of the latter (Marx 1967, 3:388–96).

Dobb in his work attempted to present a review of the concept of capitalism as defined by different authors since its inception (Dobb 1947, esp. ch. 1).

Some economists tried to identify capitalism with a system of unfettered indi-vidual enterprise. It is a system where contracts rule social and economic rela-tions, unlike in the feudal system. In this system men and women are free agents in seeking their livelihood, and legal compulsions and restrictions are absent. The free mobility of factory labor and capital is the key to the rise and expansion of industrial capitalism. "True Capitalism means an economy of free and fair competition for profit and continuous work opportunity for all" (Cromwell and Czerwankky 1947, 5). Thus, capitalism has been synonymous with a regime of laissez-faire free enterprise and free competition as well as an ultimate stage of social and economic development. Another term that has been used to signify a capitalist economy is the rule of individualism, which naturally follows.

Dobb referred to three separate meanings of the notion of capitalism, which exercised a major influence on historical research and historical interpretation of the term. Each of these three meanings results in a different causal story of the origin of capitalism and the development of the modern world.

First, Dobb mentioned Sombart's view of the essence of capitalism:

> Thus, according to him, the pre-capitalist man was a "natural man" who conceived of economic activity as simply catering for his natural wants. In pre-capitalist days, man was at the centre of all effort and all care. He was the measure of all things. But at this stage, man did not have ability neither any motivation to unveil the mysteries of nature and to unleash the unlimited natural force to enrich human society materially and in consciousness. On the contrary, the capitalist root up the natural man with his primitive and original outlook, and turn topsy-turvy all the values of life. To the capitalist the amassing of capital is the dominant motive behind economic activity and by the methods of precise quantitative calculation subordinates everything in his life to this end. To raise the rate of accumulation of capital that results from the increased productivity of labour is the aim of industrial capitalism. (W. Sombart, *Der Moderne Kapitalismus*, cited in Dobb 1947, 5)

According to Max Weber, "capitalism is present whenever the industrial provision for the needs of a human group is carried out by the method of enterprise, which is a rational capitalist establishment with capital accounting seeking profit rationally and systematically" (1961, 275).

Second, there are works that identify capitalism with the organization of production for a distant market. Market is the key to the dynamism of capitalism. However, in this definition, no distinction has been made between mercantile capitalism and industrial capitalism, and it is the latter phase of capitalism that really matters for the analysis of the dynamic development of modern economies. This definition does not include the era of the early craft guild, when the craftsman sold his products retail in the town market. While according to this definition, capitalism could be regarded as present when the acts of production and of retail sale came to be separated in space and time by the intervention of a wholesale merchant who advanced money for the purchase of wares, with the object of subsequent sale at profit. The German historical school developed this notion later, making a distinction between the natural economy of the medieval world and the money economy that succeeded it. This school laid an emphasis on the market as defining the stages in the growth of modern capitalist world (Dobb 1947, 6).

Capitalism has also been defined as a system in which some sectors of the population are engaged in making profit through the transaction of goods between producers and consumers. A certain type of profit motive characterizes the capitalist system. This is a system consisting of a substantial number of persons who rely on the investment of money, whether in trade or in production, to earn an income. P. Earl Hamilton defined it as the system in which wealth other than land is used for the definite purpose of servicing an income (1929, 339). Another author defined capitalism as "a system of exchange economy" in which the orienting principle of economic activity is "unrestricted profit" and, as an additional characteristic of the system, the author mentioned the differentiation of the population between owners and property-less workers (Nussbaum 61, cited in Dobb 1947, 6–7).

In these definitions, no attempt has been made to distinguish capital from capitalism and capitalism from capitalist transformation. Capital, pure and simple, is economic surplus produced by human labor, and when it is owned by a class of people who do not contribute to it, it becomes a capitalist system, whereas when this surplus is owned by society and used directly for social welfare, it becomes socialism. We should not forget that capital is also the vital factor in a socialist system.

In these definitions, a superficial appearance of capitalism and its functions have been presented without making any attempts to prove into the interrelationship of different factors lying behind the rise of capitalist production nor the historical process of the rise of the industrial capitalism. These definitions are silent about the effects of capitalism on the society and economy (that is, its effects of the demographic and technological changes, human resource development, economic structural change, etc.). To understand capitalism and its limits, it is essential to have a thorough understanding of these effects. Capitalism is essentially a social phenomenon involving the whole fabric of a society.

Third, according to Marx's definition of capitalism, it is a system under which labor power has itself become a commodity and, thus, capitalism is not simply a system of production for the market. Prior to capitalism, labor sold its products in the market, but now, under the capitalist system, labor itself has become a commodity sold in the market. The worker no longer owns product of his labor. He can sell only his labor and, as in following Marx, it may be defined as a system of commodity production. The concentration of ownership of the means of production in the hands of a class who has made no contribution to production on the one hand, and the consequential emergence of a class that has only its labor power to sell to the former class as the only source of livelihood, characterize the capitalist system of production. Productive activity is contributed by the worker, not by virtue of legal compulsion, as under feudal system, but on the basis of the wage contract. In this system, labor is considered equally with capital as a factor of production. The contribution of each factor is valued by the market forces. That is how apologists for the capitalist system define it. Under the merchant capital system, an artisan or a peasant sold his products to the merchant, who made a profit by selling the same product in markets near and far, at a price higher than he had paid to the artisans and peasants, the producers of the commodity. Thus, the merchant's profit is the result not of increased productivity of labor but of favorable market conditions. However, the capitalists' profit results from the increased productivity of labor, ownership of which now belongs to the capitalist. Thus, the definition above excludes the system of independent handicraft production where the craftsman owned his own petty implements of production, carried out production with the members of his family, undertook the sale of his own products and shares with members of his family (sometimes with the help of hired neighbors), and obtained the returns from the sales. There was no divorce between ownership and work. Capitalism is characterized by this divorce, which implies that the owners of capital must use its power to hire labor power in order to create surplus value in production for themselves. Last, capitalism has been defined as a system in which owners of inputs of production (that is, capital and labor) are clearly distinguished and output is apportioned to each factor according to the marginal contribution. This definition does not consider the fact that the real capital is the product of labor while the source of physical capital (i.e., the past accumulation of surplus, or savings) belongs to the owners of capital because they were the owners of money capital, with which they brought the labor of producers of capital. Under capitalism, the class system creates this class of appropriators of surplus value for capital. Under the feudal system or the mercantile capitalist system, surplus value exists but belongs to a class that did not use it for further production but for conspicuous consumption with the surplus resource.

Later, Lipson (1931), Cunningham (1916), and others tried to define capitalism in this sense. That is, the fundamental feature of capitalism is the rise of the wage system, under which a worker has no right to own the fruits of his labor, while his employer owns the materials and the labor.

In these definitions, the rise and the role of capital and capitalism have not been differentiated. Capital results from economic surplus produced by labor but appropriated by owners of capital. It thus becomes the source of economic growth, having been produced socially by human labor. When it is owned in a system by those who do not produce it and is used to increase the profits or capital accumulation for the use of owners, we call this system the capitalist system. When capital, that is the economic surplus, is produced socially by the working class, owned by it socially, and used for the interest of the society of the working class, we term it socialism.

In other words, the use of capital depends on the socioeconomic relationships that generate economic surplus and use it to fulfill that relationship. During the

period of the feudal system, there existed economic surplus which was appropriated by the landowning classes (who never contributed to the output). The merchants used the fruits of labor of craftsmen and made profits through exchange
without making any contribution to the production of surplus. The industrial capitalist system has played an important role in the accumulation of economic surplus or capital by making it always productive, in search of a higher rate of accumulation, although the actual production of this surplus was the product of
workers' labor power. Profit motives in a capitalist society help develop social
consciousness and sharpen the contradiction between the actual producers and
the owners of the production. According to Dobb, in the history of production in
a class-based society there is a relationship with a particular mode of extracting
and distributing the fruits of surplus labors over and above the labor that goes to
the supply of the consumption of the actual labor. Since this surplus labor constitutes its lifeblood, the ruling class will of necessity treat its particular relationship to the labor process as crucial to its own survival; any ruling class that as-
pires to live without labor is bound to regard its own future affluence, prosperity,
and influence as dependent on the acquisition of some claim on the surplus labor
of others (Dobb 1947, 15).
   Engles wrote:

> A surplus of the product of labour over and above the costs of maintenance of the
> labour and the formation and enlargement, by means of this surplus, of a social
> production and reserve fund, was and is the basis of all social, political and intel-
> lectual progress. In history up to the present, this fund has been the possession of a
> privileged class on which also developed, along with this possession, political su-
> premacy and intellectual leadership. (1955, 221)

Marx spoke of Capitalism itself as being:

> like any other definite mode of production conditioned upon a certain stage of so-
> cial productivity and upon the historically developed form of the productive forces.
> This historical prerequisite is itself the historical result and product of a proceeding
> process, from which the new mode of production takes its departure from its given
> foundation. The conditions of production corresponding to this specific, historical-
> ly determined, mode of production have a specific historical passing character.
> (1967, 3:1023–24)

According to Dobb, at a certain stage of social development when the productivity of labor is very low, any substantial and regular income for a leisured class
that lives on production but does not contribute thereto will be inconceivable un-
less it is grounded in the rigorous compulsion of producers. That is why in the
period of primitive communism, there existed no class system. With the growth
of population, the development of class system occurred when the increased
quantity of labor made possible the production of surplus.

LABOR SHORTAGES—PREINDUSTRIAL PERIOD
(FACTS AND INTERPRETATIONS)

This section uses a few facts and their interpretations by two eminent authors in support of the theme of the book. In the preindustrial days (i.e., in the seventeenth century and earlier) it was not expected that the proletariat would constitute any recognizable part of the population. Labor displacing capital or machinery did not arrive, and neither its presence was expected. In England, enclosures were at a very early stage and therefore had little effect in this respect. Population growth was low and sometimes negative, and thus was limited. Mobility at the same time was limited due to feudal restrictions designed to keep the labor supply steady for the interests of the feudal lords, so that they could have a cheaper supply of labor at their beck and call. A lack of easy transport and communication facilities also hampered the mobility of labor. Labor shortages in those days severely affected agriculture. It was reported that at times during the fifteenth and seventeenth centuries, the deficiency of labor for hire was most noticeable, while at the time of exceptional demands for manpower, special measures were taken such as the impressment of labor. "The most dreaded result, if the demand for hands should outrun the supply, was a rise in wages" (Dobb 1947, 231). History has recorded the fact of the alarming labor shortage that followed the Black Death, which led to the passing of laws fixing maximum wages to protect the interests of landowners, with conditions of rigorous penalties, not only to any concerted attempt by laborers and artisans to better the conditions of their employment, but even to the acceptance by a worker of any higher wages than were statutarily ordained. Any person under 60, whether of villein status or free, if found without any independent means of support could be compelled to work at the prescribed wage. Examples of this kind of labor shortages in France and the Netherlands are many (Dobb 1947, 235–39). Mandel (1968) in his work also referred to the labor shortage in those days.

In the seventeenth century, however, to stem the tide of rural exodus, legislation was passed imposing a fine on clothiers "who would not pay so much or so great wages . . . as shall be appointed" and forbidding master clothiers to serve as magistrates on any bench that was concerned with fixing wages in their own trade (Dobb 1947, 231). This marked a period when rapid inflation had reduced real wages, thus making the other wage limits meaningless, causing rural exodus, and thereby threatening the real balance between agriculture and industry. Interestingly, this was happening at a time when the number of the landless and destitute had grown sufficiently large to cause danger of rising real wages. According to Dobb, statutory minimum wage limits had little effect in protecting laborers against a worsening of their condition, due to an unchanged statutory scale of money wages juxtaposed with the rising cost of living. One author reported:

From 1563, to 1824, a conspiracy concocted by the law and carried out by parties interested in its success, was entered into, to cheat the English workman of his wages, to tie him to the soil, to deprive him of hope and to degrade him into irremediable poverty. For more than two and a half centuries, the English law, and those who administered the law, were engaged grinding the English workman down to the lowest pittance" (T. Rogers in Dobb 1947, 233).

This is a stage that provided the scope to the preindustrial capitalist to accumulate savings. However, a growing accumulation of savings in money capital is not a sufficient condition for its development into industrial capital.

This was the process of accumulation of economic surplus in the days of cottage industries and prototechnology. Throughout this period, compulsion to labor stood in the background of the labor market. Tudor legislation provided compulsory work for the unemployed, as well as making unemployment an offense punishable with characteristic brutality. Enclosure in the later period needed more labor, and in those days, agricultural machinery was more labor absorbing and, leading to the demand for labor in agriculture, especially at the initial stage.

"The number of small farms absorbed into larger ones between 1740 and 1785 [stood] at an average of 4 or 5 in each parish, which brings the total to 40 or 50 thousand in the whole kingdom" (Mantaux 1928, 177). The pace of enclosure throwing small farmers off the land went rapidly during the eighteenth century and the first half of the nineteenth in as many as 14 counties, while the percentage of acres enclosed by acts enclosing common field and some waste rose as high as 25 percent to 50 percent. In the later period, the total amount of land enclosed was some eight or nine times as large as that involved in the earlier period and embraced about one-fifth of the total average of the country (Dobb 1947, 227).

Moreover, in addition to forcible eviction, many smallholders were burdened by debts or, in the later eighteenth and early nineteenth centuries, cut off from their traditional employment in the cottage industry or adversely affected by the growing competition of larger farms. These were equipped with new agricultural methods requiring capital; therefore, smallholders had to surrender their holdings to the more well-to-do peasants or to some improving landlord without any explicit act of eviction. In regard to leases, there was evidently a widespread tendency for landlords to encourage a few large tenancies in preference to a larger number of small ones. This increased the supply of labor. In this process, a more productive use of land and labor was made possible and the ground for the future mechanization of agriculture was prepared.

According to Habakkuk (1937), "There was a very remarkable consolidation of estates and a shrinking in the number of the smaller owners somewhere between the beginning of the seventeenth century and the year 1785" (cited in Dobb 1947, 228). Dobb noted Lavorsky's study of parishes that were not enclosed in 1793, which led him to conclude that "the independent peasantry had already ceased to exist, even in unenclosed parishes, by the end of the eighteenth century" (1947, 228n). There had been apparently a growth both of the Kulak peasant and of the poorest small holders, but the middle peasantry "had become relatively insignificant" (Dobb 1947, 228).

The old system of the great feudal open fields gradually disappeared, and those that still existed by the time of the Industrial Revolution were swept away in a final wave of parliamentary enclosure acts. Economically, it was important that improvements in farm output were secured through low capital–consuming technologies and that agricultural production should not be adversely affected by contractions in the farm labor supply. Collins wrote:

> The First and most obvious shift was to utilise more fully the local labour pool. In the post Napoleonic War decades farmers were usually able to buy the services of local tradesmen, workers in household industry and the wives and children of employees at relatively low cost. Technological change when it appeared, first took the form not of mechanisation but of a switch from lower into higher working capacity hand tools. Thus more often the scythe supersceded the traditional toothed sickle and smooth reap hook as the standard corn harvesting tools. (1969, 74)

The enclosing of common waste land was done both to create "new" arable land by improved methods of clearing and draining and to facilitate animal husbandry and the raising of livestock. Initially, these new and better tools and methods required more labor and made possible its more productive use.

Rising productivity in agriculture raised the demand for nonagricultural goods and created a demand for labor. Hughes wrote: "Apart from London, it now appears that migration from the English countryside added proportionately little to the population of the new industrial towns. Most of the growth in population was due to natural increase and marginally migration from Ireland" (1970, 37). This account points to the fact that the labor shortage in those days, relative to demand, caused the danger of high wages, on one hand, while on the other, the remnants of the feudal system were acting as a hindrance to the mobility of labor, and thereby to the supply of labor for industrial activities.

According to Dobb, it is a familiar fact that during the two centuries of labor scarcity prior to the events of Tudor age, real wages in England rose considerably. However, soon this movement reversed, and what wage earners had achieved over two centuries, they were to lose within a century. The final wave of enclosures and the slow but sustained rate of population growth began to ease the situation of the labor shortage. There was no "peasant question" to wrack English social life in the late nineteenth century as agricultural wage laborers, even poor ones, were not peasants (Hughes 1970, 37). The formation of the proletariat thus emerged and played its role in the growth of industrial capitalism through the three main stages (e.g., from ground or labor rent to money rent and then to money capital, with the development of merchant capital, and from money capital to industrial capital when the sustained supply of sufficient labor became a reality). The rise of money or merchant capital, however, does not guarantee its evolution into industrial capital, which requires the backing of a sustained supply of labor.

Agricultural surplus product forms the basis of all surplus and, therefore, of industrial capital. That is why when, in England, the more powerful waves of enclosures in the late eighteenth century led to the introduction of large-scale agriculture, a supply of agricultural surplus in the form of surplus labor and their subsistence needs began to introduce capitalism in agriculture. This measure resulted in a supply of labor and a lowering of wages, dislodging as it did the army of cottagers from their last, weak hold on the fringes of the commons. Numerous small properties in land were replaced by a few large ones, which released the hitherto underutilized potential of peasants to be used more productively, and at a lower cost, forming the basis of industrial capital. However, this is only half the explanation. The other half involves the rise of population, resulting in an increasing labor surplus to be mobilized with the money capital to build industrial capital. That explained why the Industrial Revolution emerged in England, and not anywhere else like the Netherlands (an economy richer with merchant capital and accumulation of valuable metals, etc., than England but not so rich in supply of labor).

Kuznets's hypothesis of agriculture's three contributions (which was extended later to four by adding foreign exchange contribution) and the Lewis model of the development of the labor surplus economy may be supported with the help of this historial development, with the difference in that Kuznets's factor contribution (1964) in terms of labor and Lewis's (1954) explanation about labor absorption in the industrial sector, leading to a turning point in agriculture, have not materialized in India, or in most Third World economies, for that matter. Nature and sources of technological change (highly capital-intensive ones, due to the maturity of capitalism in the West, which is the source) have made this difference.

Several economists have regarded the so-called price revolution as a powerful stimulus to the transition from medieval to modern capitalist development. The influx of gold and silver from America to Europe in sixteenth and seventeenth centuries has been mentioned as the greatest influence that the discovery of America had upon the progress of capitalism. Thus, the supply of real surplus, combined with precious metals, formed the basis of merchant capital and its operations. However, there were countries in Europe that were richer in the accumulation of merchant capital than Britain. The new supply of money was at its maximum from 1585 to 1630. In Spain, the price revolution, led to a fall in real wages in the first half of the sixteenth century, but later, real wages rose and by 1620, they were higher than they had been in 1500. In Britain, real wages, on the contrary, declined throughout the sixteenth century and remained throughout the seventeenth century below the level of 1500 (E. Mandel 1968, 110–11). Differences in population growth and trends in land reforms in England account for this.

In England and other parts of Europe, including Spain, the Netherlands, Germany, Belgium, and France, the growth of commerce and the merchant capital accumulation of precious metals with an increasing supply of real surplus marked the period from 1500 to 1700 (i.e., just on the eve of the agricultural revolution in England, which spurred the industrial capitalism and the Industrial Revolution).

To evolve into industrial capitalism, that is, to inaugurate the era of capitalist production, under these circumstances, required an increasing supply of primitive accumulation of surplus in the form of labor or the growth of the proletariat in addition to money capital and real surpluses. In England in the eighteenth century, a more powerful new wave of enclosures created a favorable condition in this respect (i.e., by dislodging the army of cottagers) and thereby caused a further decline in real wages in the late eighteenth century (1760s–1800). However, what was more important part was that England began to enjoy a tremendous and sustained rate of growth of population since the mid-eighteenth century, which, as a matter of fact, was a source of growth of the proletariat acted as the catalyst for the development of Industrial capitalism (see Tables 1.1–1.3). This critical situation distinguishes England from the other European countries. The growth of agriculture and cottage industries as subsidiary employment improved living conditions therefore led to a fall in death rate. Thus, a rise in population growth rate ensued, which soon was accompanied by an increasing demand for labor along with the rise of Industrial capitalism. This later development helped maintaining the high fertility rate of the past (see Chapter 6). Besides, it was also a period when other reasons for a swelling labor reserve were most in evidence; for example, the death of the peasantry as a class and the demise of the handicraft trades. It was certainly the case, as some writers have emphasized, that once industrial capitalism was firmly established, its growing need of labor power was supplied in the main by the natural rate of increase of the proletariat (its own powers of reproduction). For example, during the nineteenth century, the population of Europe increased by nearly two and a half times. However, over the three centuries in which capitalist industry was gaining a foothold (between the mid-fourteenth century and the time of Gregory King's estimate), the population of England probably grew by no more than 2 million, from 3.5 to 5.5 million i.e. a very low rate of growth of population led to a slow growth of industrial capitalist production.

The factors responsible for the growing army of the destitute in England in the century that followed the Battle of Bosworth are as follows: the disbanding of feudal retainers, the dissolution of the monasteries, the enclosures of land for sheep farming, and changes in methods of tillage each played its part. Between

1455 and 1637, the number thrown out of employment was between 30,000 and 40,000 (Johnson, 58; c.f. Dobb 1047, 224–25). "A figure of 50,000 [is] the number directly made destitute by the dissolution of the monasteries" (Rogers, 8; c.f. Dobb 1947, 225).

The total may seem small today but as a proportion to the demand for hired labor at that time, it was substantial. However, for a century following the Restoration, complaints of labor shortage abound, and the weak development of the proletarian class at this point must have exerted a retarding influence upon the further growth of the industrial investment between the last of the Stuarts and the closing years of George III (Dobb 1047, 226–27). Mandel's *Marxist Economic Theory* (1968), regarded as another pioneering work on the development of capitalism, has dealt with this problem of supply of labor during the preindustrial days in the West. A brief summary of his study is given below.

Mandel (1968, 114–15) wrote about the seventeenth-century condition of labor supply in Continental Europe, particularly Italy and the Netherlands. Preindustrial manufacturing made it possible to subdivide each craft and each production process into an infinite number of labor operations. This process of division of labor served, at one and the same time, to increase output and the number of finished products completed in a given period of time. The labor shortage condition of the period was expected to raise the cost of production, but the solution to this problem was found in the availability of a labor force of women, children, sick and old persons, and even the mentally ill. The labor force was largely composed of those people, particularly in the manufacture of textiles. This was also applicable to Britain in the sixteenth and early seventeenth centuries.

Mandel wrote: "The utmost brutality, together with an amazing hypocrisy, were normally employed to compel these unfortunates to furnish a cheap supply of labour to young manufacturing capital" (1968, 115). In a Floretine woollen industry, where the wage earner was tied to his employer by debts, a whole set of laws was introduced in order to compel him to do overtime. He was, in particular, forbidden by a law of 1371 to repay his debt in money; he had to do this in the form of work (Mandel 1968, 115n). In 1721, it was decided to set up a cloth manufactory in Graz; in order to provide the necessary labor force, a suitable number of persons had to be "caught and locked up" from among the beggars who crowded the streets of the town. Sombart (1928, 814–17, in Manod 1968, 116) quotes numerous examples of the state's compelling the population to carry out veritable forced labor in manufactories. Because of the labor shortage, these manufactures could not graduate into industrial manufacture. Only in England, enclosures and the accompanying demographic change gradually made possible the supply of an adequate number of hands for the growth of industrial production. Mandel's comments (1968, 122) on India, China, and Japan, that the competition of cheap labor due to "considerable growth of population" prevented, for thousands of years, any attempt to introduce machinery into the crafts, cannot be supported by historical facts and economic reasonings. We have already taken note of the population growth in China and India in those days, which was low compared to the West. In terms of economic reasoning, if China or India had a high population growth, it would have been easier for either of these economies to transform their proverbially rich prototechnology into industrial capital (see Chapter 5 for a detailed analysis). In those days, quantity labor was the only effective factor of production (see also Chapters 1 and 2).

3

ECONOMIC STRUCTURAL CHANGE AND CAPITALIST TRANSFORMATION

For developed capitalist economies, since the works of Fisher (1939) and Clark (1957), economic activity has often been classified along structural lines into agricultural, industrial, and service sectors (or primary, secondary, and tertiary sectors). It has been argued that the roles of these sectors change with the level of development. This book argues that this change indicates the dynamicity in sectoral allocation of the labor force to meet the requirements of increasing capital accumulation and technological change so that a higher rate of return from investment of resources may be realized. Capitalist development of an economy is expected to bring about these changes in economic structure. The need for an increasing capital accumulation stimulates economic structural change, which in its turn generates the process of capitalist transformation of the economy. This process takes the form of dynamic changes in sectoral distribution of the labor force and, thereby, induces a demographic transition and introduces wage labor (see, for detailed discussion, Chapter 6).

All developed capitalist economies have undergone this process of transformation, but not the developing countries (despite the remarkable growth in capital accumulation and increasingly diversified industrial growth, which is unlike what happened in the developed countries at the comparable period of their capitalist development (see Bairoch 1976, chs. 9, 10). Today, the capitalist development of the Western economies, with increasing capital accumulation and dynamic economic structural change, has resulted in the present dominance of the service sector in the place of the primary sector, as at the early stage of the Industrial Revolution (followed by the preponderance of the secondary sector since about the 1850s). With the progress of the Industrial Revolution and the advancement of capitalism, agricultural dominance gave way to the dominance of the industrial sector between the mid-nineteenth and twentieth centuries, which in due course began to relinquish its leadership to the service sector.

Thus, the agricultural society first became the industrial one, which soon evolved into the postindustrial one of today. This can be easily understood with the help of data showing the transition over the last 200 years (see Tables 6.1–6.5). This has been the course of development in all developed capitalist countries, but in the cases of the latecomers of the nineteenth century (e.g., in the Continental Europe and Japan), the dominance of the agricultural sector continued longer than in the countries of the Industrial Revolution (see Maitra 1980). However, this process of historical development has not happened in most Third World countries in general and in India in particular, despite the fact that these economies have achieved tremendous growth in capital accumulation as a proportion to their GDP, as well as in industrial production and its diversification. South Korea and the other three South Asian countries, Singapore, Hong Kong and Taiwan, are today called newly industrialized economies. We will exclude the latter three countries from our consideration because if we take them historically as parts of their mother countries, China and Malaysia, then they have done no better than Calcutta, Bombay, Kualalampore, or Brasillia. True, South Korea has 26 percent of its labor force in agriculture, contributing only 14 percent of GDP (*World Development Report* 1948), with over $3,000 per capita income, while most latecomers of the nineteenth century had a much smaller proportion of their labor force in agriculture and a much larger proportion in industry, with less per capita income. These differences in economic structural changes could be explained by taking into account the sources and phases of technological change when it is transferred.

The extensive phase of the capitalist mode of production began its triumphal march with the development of coal, iron, and steel industries, which gave rise to, first, the most important consumption of manufacture of the period, cotton textiles (from the early 1800s), followed by the basic transport industry, railways, in 1825. This development of energy, basic and heavy industries, consumption goods industries, and transport services was further facilitated by a rapid extension of cheap transport services binding whole countries through networks of railways. Markets for products of industries and agriculture got a tremendous boost, and the demand for labor by various nonagricultural activities increased, breaking down the feudal structure.

> By closely linking town and country, this new development of transport industry facilitated the penetration of commodities produced at low prices by big factories into the remotest corners of all countries. At the same time, the building of rail transportation constituted the chief market for the products of heavy industry (coal,

iron and steel, metal, etc.) first in Great Britain, then on the continent, later in America and throughout the world. (Mandel 1967, 119)

This development also helped enormously in the mobility of labor force, to the advantage of entrepreneurs. This progress has brought about gradual economic structural change by drawing the labor force into the capitalist industrial sector and thereby causing capitalist transformations of agriculture. This process has been defined in economics development textbooks as the turning point—the point at which wage or factor labor prices are paid according to the marginal product of labor ensuring profit or capital accumulation, which is to be reinvested subsequently. In the precapitalist days, workers were paid according to the average product of labor, that is, under noncapitalist family labor production, all members of the family share the output in terms of clothing, shelter, and foods, after what is left as payment to landlords. The textbook analysis says that the rate of capital accumulation rises with the increasing profit proportion of the firm, or national income; profit did not accrue during the precapitalist stage, when rental income was the predominant factor income and the rest was meant for subsistence, while the merchant's income was his profit, which was essentially a rental income that accrues as a result of supply scarcity. Household production aimed at maximizing subsistence living, while capitalist production aims at maximizing profit and thereby, capital accumulation. Mandell wrote:

> Under petty commodity production the producer, master of his means of production and his products, can live only by selling these products of his labour in order to acquire the means of life. Under capitalist production, the producer separated from his means of product is no longer the master of products of his own labour and can service by selling only his labour.

Thus, he has lost ownership of the means of production produced by his labor; on the contrary, he himself became the commodity as he sells his own labor power in exchange for a wage, which he uses to buy these products of his own labor at much reduced quantity. In other words, the surplus he produces takes the form of profit, reinforcing the growth, or increase, of capital in the hands of the owner. These two simultaneous transformation phenomena have occurred from the late eighteenth century onward mainly in Britain, but later in Western Europe. This process is marked by two parallel phenomena: on the one hand, the transformation of labor power into a commodity, and on the other hand, the transformation of the means of production into capital. The logical culmination of this dual process of transformation is the capitalist transformation of the entire society and economy. These two processes of transformation invariably bring about structural change in terms of shifting subsistence labor that was engaged in production of the primary needs to labor designed to transform the means of production into capital and, thereby, transforming itself into a commodity. When this

TABLE 3.1 Five Countries' Agricultural Employment as a Proportion of Total Employment (Percentages)

Country	Year	Proportion
England and Wales	1841	24
	1861	19
	1881	12
	1901	9
	1950	5
	1962	4
	1973	3
France	1788	75
	1845	62
	1866	52
	1886	48
	1906	43
	1926	39
	1951	27
	1962	20
	1973	12
Japan	1877-82	83
	1887-92	76
	1897-1902	70
	1907-12	63
	1920	54
	1940	42
	1953	42
	1962	30
	1973	13
India	1960	74
	1965	73
	1981	69
	1983	70
China	1952	83.5
	1957	81.2
	1968	81.7
	1978	70.7
	1987	60.1
	1990	60.0

Sources: Kuznets (1957, 1971); Table 3.5; Jia (1992).

transformation begins to take place, a rising rate of capital accumulation brings about a dynamic transformation of the entire economic structure and, thereby, transformation of feudal social consciousness into a humanistic or secular social consciousness (see Table 3.1).

Capitalist transformation of an economy needs production to be based on science, so that output can be increased and diversified at a diminishing cost (i.e., a diminishing rate of labor, and thereby, raising the rate of capital accumulation). Increased productivity with a reduced quantity of labor ensures the increasing rate of capital accumulation. This is what all developed capitalist countries have shown throughout their long history of capitalism. In the Third World countries, the process of transformation has been half-baked, which negates in reality the capitalist transformation of their economies and the transformation of their pre-capitalist social minds. I will discuss this aspect in terms of effects of capitalist development, demographic change, development of human capital, and economic structural change in later chapters.

Marx was essentially concerned with the concept of capital, the rise and development of the capitalist mode of production, and how it reaches its maturity, with its effects on technological change and labor power. In his analysis, Marx emphasized the economic mode to generate economic surplus as the source of capital accumulation with profit. Bourgeois economists today also are similarly concerned with the growth of capital and profit, but unlike Marx, also focus on the growth in productivity and diversity in production as the source of profit and, thereby, capital accumulation.

ECONOMIC STRUCTURAL CHANGE, CAPITALIST TRANSFORMATION, AND TECHNOLOGICAL CHANGE: THEORIES AND MODELS

By economic structural change is meant the transfer of resources between the three sectors—the primary (agriculture), the secondary (industry), and the tertiary (services)—so as to alter their percentage shares of employment and output. It is common knowledge that with the growth of the economy, an increase in agricultural productivity begins to take place, resulting from the increased use of capital in agriculture, on the one hand. On the other, with the rise in income resulting from growth, income elasticity of demand for food and, later raw materials gradually tends to be less than one employing increased efficiency and the use of science-based technology generated by rising capital accumulation. These are the real forces on the side of demand and supply, which cause a reduction in the real labor done in farming. Again, with economic development and expanding national and international markets necessitating rapid changes in technology, the real product per man hour in manufacture nearly always increases at a faster rate than the real product per man hour in other sectors of the economy. This is with regard to the supply side. On the demand side, with industrialization, the service sector invariably expands at a faster rate, responding to an increased demand for its products by government departments, teaching and research, medical services, entertainment of various kinds, transportation and communication services, commerce, trade and finance, and welfare services. Per capita availability of these services is regarded as an important index of economic development. The surplus created through increased productivity in the agricultural and industrial sectors with an increasingly smaller labor force (according to the *World Development Report*, 1987, less than 30 percent of the total labor force are engaged in these two material production sectors taken together in developed capitalist economies today, and the rest are in the service sector) helps in the rapid expansion of the service sector because of the rapidly growing demand for its products. Developed economies are, therefore, called postindustrial economies, with the service sector becoming dynamic sector and supplying the major inputs, like technology, skill, human capital, knowledge, and information. Even when the relative demand for manufacturers is increasing, in the long run, a decreasing proportion of the labor force is engaged therein. Colin Clark wrote in 1940, "Studying economic progress in relation to the economic structure of different countries, we find a very firmly established generalisation that a high level of real income per head is always associated with a high proportion of the working population in tertiary industries" (Clark 1940, 176). S. Kuznets, in his elaborate study, "Industrial Distribution of National Product and Labour Force" (1957, 84, 88, 89) has analyzed the trend in structural change since the 1870s, and his findings show the ever-increasing importance of the service sector in output and employment.

Fisher (1939) first popularized the conceptual breakdown of the economy into three sectors, primary, secondary, and tertiary, and noted that economies could be classified structurally according to the proportion of population employed in agriculture. Karl Marx clearly mentioned the economic structural change more than a century ago when he wrote:

Given an advance of industrial productivity to the point where only one-third of the population takes a direct part in material production, instead of two-thirds as before then one-third furnish the means of life for the whole, whereas before, two-thirds were required to do so. Disregarding the class constriction, the whole nation would now need only one-third of its time for direct production, whereas earlier it had needed two-thirds. With equal distribution, everyone would now have two-thirds of his time for unproductive labour and for leisure. But in capitalist production everything appears, and is, contradictory. As productivity rises, the number of unproductive labourers required to service and maintain the growing capital establishment also rises, for example, members of traditional unproductive workers like clerks, bookkeepers, also increase. This process in due course calls into being entirely new branches of unproductive work such as the banking system, the credit system, insurance empires and advertising, but the growth of scientific and technological establishments, as well as an increase in public education generally, are also included in his category. (Marx 1978b)

Marx wrote in *Grundrisse*:

As large-scale industry advances, the creation of real wealth depends more on the labour-time and the quantity of labour expended than on the power of instrumentalities set in motion during the labour time. These instrumentalities, and their powerful effectiveness, are in no proportion of the immediate labour time which their production requires; their effectiveness rather depends on the attained level of science and technological progress; in other words, on the application of this science to production. Human labour then no longer appears as engaged in the process of production—man rather relates himself to the process of production as supervisor and regulator. He stands outside of process of production. In this transformation, the great pillar of production and wealth is no longer the immediate labour performed by man himself, or his labour-time, but the appropriation of his own universal productivity, i.e. his knowledge and mastery of nature through his societal individual. As soon as human labour, in its immediate form to be the measure, has ceased, and must of necessity cease to be the measure of use value. The mode of production which rests on the exchange value thus collapses. (1964b, 31)

It appears from this statement that Marx was aware of the rise of the postindustrial society, with technological change and the emergence of the internationalization of production phase of capitalism (see Chapter 4). Postindustrial economies are those that are characterized by the dominance of service sector activities, particularly research, technology, knowledge, and information, and obviously at this stage, mass consumption or consumerism is fueled by constantly improving technological innovation. Thus the stage is set for the internationalization of investment and production. This book tries to show why a complete capitalist transformation of the Third World economies will not materialize, despite a tremendous growth of capital accumulation as a result of these economies being an integral part of global capitalist production.

In all developed countries the rate of growth of the service sectors since 1945 has been faster than that of employment (Organization of Economic Cooperation and Development 1966). According to Kuznets (1957) on structural change in terms of changes in employment, there has been an unambiguous secular tendency for the share of total agricultural employment to fall and for the share of manufacturing employment to the rise and later to fall with the rise of service employment, when the service sector rose to dominance in the economy. These changes in economic structure are functionally related to the rise of the rate of capital accumulation as a proportion of GDP and rapid technological change from the extensive phase to the mature, intensive phase. The process of capitalist transformation of an economy inevitably generates this pattern of technological change. Classical economists did not believe that a phenomenon like the rise of postindustrial economy could happen, which largely represents their misperception of the nature and importance of technology: technology has provided both capital- and labor-saving devices to the manufacturing industries. As a consequence, manufacturing, like agriculture before it, has become enormously efficient and productive, requiring a much smaller input of labor. The service sector now has become the largest sector and supplies technological inputs, knowledge, and information, on the one hand, and on the other, infrastructural services (e.g., easy and less time-consuming, almost instant communication facilities to facilitate the internationalization of the production process).

Fisher (1939), Kuznets (1966), and Clark (1957) do not mention the term *capitalist transformation* in their analyses of the economic structural change that is expected to take place under the capitalist mode of production. Marx mentioned this kind of economic structural change as a result of growth of capitalist mode of production. It is interesting to note that both Marx and bourgeois economists more or less came to the same conclusion with regard to structural change.

It is understandable why Marx did not explicitly deal with the capitalist transformation of an economy that was undergoing the process of capital accumulation. During Marx's time, in the nineteenth century, with the rise of the industrial capitalism, growing capital accumulation automatically brought about the capitalist transformation. The need for raising the rate of real capital accumulation induced reorganization and the transference of resources from less productive sectors. The surplus labor of these sectors began to be absorbed in the growing productive industrial sector, which in turn began to supply the lagging sector with more productive inputs. Thus, the growing capital accumulation enabled the lagging sector to release increasingly the redundant labor to more productive sectors—the industrial and service sectors—which resulted in cheaper labor, the main ingredient in capital accumulation. Using this cheaper labor, the industrial sector produced capital inputs for both agriculture and industry and thereby increased capital accumulation.

The objective of increasing the rate of capital accumulation needed, in the course of time, high-level, quality labor (human capital), better communication, better information, improved technology, and so forth, so that the horizon of production and market needed to generate the possibility of a constantly rising rate of capital accumulation widens as the days go by. In this process, labor needed to be more productive to promote technological improvement based on science for developing better skill, more efficient communications and transport systems, more productive energy (from labor-intensive coal to oil and, gradually, to nuclear and backstop fuel), better information, and so forth. This was possible only by the development of education to promote human capital. The tremendous expansion possibility of capitalist production using science could materialize only by improving the quality of labor and reducing the quantity. Because of the increased productivity of labor wages tended to rise, cutting into profit; this resulted in the need to reduce the quantity of labor and, thereby, ensure rising profit. This basic need of the capitalist system generated gradual changes in the economic structure, from industry-dominated to service sector–dominated. Thus, economic structural change results from the process of capitalist transformation of the economy, which began with the Industrial Revolution in England, followed by industrial growth in Western Europe.

Today, the productive systems themselves have become increasingly multinational and automated. Postindustrial production systems are highly technologized, require little labor, and involve numerous steps, components, and processes which are scattered across a transnational web of technological specialization. Much of the shift represents the enormous growth of transportation and communication facilities. This development characterizes the process of the globalization of production (see Chapter 4). Whether a mature industry moves to a Third World country or becomes mechanized or automated, the results are same: a loss of jobs in that industry. This has become evident in developed countries for over a decade. In the meantime, there have emerged new kinds of industries (chemicals, pharmaceuticals, electronics, computers, etc.), which are characterized by the following features: they are knowledge-based, highly technologized, multinational, and require only a small labor force (see, for detailed discussion, Folker Frober, J. Heinrichs, and O. Keys 1980). The unemployment that has resulted does not reflect a temporary decline in business activity but rather a technological displacement of labor. Many of these unemployed will be, in the course of time, absorbed in petty businesses run by family members, low-wage occupations, small shops, restaurants, pavement vending, and so forth. These underemployed, in the postindustrial stage, will swell the number in service sector occupations. Large-scale, organized manufacturing and service activities run by high-wage employees using high technology will decline (see Chapter 5).

Table 3.2 shows a trend in changes in manufacturing and nonmanufacturing employment in Great Britain at the early phase of the rise of the service sector (i.e., 1950–1978):

The knowledge industry has become the most rapidly growing industry in

TABLE 3.2 Changes in Manufacturing and Nonmanufacturing (Mainly Service) Employment in the United Kingdom, 1950–1978 (percentages)

Sectors	1950	1959	1966	1974	1978
Manufacturing	40.9	37.7	36.9	34.6	32.2
Nonmanufacturing	59.1	58.6	63.7	65.4	67.8
Changes	1948–49	59–66		66–74	74–78
Manufacturing	+0.5	−0.8		−2.3	−2.4
Nonmanufacturing	−0.5	+0.8		+2	+2.4

Source: P. Thornton and V. Wheelock. (1980) Technology and Employment. *International Journal of Social Economics*. Vol. 7, 1:25

postindustrial economies and, consequently, employment in research, technology, and information activities has expanded rapidly, at the cost of employment in direct production, which has become highly technologized and supplied with most sophisticated inputs by the service sector. As a result, recent employment statistics of Great Britain indicate that between 62 and 65 percent of the working population can now be classified as information operatives. (This was in late 1970s and early 1980s, and we can imagine what the percentage has become since.) The largest proportion of workers in this category are located in the service sector of the economy, but an important and growing percentage of workers in manufacturing industries are, in fact, information operatives. Indeed, without the growth of this type of worker, the decline of manufacturing would have been more pronounced (Thornton and Wheelock 1980). This pattern of economic structural change has been accompanied by rapid growth in the rate of capital accumulation, which has risen from about 15–17 percent in the 1950s to over 30 percent in the 1980s.

According to Kuznets (1966), in most countries the substantial decline in the share of the agriculture sector is compensated by a substantial rise in the share of service sector, not by a rise in the industry and manufacturing sector. Kuznets's observation is particularly true of the Third World countries but is not applicable to the latecomer Western European economies of the nineteenth century, where capital accumulation and technological change at the early phase of industrial development resulted from a more productive use of quantity labor under large-scale organization and based on an increasing division of labor. Hence, in this process, more quantity labor was absorbed from the surplus agricultural sector. Commerce and trade in such products were mainly localized and gradually became national. However, because of a heavy demand for labor, both in agriculture and industry, where the technology was at its extensive phase and absorbing increasing amounts of labor, not much surplus was left for commerce, trade, and other service activities (see Jones and Wolfe 1969, and Collins 1969).

> Following Fisher (1939, 116) the most firmly established empirical generalisation about economic growth has related to the decline of agriculture, to the secular decline of both rural population and agricultural labour force and to the agricultural sector's declining share of the national product. In Clark's (1940, 341) view, switching of resources between sectors is an indicator of, and a cause of, increasing productivity.

Lewis's (1954) model of the growth of economies of latecomer countries pictures a dualistic economy with a large and overwhelming subsistence sector, which is characterized by production that is for self-consumption, is unorganized, and without wage labor and is shared by participants without reference to the particular contribution of each. The market and money exchange have very little to do with production. A modern or capitalist sector that used wage labor initially at the subsistence level, was organized on the basis of money, market, and capital, with profit as the target of production. In the West (France, Germany, the Netherlands, Italy, etc.) in the nineteenth century, with borrowed technology and capital from the original country of the industrial capitalism, the United Kingdom, a modern sector was established which, in due course, drew the traditional subsistence sector into the capitalist sector and thus brought about an integrated capitalist transformation of the entire economy. The capitalist sector is comprised of the industrial production sector and the tertiary sector, which services the production sector in the form of developing markets of its products via trade and commerce, providing transport and communication, and supplying education and skills, health (particularly, eliminating epidemics to keep production and marketing uninterrupted), finance, credit, and banking systems to mobilize economic surplus for further capital accumulation.

According to Clark, the first cause of economic progress was improvement within sectors rather the transfer of resources between sectors of differing productivity. Clark's observation is true as far as the agricultural revolution as the condition for the industrial capitalist revolution phenomenon is concerned. In the case of the latecomer countries, resource transfers between sectors, particularly of industrial inputs and service inputs, have played the dominant role in achieving growth. However, agriculture supplied mainly the food and raw materials, with little supply of labor to industrial and service sectors, rather a very large part of the labor has gone to unproductive and unorganized parts of the service sector (i.e., petty trade, street vending, domestic service, etc.).

The dominant belief among the development economists and economic historians is that the industrial sector, with increasing physical capital formation embodying improved technology, has played the role of prime importance in economic growth. This is, of course, true and applicable to all latecomer countries, where this sector has acted as a market for agricultural and service products and, on the other hand, served as a source of physical capital to enhance the productivity of all three sectors. However, the supply of labor to industry has been negligible, and the demand for labor in the industrial sector has always been extremely limited as well. This is evident from India's economic structural change and the demographic transition (see Chapter 5).

Traditionally, the migration of labor from agriculture to industry during the Industrial Revolution was seen as a *push* factor, the result of changes in agricultural technology and organization that reduced the demand for labor. However, we should also take note of the stronger factor in its process, that is, the *pull factor.* Technological change in the industrial sector initially was at its extensive phase of absorbing labor and thus created a demand for labor, hence, the dynamic process of capitalist transformation ensued. It is well known that industrial capital grows out of the availability of cheaper labor. Again, in the case of the Third World, industrial growth did not have any pull effects, while the push effects have been very strong and are becoming stronger with the growth of population. Therefore, the surplus labor force that was pushed out of agriculture due to overcrowding migrates to towns to become street vendors, hawkers, servants, porters, and sex industry workers. This swells the rank of the service sectors, but these workers become the source of consumption only and not of productivity. Therefore, in the Third World countries, the service sector has expanded much faster than the industrial sector. Moreover, the industrial sector, as compared to the service sector, absorbs a very tiny portion of the labor force but contributes a much larger proportion to GDP than the other two sectors, unlike in the first world.

One point must be made clear here: when change in agricultural technology and the organization of production through enclosures was taking place, leading to the Industrial Revolution, it increased rather than decreased the demand for labor and, generally, was labor intensive; in other words, prior to this change there gradually accumulated surplus labor with which this change (i.e., large-scale farming with better tools, etc.) was put to more productive use in farming and generated a higher rate of capital accumulation. Besides, logically, this should happen because in those days, a higher rate of output and capital accumulation was only made possible by bringing about organizational change and, thereby, making more efficient use of labor. The incentive on the part of investors was the supply of cheap labor.

The service sector gradually became important because of the need of capitalist production for an expanding market which stimulated the growth of trade, commerce, law enforcement, government administration, and the development of skills and education as a source of human capital to reduce the labor costs of production. It was the improved quality of labor in industry and agriculture that made possible the expansion of capitalism, making products competitive, costs of production cheaper, and production diversified through constant technological innovation and, thereby, promoting the worldwide expansion of capitalism from its start in the United Kingdom in the nineteenth century. When Western capitalism became internationalized, particularly after the end of World War II, the improvement in human capital depended mainly on the expanding service sector, particularly in the fields of medicine, education, and research and development.

The developed capitalist countries today have reached the stage of postindustrial economics—a stage dominated by the service sector with research and development in technology and innovation as the key to bring about a higher rate of capital accumulation. This is achieved, as has been the practice with capitalism in the past, through reductions in labor costs by making labor increasingly productive, on the one hand, and making its supply greater than the demand via introducing the policy of free market economy, on the other (see Chapter 4).

All economic theories—classical, neoclassical, Marxist, and Keynesian—lay emphasis on capital accumulation as the cause of economic development from the feudal-mercantile phase. None except Marxist analysis (which does so only indirectly), deals with the question of capitalist transformation as the necessary condition for the development of the Third World. We notice, despite the rapid growth of capital accumulation, that no or negligible capitalist transformation has accompanied the capital accumulation. Some development models (Lewis 1954, for example) have advocated the need for the monetization of economic activities as a step toward organizing economic surplus or savings into capital accumulation. This approach has played a dominant role in Lewis model and in government policies of most Third World countries.

In other words, the introduction of money into the economy is considered the key to the growth of money capital that characterized the period of mercantile capitalism. Money capital, according to economists, develops into industrial capital with the fulfillment of two basic conditions:

1. Sufficient money capital
2. Sufficient supply of labor

The existence of one condition without the other will not be sufficient for the development of industrial capitalism. Many economists like Fisher (1939), Clark (1957), and Kuznets (1966), have suggested the measurement of economic development in terms of the sectoral distribution of the labor force and GDP. This is an important indicator of capitalist transformation. However, Fisher, Clark, Kuznets, and subsequent analyses of their models have not shown how the sectoral distribution of labor force is functionally related to technological change and the capitalist transformation of the economy. However, Clark has explained the causes of this change.

In this sense, development becomes synonymous with economic structural change as measured in terms of dynamic changes in the distribution of the labor force. Terms like negligible or "limited capitalist transformation" sound contradictory. That is, the capitalist transformation of an economy can not stop halfway. It is a dynamic force, and when it emerges in a society, it penetrates into every corner of economic activities and thus purges all elements of precapitalism from social and economic life. In this sense, the development of capitalism in a society acts as a progressive force in social and economic life. A human being establishes himself in this process as the master over his environment and controls and organizes resources to develop his full potential, which widens with every stage of his progress. In this book, we will confine ourselves only to economic aspects of the capitalist transformation of a society and its effects on society in terms of population growth, the development of social conscience, and productivity (i.e., technological change), with levels of growth and their relationship with capitalist transformation as criteria.

Kuznets (1966) related structural change to per capita income increase. In his quantitative work he grouped countries according to per capita income and showed that with the rise of income per capita, there is:

1. a constant decline in the share of agriculture in national product
2. a consistent rise in the share of the industrial sector in national output
3. no clear pattern in the share of the services sector

Clark (1957) defined the process of this change in terms of production and consumption effects. With respect to labor force distribution by sectors, he also demonstrated that there was a decline in the proportion of the labor force engaged in the agricultural sector, while that of the industrial sector showed a slight rise, which was much less pronounced than the rise in its share of national output. However, in the case of a developed capitalist economy, the rise in the share of the industrial sector of the total labor force was spectacular for the period, as in Britain in the 1850s, when its proportion rose to 40–42 percent while that of agriculture fell from 65 percent in the 1870s to 20 percent (see Hartwell, 370, Table on Sectoral Change in British Economy). The Kuznets and Clark studies also reveal that there has been a continuous rise in the service sector in the Western economies since the Industrial Revolution, with transport communication and commerce dominating it initially, later followed by a rapid rise in education, research, information, and technology development activities since the beginning of the twentieth century. In the postindustrial stage, the latter activities became the dominant sector of employment. However, since the 1990s, a small business sector, consisting of small shops, takeaway food shops, street vending, and various self-employment service activities (housekeeping, gardening, fruit gathering, plumbing, house painting, etc.) have been increasing rapidly as source of employment requiring a relatively low level human capital (i.e., with school certificates, high school, and degree holders) and money capital. One interesting aspect of this type of development is that the predominance of this latter kind of service activity (i.e., small-scale, low-income, self-employment activities) was also visible in the preindustrial as well as industrial days in developed economies. On the other hand, this kind of employment has always been the case with developing economies, even when there has been a tremendous growth of large-scale industries and manufacturing. Employment in the agricultural sector in these economies still absorbs, in contrast with the developed capitalist economies, about 70 percent of the labor force and contributes less than 40 percent of GNP, while in developed capitalist economies like the United Kingdom and United States, only about 2–3 percent of the labor force is engaged in agriculture, contributing 5–6 percent of GNP (World Bank 1987).

Lewis's (1954) classical model, as modified to suit the case of the Third World economy, may be used to interpret the expected changes in a stagnant economic structure, as a result of the introduction and expansion of the capitalist sector, which absorbs surplus labor at a subsistence wage and thereby brings about a turning point in the economy when subsistence agriculture becomes exhausted of its surplus labor. Lewis also included in his model the policy of credit creation or monetization as the principal instrument of mobilizing surplus labor and nonmarketed resources for further investment. He advocated strongly the case for transplanting the capitalist sector to bring about this transformation. He and other development economists ignored in their models the different effects that capital and technology transfer produces at different stages of their development. All these models have developed at a time when world capitalism has reached the stage of internationalization of investment and, therefore, advocated the case for development with foreign investment and capital via the supply of finance and credit. This process also helped the underdeveloped economies to extend monetization of their economies and thereby prepare the ground for import-substituting industrial (ISI) growth. The ISI policy dominated the development policy of these economies (see Chapter 4).

Fei and Ranis (1963), in their modification of the Lewis (1954) model, advocated the case for the simultaneous development of agriculture and industry. Otherwise, expansion of the capitalist sector would be halted halfway because of the lack of supply of surplus from the subsistence sector. Neither of these two models discussed the role of the transformation effects of technological change at its different phases. In this sense, the Lewis model, historically may explain the effectiveness in bringing about the capitalist transformation of the latecomers of Europe in the nineteenth century, while that of Fei and Ranis may explain the case of Japanese development; that is, the capitalist transformation of its economy took much longer time than that of the latecomers of Europe. The Japanese approach of a dual production function, one for the agricultural sector and the other for the modern industrial sector, was meant to bring about a simultaneous development of agriculture and industry (see also Maitra 1980, 1986).

The neoclassicists viewed the process from a different angle. Wages in the subsistence sector are determined by the equilibrium of the supply of, and demand for, labor, and as the technology is of a low level, the wage or factor price for products is also low. The only way out is to raise the level of technology and, thereby, make available for the industrial sector surplus labor generated by improved technology. Technological change depends on investment and the creation of capital. In this way, the capitalist transformation of the entire economy is achieved. In the case of the Third World, emphasis has been laid on the development of the capitalist or industrial sector as the engine of growth, at the neglect of agricultural sector, which is the largest sector in the economy at that stage of development; hence, the problem of transformation of a feudal economy into a market-oriented, capitalist economy.

In the case of the United Kingdom, land reform policy played a vital role in bringing about the rise of industrial capital from merchant capital, while in India and other Third World countries, land reform policies were adopted long after the introduction of industrial capital.

We may mention the case of the Green Revolution technology introduced in the Third World in the 1960s as an example of the neoclassicist approach toward agricultural growth. This case created demand for quantity labor as the technology and was essentially land productivity augmenting; in short words, it was a land intensive technology. When productivity of labor is increased, as a result of tracttorization, decreasing amount of labor is required per unit of output. True, there has been a tremendous growth of agricultural output with the land-intensive approach, which has created a demand for labor in agricultural activities with little effect of a productivity increase in these labor force. Had labor productivity growth effects been created instead of creating a demand for labor in agricultural pursuits, more and more labor would have been released for the industrial sector. However, with the industrial sector ineffective in absorbing labor, the effects would have been worse. The high population growth rate has resulted in a strong drift of migrants to the urban sector and a rise and expansion of shanty towns offering cheap labor.

One important lesson that we could learn from the Green Revolution technology was that had the inputs used in its land-intensive approach (e.g., fertilizers, improved seeds, water supply, etc.) been produced locally using labor more productively, it would have improved traditional technology in this respect. In the case of Japan, at the initial stage of Japanese development, the potential of traditional technology was fully utilized. Unfortunately, however, with the growth of population and the industrial sector absorbing very little of the labor force, when small-scale agriculture began to face the growing pressure of surplus labor, modern inputs for the land-intensive approach were imported from the West. This resulted in differential development in Japan, with agriculture lagging far behind the industrial sector. According to Ohkawa (1965, 473–75), Japan opted for rapid growth in the agricultural sector to supply resources for its rapidly growing industrial sector. That led to a cleavage between the two sectors, which continued until the 1950s. The sectoral distribution of the labor force justifies this conclusion (see Table 3.3). Moreover, later development studies agreed to consider the 1950s as the period of take-off or turning point in agriculture in Japan, which also implies a capitalist transformation following the Lewis (1954) and Fei-Ranis models (1963).

The capitalist transformation of an economy is reflected in economic structural change in terms of a dynamic sectoral shift away from agricultural through industry to the service sector. In the nineteenth century, Western countries recorded the beginning of the decline in size of agriculture in terms of the proportion of labor depending on it and its contribution to total output, which is still continuing. With this decline of agriculture at the beginning, the industrial sector expanded rapidly over the last hundred years on both counts (i.e., share of labor and output). Since the early nineteenth century, it was accompanied by a growth in the service sector. This is the period characterized by the extensive phase of technological change absorbing the unskilled and less skilled labor force through rising productivity. A slow growth of the rate of capital formation as a proportion of GNP accompanied this period and began to create an increasing demand for labor at a cheap rate. Exports and domestic income grew, creating an increasing

TABLE 3.3 Composition of Japan's Working Population by Industry (Percentages)

	Primary	Secondary	Tertiary
1878-1882	82.3	5.6	12.1
1898-1902	69.6	11.8	18.3
1913-1917	59.2	16.4	24.4
1920	53.6	20.7	23.8
1930	49.4	20.4	30.0
1940	44.0	26.1	29.2
1950	48.3	21.9	29.7
1955	41.0	23.5	35.5
1960	32.6	29.2	38.2
1965	24.6	32.3	43.0
1970	19.3	34.1	46.5
1975	13.9	35.1	50.7

Source: For 1878 to 1917, Ohkawa (1956), and for 1920 to 1975, Bureau of Statistics, Prime Minister's Office, population census, Government of Japan for each year.

demand for labor, which needed a rapid mechanization of agricultural and manufacturing activities to economize its use, as well as the supply of relatively formally skilled labor instead of unskilled or quantity labor. This is reflected in the development of education from the literacy level to primary and high school education (see Chapter 7), or in other words, from quantity labor to a gradually improving quality labor. This implies that, with the growth in productivity and capital accumulation, an increasing proportion of income begins to be invested in the development of more productive technology (i.e., the days of physical capital and more productive labor raising the level of human capital emerged).

The expansion of capital-intensive products needed expanding markets, within and outside the country, requiring improving communication and transport systems, widening and raising the quality of education facilities, and better law enforcement; in other words, the development of an infrastructure that began to draw the labor force from the industrial and agricultural sectors which were being turned increasingly capital-intensive to release labor force. An increased supply of labor helped keep wages under control, thereby raising the rate of profit and capital accumulation. The need for more productive labor to reduce the cost of production with expanding competition and world trade (see Table 3.3) stimulated research and development activities and improvements in information regarding better resources, markets, and so forth. These were becoming increasingly the greatest user of human capital released by the physical production sectors, agriculture, and industry. This is evident in today's highly developed capitalist economies, with less than 30 percent of the labor force depending on physical production sectors and the remaining on the service sector, which includes information, knowledge activities, and so forth. I took note earlier of the recent experience of the British economy. Electronic technology and its network has replaced the iron and steel industry of the nineteenth and early twentieth centuries in capitalist development. This also reflects the changes in the energy use pattern, from labor-intensive energy sources like fuel wood through coal and to the present-day nuclear and backstop fuels. (Backstop fuels are available in super abundance which do not cost e.g. wind power, solar power.) The intention is to reduce the cost of production and make it competitive by reducing its most expensive factor, labor and human capital, with the competition becoming concentrated and international (discussed in Chapter 4).

Recent studies (Gemmel 1986, 15–19) have highlighted the decline in either the absolute or relative size of the industrial sector in most developed countries. A decline in the manufacturing sector's share of employment over the decade has been identified most frequently, though a similar decline in the sector's share in output is also confirmed, the reason being that the service sector's output, particularly of knowledge, information, communication, education, and research (using the output supplied by the productive sector) has become enormous. Constant technological innovation in the service sector (e.g., R and D activities), accompanied by cheaper and more immediate communication systems, has played the key role in this development of capitalist sector. Gemmel wrote (1986, 14): "This decline is almost always accompanied by a rising share of the service sector, public and/or private, and has created renewed interest, in developed countries, in the sector's economic characteristic." It is to be noted here that the service sector is playing the key role in the globalization of the production phase as the heavy and producer goods industries (e.g., machinery producing industries) did at the earlier phase of the globalization of investment. These phases of the development of capitalism will be discussed later (see Chapter 4).

Gemmel (1986, 17), in support of economic structural change that takes place with economic development, wrote: that agricultural employment falls most rapidly in the early stages of development, giving rise to rapid increase in the shares of industry and services in total employment. However, the decline in the share of agriculture slows with increasing development, approaching asymptotically a share of about 3 percent (with industry 25 percent and services 72 percent).

According to development theory, not only should a relative transfer of resources from agricultural to nonagricultural sectors be expected as per capita income rises, but also (under the assumption of diminishing marginal returns), the pace of resource transfer will slow as income rises. This is based on the following arguments. At low income levels, when the economy is entirely agrarian and marginal productivity in agriculture is low, a larger reduction in the labor force is possible for a given rise in productivity than when the share of the agricultural sector in the economy is smaller and marginal productivity is higher. Since it has been observed that income and productivity tend to rise together over time, equal and successive rises in income can be expected to be associated with successively smaller decrements in the resource share of the agricultural sector (Gemmel 1986, 17).

This observation applies to developed economies where economic structural change became dynamic along with economic development and a growth in productivity. However, in India and most Third World countries, growth in productivity and rises in per capita income have never been accompanied by substantial economic structural change and have remained more or less stagnant, as evident from Tables 6.1 and 6.4. In the Third World countries, whatever shift of resources has taken place has been biased toward the service sector (mainly in low-income, self-employed, and distributive activities, etc.) than toward the industrial sector. The development of organized sectors in industrial, manufacturing, and service activities has been taking place, with little absorption of the labor force from the agricultural sector.

The dynamic changes in economic structure in the United Kingdom and, later, other developed countries support the consequent trend of relative resource transfer from the secondary to the service sector for entirely economic reasons.

World capitalism emerged in the West and, in its quest for a market, spread all over the world, riding on its basic characteristic (i.e., the force of competition). The rapid expansion of markets to fulfill the motivation of the capitalist toward earning higher rates of profit and levels of capital accumulation has always resulted in deepening competition among capitalists, which has made a reduction in the costs of production imperative. This is being achieved by reducing the labor cost (which has been rising with the increase in labor productivity), by trying to raise its productivity all the time through constantly improving technology and diversifying production via technological innovations. This has meant, since the beginning of the use of modern science in production in the late nineteenth century, constant changes in technology (see Chapter 7). Thus, the need for achieving capitalist transformation to diversify output and reduce the costs of production by raising labor productivity results in dramatic effects:

1. (a) a release of the labor force from the production sectors to the expansion of service sectors, which become dominated by education, research and development activities, information and communication activities, and so forth; (b) limited employment possibility in this sector;
2. a rapid growth of the low-income self-employment sector, with increasing numbers of underemployed individuals.

A study of the development of education and growth of human capital (see Chapter 7) would prove this contention and also the fact that in the long run, with the growth in the level of human capital and technological sophistication, labor productivity and, therefore, wages will rise. This latter development will cost jobs in the organized sectors and force the workers to self-employment occupations in various kinds of service activities, mainly, and small-scale, light manufactures, marginally. This latest trend has already become evident in most of the developed economies that are at the phase of globalization of production. This shift of resources can also be looked at from the point of view of technological change and productivity growth effects on production, employment, and consumption, as discussed at the beginning of this chapter. Moreover, income elasticities of demand for service products were higher than for industrial outputs, as those for industrial output were higher than agricultural output in the past, so that, ceteris paribus, with the rise in per capita income, demand for industrial output will rise faster than service at first but slow down later (assuming the coincidence of higher elasticities with higher income levels), proving higher than industrial output.

Second, the evidence suggests that at the early stage of expansion of the service sector in developed capitalist economies, its productivity in aggregate terms will increase more slowly than industrial productivity as it needs more labor in its process of expansion (also due to the fact that the service sector as a whole is labor intensive by nature when we include the large segment of teaching, health service, research and small-scale business, e.g., takeout shops, street vending, housekeeping, jobs in offices, kindergartens, child care centers, etc.). Moreover, the globalization of investment phase characterized by expanding social welfare activities of the state creates tremendous employment opportunities and rises in income, which in turn stimulate commercial activities requiring more hands. However, the fuller employment conditions raise the wage higher than their marginal production, which induced technological change in service activities. Gemmel wrote: "The industrial and service employment shares both grow initially at the expense of agricultural share as income rises, but once the agricultural share becomes fairly small the service sector shares begin to expand at the expense of the industrial sector share" (1986, 19). According to Baumol (1967), at higher income levels and with agricultural surplus all but exhausted (in the United Kingdom, about 2.5 percent, and the United States, 3 percent of the labor force is in agriculture), a transfer of labor from the industrial to the service sector will be required to maintain relative output growth rates between sectors. Capitalist expansion needed this kind of mobility to maintain and raise its rates of profit and capital accumulation. As the labor becomes increasingly productive with technological change, it becomes increasingly costly to entrepreneurs, on one hand, and on the other, it makes itself redundant (i.e., cheaper). The service sector takes advantage of this situation and uses it in making technology improvements all the time and making product diversification possible, thereby making them redundant or available at lower wages, as is evident today. However, a limited area of activities in the service sector like education, research and development, information, and communication needs highly skilled labor and high wages because of the high productivity and skill level involved.

The reason behind it is that science and technology evolved in the United

Kingdom as a consequence trials and errors to develop them cost the economy. Moreover, Britain had a vast assured market in her Colonies all over the world which with its cheap labor served as an enormous source of agricultural products e.g., food from newly settled countries and raw materials from underdeveloped countries. True, the United Kingdom reached a low share of its population in agriculture at low levels of per capita income compared to other developed countries. We should also take into consideration the level of technological change and the rate of capital accumulation at that stage of the Industrial Revolution. The extensive phase of industrial technology emerged and evolved in Britain, absorbing labor in industry from agriculture at a relatively high rate. While the other Western developed economies began industrializing their economies with borrowed capital and technology from Britain when its technology reached the last stage of the extensive or the first stage of the intensive phase (i.e., around the 1860s, when modern science began to be used in production) and therefore, dissimilar effects are expected (see Tables 3.1 and 6.4). This is more glaring today in the case of Japanese development and development of the Third World countries. However, these explanations cannot throw light on the continuous absence of dynamic change in economic structure in the Third World economies since the introduction of industrial capitalism in the nineteenth century or the recent rapid rate of industrial growth, capital accumulation, productivity, and per capita income. Therefore, to explain these negative effects we would have to look into the capitalist transformation effects of capital accumulation. In India, capital accumulation as a proportion of GNP has gone up remarkably, from about 5 percent in the 1950s to over 21 percent in the 1980s (i.e., over four times in 30 years), while the economic structural change has shown little change, with over 70 percent in agriculture. In other words, capitalist transformation effects have failed to materialize, despite the growth of capital accumulation, rises in industrial and productivity growth, and growing technological sophistication. The demographic transition effects of capitalist transformation are also absent in India (see Tables 6.1 and 6.2). I will now sum up briefly the factors responsible for the reallocation of resources (i.e., labor).

It is common knowledge that with the growth of the economy, an increase in agricultural productivity begins to take place, resulting from the increased use of capital in agriculture, on the one hand, while on the other, with the rise in income resulting from growth, income elasticity of demand for food gradually appears to be less than one e.g., when demand for food does not increase at the rate income increases. These are the real forces on the side of demand and of supply that cause a reduction in the real labor done in farming. Again, with economic development and industrialization, the amount of real product per man-hour in manufacture nearly always increases at a faster rate than the real product per man-hour in other sectors of the economy. This is with regard to the supply side. On the demand side, with industrialization, the service sector invariably expands at a faster rate due to an increased demand for its products by government department, teaching and research, medical services, entertainments of various kinds, transportation services, commerce, trade, and finance and welfare services. The per capita availability of these services is today regarded as an important index of economic development. The surplus created through increased productivity in the agricultural and manufacturing sectors with relatively small labor helps in the rapid expansion of the service sector because of the rapidly increasing demand for its products. Thus a stationary relative demand for manufactures would lead to a decreasing proportion of the labor force employed therein. Even when the relative demand for manufactures is increasing, in the long run, a decreasing proportion of the labor force is engaged therein.

This is also to be noted here that with industrialization, all sectors of the economy become relatively organized, and thus the proportion of independent workers, which had a dominant position among the different categories of workers in the unorganized condition of the economy, declines, while the number of employees increases (Maitra 1977, 14). However, in developed capitalist economies, this is coming back, while in India and other Third World economies, the unorganized sector, is increasing with a growing number of low-paid workers like street vendors, tea shop boys, railway and bus station porters, takeout shop employees (mostly family members), rickshaw pullers, and so forth.

CONCLUSION

This chapter attempts to revisit the meaning of capital, the process of capital formation and capitalist transformation of an economy, and their relevance for India as a Third World economy. The failure of the present-day approach to economic development, which was essentially based on imported capital and technology used to bring about the capitalist transformation, has made it imperative to analyze the causes of the failure. India and most other developing countries have accumulated huge amounts of capital, and the proportion of capital formation in these economies has reached more than 20 percent of their GNP. However, these economies have basically remained preindustrial in economic structure and in terms of social consciousness. When we look at the stagnating economic structure side-by-side with rapid industrial growth in these countries (see Table 6.1) and compare them with the already developed capitalist economies of the West at the time of the Industrial Revolution and rise of industrial capitalism, we find a paradoxical development. In the latter countries, the rate of growth of capital accumulation took place at a meager rate of about 5 percent of GNP in the nineteenth century but was accompanied by rapid economic structural change indicating the dynamic process of capitalist transformation. The latter process continued with a shrinking of the agricultural sector and the rise and dominance of the industrial sector which, by the mid-twentieth century, lost its dominance to the service sector. The entire process results from the effects of the rising rate of capital accumulation. In the case of India, this process has failed to materialize despite the fact that the rate of capital accumulation to GDP has assumed a proportion comparable to developed capitalist economies of 1950s. The demographic transition and the capitalist transformation effects of capital accumulation, however, have been utterly negligible (see Chapter 6).

This lack of capitalist transformation is also evident in its effects on three basic factors in the supply of labor in economic development:

1. the demographic effects that have failed to follow the Demographic Transition and thereby acted as a hindrance to development (see Chapter 6);

2. the failure to materialize human resource development into human capital, unlike in the developed capitalist economies;

3. the technological change and energy use patterns have no relationship with the state of capitalist transformation and economic structural change in India's economy, unlike in the developed capitalist economies. These topics are discussed in Chapters 6 and 7.

4

THE INTERNATIONALIZATION OF CAPITALISM

Industrial capitalism first evolved in Britain in the nineteenth century, with the Industrial Revolution (see Chapters 1 and 2) and, later in about the mid-nineteenth century, it was introduced to mainland Europe, and particularly Western Europe (see Henderson 1954; Maitra 1980). This was the beginning of the expansion of world capitalism, which was led by the West since the late nineteenth century, under the flag of international trade of goods and commodity capital. This first stage of the internationalization of capitalism continued by bringing under the orbit of capitalist production the rest of the economies of latecomer countries, mostly colonies of the Western colonial powers (see Tables 4.1, 4.2, and 4.3). This was regarded as the first stage of introduction of industrial manufacturers to these economies—mainly consumer goods, which were imported by these economies against their exports of cash crops. In this process, when the imported industrial goods of mainly consumer goods created sufficient markets so that it was economical to produce locally, market-determined, import-substituting industrial production began. Needless to say, inputs for import substitution were imported in exchange for the traditional exports of cash crops.

The second stage of the globalization of capitalism is marked by a massive transfer of interest-earning finance via foreign investment loans and credit. The Western capitalist economies accumulated huge amounts of finance and productive capital during the first stage of transfer of goods and commodity capital. Markets of these products beyond their borders stimulated the rapid growth of productive industrial capital in the West. The Third World, now equipped with

TABLE 4.1 British Foreign Investment, 1865–1914

Year	Europe	North America	Asia
1865	7.5	7.1	11.2
1866	4.5	4.4	4.5
1867	4.6	1.5	7.5
1868	11.7	3.5	8.1
1869	8.0	4.8	6.3
1870	18.6	10.0	7.1
1871	29.2	13.0	3.7
1872	34.9	30.8	2.2
1873	25.4	26.8	4.1
1874	24.7	33.1	5.9
1875	10.1	12.2	4.0
1876	5.0	9.3	5.1
1877	3.7	4.3	6.7
1878	6.1	6.2	5.0
1879	3.3	7.2	0.7
1880	2.7	18.3	3.2
1881	20.6	22.2	10.6
1882	12.1	28.6	9.4
1883	4.7	16.6	4.6
1884	7.3	15.1	5.8
1885	3.4	14.1	11.0
1886	5.0	14.0	9.6
1887	12.9	23.9	10.5
1888	10.1	37.2	10.7
1889	11.2	37.2	11.2
1890	12.3	52.8	10.8
1891	5.0	18.7	5.7
1892	2.7	14.9	4.1
1893	1.7	13.1	2.5
1894	1.8	17.0	13.1
1895	3.6	26.0	10.4
1896	2.7	13.2	15.4
1897	8.1	16.7	27.2
1898	10.1	19.8	21.1
1899	8.6	12.1	21.7
1900	6.9	10.7	11.9
1901	5.8	14.1	4.6
1902	5.2	37.3	10.8
1903	2.1	17.3	6.6
1904	0.8	31.3	15.2
1905	3.0	43.9	35.6
1906	14.7	19.1	15.8
1907	7.0	42.7	23.4
1908	10.4	62.7	29.6
1909	13.6	68.4	25.4
1910	18.8	82.5	32.9
1911	14.5	73.5	24.7
1912	22.8	89.9	21.5
1913	18.9	116.9	17.4
1914	43.5	82.5	16.4

Source: Matthew Simon, *The Pattern of New British Portfolio Foreign Investment* in *The Export of Capital from Britain 1870–1914*, edited by A. R. Hall (London: Methuen & Company), 39–40. Used with permission.

TABLE 4.2 Shares of Primary Products and Manufactures in Total Trade of Each Region, 1876-1913 (Percentages)

Region	1876–1880		1896–1900		1913	
	Primary products	Manu-factures	Primary products	Manu-factures	Primary products	Manu-factures
Export Trade						
U.K. and Ireland	11.9	88.1	17.2	82.8	30.3	69.7
N.W. Europe	43.8	56.2	50.5	49.5	48.0	52.0
Other Europe	78.1	21.9	74.9	25.1	75.6	24.4
U.S. and Canada	85.7	14.3	81.0	19.0	74.1	25.9
Underdeveloped countries and rest of world	97.6	2.4	91.6	8.4	89.1	10.9
World	61.9	38.1	62.8	37.2	61.8	38.2
Import Trade						
U.K. and Ireland	85.8	14.2	82.6	17.4	81.2	18.8
N.W. Europe	60.9	39.1	62.0	38.0	59.9	40.1
U.S. and Canada	63.5	36.5	63.0	37.0	63.4	36.6
Underdeveloped countries and rest of world	30.9	69.1	29.2	70.8	40.2	59.8
World	61.9	38.1	62.8	37.2	61.8	38.2

Source: Kenwood and Lougheed (1971), 44.

TABLE 4.3 Trade in Manufactures: Regional Shares, 1876-1913 (Percentages)

Region	1876–1880		1896–1900		1913	
	Imports	Exports	Imports	Exports	Imports	Exports
Export Trade						
U.K. and Ireland	9.1	37.8	10.4	31.5	8.2	25.3
N.W. Europe	18.1	47.1	20.3	45.8	24.4	47.9
Other Europe	13.3	9.2	12.2	10.3	15.4	8.3
U.S. and Canada	7.7	4.4	9.6	7.4	12.1	10.6
Rest of World	51.8	1.5	47.5	5.0	39.9	7.9
World	100.0	100.0	100.0	100.0	100.0	100.0

Sources: Kenwood and Lougheed (1971), 44.

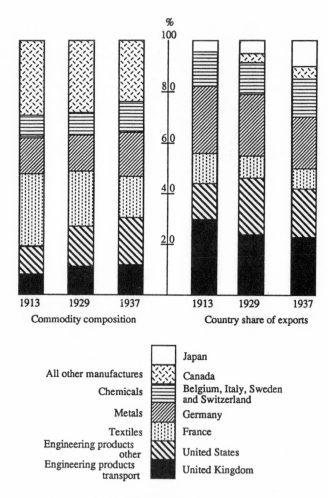

Figure 4.1 World Trade in Manufactures, 1913–1937 (Commodity Composition and Country Share)

Source: A. G. Kenwood and A. L. Lougheed, *The Growth of the International Economy, 1820–1900*. (London: Allen and Unwin, 1971). Used by permission.

foreign loans, bank credits, and foreign investment, is capable of undertaking a vigorous program of import-substituting industrialization based on imported capital and producers' goods as a strategy. This was also the period (1950s–1970s) of Keynesian social welfarism in the West and the ISI policy in developing countries, including India, which was a strategy of planned economic development led by a version of the Keynesian model suitable for the Third World. This strategy of ISI in the economy of the rest of the world (70 percent of the population) created a tremendous outlet for the huge amount of capital accumulated in the West over 100 years through trade in goods and commodity capital. Market-determined, piecemeal ISI has taken place in India and some other Third World economies since the late nineteenth century, with the help of loans and foreign investment via the supply of credit. However, after World War II, a planned attempt to industrialize these economies began (1950–1970), which created tremendous demand for products of the First World. I will discuss this aspect in more detail using the case of India's economic planning and the role it played in the transplantation of the capitalist industrial production in India (see Chapter 5).

The third stage of the internationalization of capitalism via the globalization of production dates to the mid-1970s and onwards. This stage, like the other two, is an inevitable culmination of capitalism's quest for profit, stage by stage, by unleashing limitless productive forces over the last 200 years. However, in doing so, capitalism has created an enormous problem in terms of creating environmental crisis, stagnating outlets for its increasing productivity and outputs, and, thereby, social crises. Capitalist social consciousness (i.e., produced by market-determined factor and product pricing and by employment conditions in a capitalist system) is indicated by utility-seeking individualism, which is best served by the market. Market results are clearly the results of the expressed wishes of utility-seeking individuals. The market facilitates the release of limitless productive forces hidden in nature and thereby, as is claimed, creates the condition of maximum welfare for members of a society. In the next section, capitalism's progress in three stages and the crisis capitalism is facing will be discussed.

The classical international division of labor theory as the basis of the international trade between industrial and agricultural countries was later, particularly after World War II, remodeled to state that the trade resulting from the international division of labor based on differences in factor endowments (i.e., between countries with cheaper labor and cheaper capital) would bring about a maximization of output, in the present, changed world situation, of a huge accumulation of capital, on one hand, and on the other, growing surplus labor accompanying rapid population growth in the Third World. We must note here that these conditions evolved because of the operation of international trade based on an international division of labor between countries with so-called differences in natural endowments (i.e., the countries that were blessed with initial ability and efficiency to industrialize and those that were blessed with rich natural resources but were poor in numbers of people). Arguments in favor of this trade theory are based on the fact that industrial production is subject to the law of increasing returns while the agricultural production is subject to the law of diminishing returns and, therefore, the exchange of goods between the two groups of countries will benefit global output and, more so, the groups of agricultural countries.

The import-substituting process arises from the close relationship between income level, consumption, and production patterns. Consumption patterns, it is

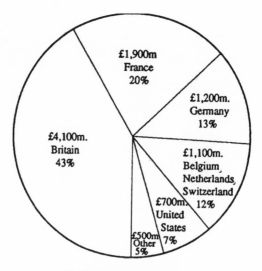

(a) By Investing Regions

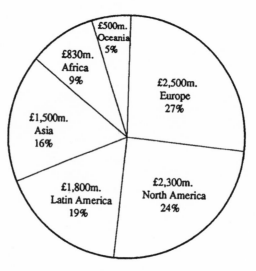

(b) By Recipient Regions

Figure 4.2 Distribution of Foreign Investment, 1914

Source: W. Woodruff, *Impact of Wastern Man* (London: George Allen and Unwin and Sydney Australian Publishing Company, 1966), 154–155.

TABLE 4.4 Trade in Primary Products: Regional Shares, 1876–1913 (Percentages)

Region	1876–1880 Imports	1876–1880 Exports	1896–1900 Imports	1896–1900 Exports	1913 Imports	1913 Exports
U.K. and Ireland	29.7	3.1	25.8	3.9	19.0	6.2
N.W. Europe	39.3	22.6	45.0	27.6	43.1	25.2
Other Europe	11.2	20.2	10.4	18.1	12.3	14.7
U.S. and Canada	7.2	16.1	8.5	18.7	11.3	17.3
Rest of World	12.6	38.0	10.3	31.7	14.3	36.6
World	100.0	100. 0	100.0	100.0	100.0	100.0

Source: Kenwood and Lougheed (1971), 44.

argued, depend on income levels, with different types of product consumed at different income levels. In this respect, the argument is very similar to that about the relationship between products and income level. Countries that are at a similar stage of development, therefore, consume similar goods. Innovation and production initially take place in order to supply the home market. Once a product is established on the home market, the industry widens its horizons to markets in countries with similar income levels, since the product was designed for that type of consumption pattern (Linder 1967). In import-substituting industrialization, production for consumption in the home market precedes exporting, which means that any goods that are exported are first designed for home consumption. Export markets arise in similar economies. The Heckser-Ohlin theory (Heckser 1949; Ohlin 1967 in Samuelson and Storper 1941) divorces production from consumption, so that a country produces whatever it has a comparative advantage in, irrespective of whether the good is consumed domestically. The latter view is reasonable in a world of unchanging technology, perfect knowledge, and perfect markets. In such a world there is no need to seek the security of the home market for new processes and products before venturing on the world market.

The new version of the theory of international trade (known as the Heckser, Ohlin, and Samuelson version) has been the result of the critical need of a huge accumulation of money and productive capital in the world's center of capitalism (the Western countries), which the first phase of the internationalization of capitalism has brought about in the last 100 years of its application. This phase of capitalism has been supported by the original version of the international division of labor theory. Therefore, the new version is an attempt to bring about the internationalization of finance and investment, so that this accumulated productive capital may be used to create further accumulation. Therefore, a strategy of import substitution industrialization became inevitable in the Third World. On

TABLE 4.5 Stock of Outward Foreign Direct Investment (FDI) of Selected Countries Compared to GDP, 1967 and 1988

	1967		1988	
	Stock ($bn)	% of GDP	Stock ($bn)	% of GDP
Western Europe[1]				
Germany	3.0	1.6	0.34	8.6
France	6.0	7.0	56.2	5.9
Italy	2.1	2.8	39.9	4.8
Netherlands	11.0	33.1	77.5	34.0
Sweden	1.7	5.7	26.2	16.4
Switzerland	2.5	10.0	44.1	23.9
Other				
UK	15.8	14.5	183.6	26.1
US	56.6	7.1	345.4	7.1
Japan	1.5	0.9	110.8	3.9
Total[2]	112.3	4.0	1,140.5	6.7

Source: Jones and Schroter (1993), 22. Calculated from Dunning (1991).
[1]Separate data for Belgium is not available in this source.
[2]This is total world outward direct investment. The percentage is calculated against world GDP.

the other hand, technology up until 1960 was largely scale-intensive and, therefore, its productive and efficient use required a larger organization of production and larger market. Products like vehicles, aviation equipment, chemicals, and metals are examples. Later, capitalism's production became scope intensive and flexible in operation. This is the emerging characteristic of the internationalization of production phase of capitalism. "The emerging economy of flexible production has brought into existence a series of new core production regions, and these are typically quite different from those of the mass production" (Storper and Scott (eds.) 1992, 8). Three groups of contemporary regions of flexible production can be recognized.

The first group, craft-based, design-intensive industries, such as clothing, textiles, furniture, jewelry, ceramics, sporting goods as well as precision metalworking and machine building, may be found in two main types of location. One coincides with inner-city areas in large metropolitan regions such as New York, Paris, Los Angeles, and London, with their large immigrant populations. The other coincides with old centers of craft production, as in Emilia-Romagna and Tuscany in Italy, parts of the Rhone Alps and Mediterranean regions of France, and certain parts of southern Germany and Scandinavia (Ganne, Saglio, Courault and Romani, Bianchi).

Second, high-technology industry has tended to locate above all at selected suburban locations close to major cities and in formerly nonindustrialized areas such as Cambridge in the United Kingdom, the French Midi, and especially the U.S. Sunbelt, with its major new, high-technology growth centers in such places as Orange County, Silicon Valley, Chatsworth-Canoga Park, Dallas–Fort Worth, and so on (Saxenian).

Third, advanced producer and financial service agglomerations are found in or close to the central cores of large cities, such as Tokyo, New York, and London, or La Defense in Paris (Storper and Scott 1992, 8). (See Tables 4.5–4.19).

The internationalization of production phase of capitalism of today has led to the transformation of import substitution all over the world, and the Third World in particular, into export-substituting industrialization. The emergence of the economy of flexible production became the most effective instrument in the internationalization of production (see Storper and Scott 1992, 8–11).

Two economists wrote:

The phenomenal growth in the internationalisation of production, the intrinsic need to go beyond the boundaries of national states, and to relocate production sites in markets across the world on the one hand, and the third world struggle against the

TABLE 4.6 FDI in Developing Regions and Countries, 1980–1989

	Percentage Share of Global FDI	
Host Region and Economy	1980–1984	1988–1989
Developing countries	25.2	16.9
Africa	2.4	1.9
Latin America and the Caribbean	12.3	5.8
East, South, and Southeast Asia	9.4	8.8
Least developed countries	0.4	0.1
Ten largest host countries	18.1	11.1
Argentina	0.9	0.6
Brazil	4.2	1.5
China	1.1	1.9
Columba	0.8	0.2
Eygpt	1.1	0.8
Hong Kong	1.4	1.2
Malaysia	2.3	0.7
Mexico	3.0	1.4
Singapore	2.8	2.0
Thailand	0.6	0.8

Source: United Nations Development Program (1992), Table 4.6.

economic problems emanating from the colonial division of labour, on the other, gave rise to import substitution industrialisation (ISI) as a common strategy in the immediate post-war era. (Bina and Yaghmaian 1990, 79)

ISI is essentially an offshoot of this phase of internationalization of investment via finance, loans, and credit, which enabled the Third World to initiate industrialization with imported inputs (i.e., capital, technology, knowledge, and skill) from the Capitalist West. Economic planning led by state played the key role in this process, unlike the piecemeal, market-determined import substitution efforts in the past. However, the internationalization of the production phase proper through the multinational corporations (MNCs) and flexible production systems took the form of the transfer of direct production plants all over the world (see Tables 4.5–4.21). At this stage, obviously, export substitution industrialization becomes the principal tool, requiring the dismantling of the state-planning or public sector, which is replaced by the policies of privatization, a free market, and the unrestricted movement of products and factors. We must be aware of the distinction between these two phases, which most authors have ignored. This stage-by-stage expansion of world capitalism results from the gradual unleashing of productive forces, on the one hand, and on the other, its acute crisis of accumulated huge productivity, with the resultant lack of effective employment opportunities in the organized capitalist sector in order to clear the markets of increasing output.

Only after World War II did the capitalist tendency to transform the system into a world system become historical reality, as all functional forms of capital, commodity capital, interest-bearing capital, and productive capital, were globalized. With the gradual internationalization of capitalism via trade, a supply of finance capital, and the current international transfer of productive capital and direct production, a basic and determining contradiction arose: the capitalist state is, by its

TABLE 4.7   Real Growth of U.S. FDI and GNP, 1950–1985

Period	FDI	GNP	FDI rate GNP rate
1950-55	7.7	4.2	3.5
1955-60	7.8	2.3	5.5
1960-65	7.5	4.7	2.8
1965-70	4.4	3.2	1.2
1970-75	3.7	2.6	1.1
1975-80	4.6	4.7	−0.1
1980-85	1.5	2.5	−1.0
1985-88	12.3	3.7	8.6

Source: Cited in McIntyre (1990), 143–44.

very origin, a national state, whereas the production process is internationalized, and hence arises a contradiction between the nation's political decisions versus economic decisions, which is determined by the international factors arising from the globalization of the production process. In this contradiction, which has become marked in these days of globalization of capitalist production, the national political decisions of the state are being put in the backseat to facilitate the capitalists' quest for globalization of production and thereby help lead the flourishing productive forces to an unlimited horizon. However, this advancement of capitalism worldwide is creating a contradiction in the form of growing unemployment, low-wage unemployment, and severe environmental crises. The basic factor in capitalism's effort to increase the profit rate is to reduce costs, that is, by reducing labor content and, therefore, indirectly limiting the market for its products. Competition among capitalists, with their unlimited capacity to produce, innovate, and diversify output with a reduced market capacity due to unemployment and low wages is forcing constant technological improvements and innovation, with further cuts in marketability. To reduce environmental crises, the production process requires higher costs and, to compensate, involves a further loss in jobs. In a market system, to reduce environmental crises, more productive and better natural resources are needed which, in turn, requires more sophisticated but limited number of workers, adding fuel to the vicious circle of intense competition, technological sophistication and innovation, increased output and consumerism, growing pollution costs, more technological change to reduce costs and diversify output, further reduction of the market, and more intense competition, completing the circle.

Socialist industrialization and capitalist industrialization are two fundamentally different sides of the economic process, but in both cases, production is based on surplus produced by labor. In the former case, the aim of production is to

TABLE 4.8 U.S. FDI by Area (Percentage Composition)

Area	1950	1960	1965	1970	1975	1980	1985	1988
Canada	30.4	34.2	30.9	29.4	25.0	20.9	20.4	19.6
Europe	14.6	20.4	28.4	31.1	39.7	44.9	45.7	48.8
Japan	0.2	0.8	1.4	1.9	2.7	2.9	4.1	5.4
Australia, N. Z., and South Africa	3.1	3.6	4.6	5.6	5.6	4.9	4.7	4.9
Brazil, Mexico	9.0	5.3	4.6	4.6	6.3	6.3	6.1	5.6
Other America	29.8	22.3	17.6	14.2	11.6	11.6	6.2	5.3
Other Africa	1.2	2.4	2.8	3.3	1.9	1.7	1.9	1.5
Other Asia	2.5	2.7	2.8	3.1	4.6	3.9	6.7	6.0
Other	3.3	4.7	4.2	4.6	5.7	1.7	2.3	1.5

Note: McIntyre (1990), 143-44.

bring about social development using labor. Under this system, labor is also a commodity and a source of capital, but the laborer owns his product collectively or socially, while in a capitalist system, labor is a commodity, the source of capital, and its output is owned by the owners of capital, who do not produce it, and not by labor socially; nor is production socially shared. That is why the future growth of the productive force with social labor–made capital (i.e., instruments of production) can be unlimited. I have discussed the case of capitalist production, which is the main concern of this book (see Tables 4.1 and 4.2).

However, with an increasing accumulation of finance capital in the center and its transfer to the Third World to push the import-substitution industrialization strategy, the latter was further and more strongly integrated into the international capitalist system. Most Third World countries were at the precapitalist, semifeudal stage when they gradually became integrated to the world capitalist system, particularly in the period after World War II.

During the earlier stages of internationalization, capitalist states retained their national role. We should be particularly aware of the great achievement of the Keynesian revolution, which established the "lender of last resort" and "big government" on the level of the national economic system in order to avoid a future crisis like the 1930s Depression. Besides, this period was also marked by tremendous progress in the development of productive forces and productivity, accompanied by social welfarism, affluence, and a full employment condition in the developed capitalist economies. Meanwhile, in the Third World, Keynesianism in the form of state planning and public sector investment contributed to the growth of a stronger industrial capitalist sector. Needless to say, this was done to help prepare the world economy for the onward march of the globalization of production phase of capitalism that followed the phase of investment via supply of credit (see Chapter 5).

TABLE 4.9 U.S. FDI in Manufacturing by Area (Percentage Composition)

Area	1950	1960	1965	1970	1975	1980	1985	1988
Canada	49.5	34.6	35.5	28.9	26.3	21.1	23.0	21.0
Europe	24.3	34.4	39.3	44.5	46.5	51.0	47.9	50.9
Other developed	4.1	6.3	7.6	9.0	8.4	8.1	8.8	9.6
Latin America	20.4	13.8	15.2	14.6	15.3	16.3	15.6	13.17
Other developing	1.7	1.9	2.4	3.0	3.4	3.5	4.6	5.3
All developed	77.9	84.3	82.4	82.4	81.2	80.2	79.7	81.3
All developing	22.1	15.7	17.6	17.6	18.8	19.8	20.3	18.7

Source: U.S. Department of Commerce, *Survey of Current Business*, various issues. Cited in McIntyre (1990), 143–44.

However, in the current stage of internationalization of production, (a) when international money and product markets determine national monetary and fiscal policy; (b) when mobilization and the pricing of factors of production become subject to international market conditions; and (c) when the transnational organization of production dominates local policy and capitalist organization, national institutional networks and policy lose effectiveness. Therefore, international institutional networks like the World Bank, International Monetary Fund (IMF), General Agreement on Tariffs and Trade (GATT), and so on, with the superpower United States become the dominant factors in determining the economic policies of all nations belonging to the world capitalist circuit. Recent World Bank, IMF, and GATT advice to the Third World provides ample proof (see Cline 1976).

The capitalist system prospers by raising the rate of capital accumulation and developing productive forces all the time, but paradoxically, because of the nature of the system, the more developed the productive forces, the more intensive become the crisis this generates. We are witnessing today the extent and depth of this crisis.

The internationalization of production is the highest point of development of three historically distinct phases of the internationalization of goods and commodity capital, money capital, and productive capital. In these three stages of the expansion of capitalism, productive forces are also developed to the maximum possible under the system. We see today the signs of contradictions between the system and the onward progress of the productive forces, as reflected in an acute inequality and concentration of wealth; worldwide, giant organizations of production; highly developed, science-based technology, and an extreme form of consumerism, on the one hand, and on the other, growing and disguised unemployment; millions of small, self-employed, low-income units of production, and growing poverty confronting the mass of the population.

The internationalization process has been the result of a series of interrelated and mutually reinforcing developments dating from the last part of the nineteenth century, which include the concentration and centralization of capital, the formation of joint stock companies in banking and manufacturing, the expansion of a credit system and its growing importance in capital accumulation, and consequently, the formation of finance capital. The financial capital of large banks with the productive or physical capital of very large conglomerates of industrial concerns became interlocked in the course of time. C. Bina and B. Yaghmaian wrote: "Finance capital and the internationalisation of all circuits . . . are historically specific developments that have left unprecedented effects on pre-capitalist socio economic formations of the rest of the world" (1990, 21).

Some Marxist economists concluded that the internationalization of the circuit of money capital through loans and the circuit of productive capital strengthened the political position of the precapitalist ruling classes and while it also served as a "leading wedge" in the capitalist transformation of precapitalist social relations

(Weeks 1955). However, according to Bina and Yaghmaian, "Although the export of money capital and the internationalisation of commodity capital did not result in the capitalist transformation of the colonies, nevertheless, in some cases, it contributed to the development of their productive forces" (1990, 83). It is hard to accept this conclusion. It is true that these two phases prepared the stage of the transition towards the fully integrated global capitalist economy of the mid-twentieth century. However, it is perhaps not correct to say that these processes of the internationalization of capitalism have contributed to the development of nations' (i.e., the Third World's) productive forces. The question remains, what should be the criterion? True, increasing capital accumulation results in the development of productive forces in the countries of its origin; in this case, the West. This was evident in the dynamic changes in the economic structure of these economies, the demographic effects of the capitalist transformation, the development and dominance of the factor-pricing system, and so forth. What has happened in the case of India or the Third World is that the transfer of money capital to facilitate the supply of commodity capital to India and other countries has led to the development of industrial growth with little absorption of the huge surplus of labor and without generating any of the social and economic reorganization that the growth of productive forces inevitably brings about. These economies remained predominantly precapitalistic, not only in economic structure but also in social consciousness; India is an example. The primitive accumulation of money capital and economic surplus via a growth in productive forces from overseas has been transplanted from the Western capitalist economies and

TABLE 4.10 Private U.S. Investment Abroad, Assets Held at Year End, 1950–1987 (billions of $ U.S.)

Year	Direct investment	Bonds	Stocks	Total
1950	11.8	3.2	1.2	17.5
1955	19.4	3.0	2.4	26.7
1960	31.9	5.5	4.0	44.4
1965	49.5	10.2	5.0	71.0
1970	78.2	13.2	6.4	105.0
1975	124.0	25.3	9.6	174.4
1980	215.4	43.5	19.2	516.6
1985	230.3	73.0	39.8	819.5
1986	259.6	81.8	51.4	933.4
1987	308.9	91.0	55.7	1033.6

Source: Root (1984).
Note: Total column includes categories in addition to direct investment, bonds, and stocks; therefore, components do not sum to total.

combined with a tiny fraction of the surplus labor of these host countries. The result has been tremendous growth in output but with little growth in the productive force in host countries and little impact in bringing about fundamental changes in precapitalist economies, like that of India. Therefore, when Bina and Yaghmaian wrote that industrialization and the capitalist transformation of less developed countries (LDCs) have been the result of the internationalization of productive capital and the globalization of production beyond the national boundaries in the postwar era, this sounds devoid of an objective assessment of the process of capitalist transformation. It is undeniable that there has been remarkable growth in industrialization and capital formation, but the economic structure, pattern of demographic transition, and economic organization show little sign of capitalist transformation. We should ask ourselves, can we expect the transfer of highly resource-intensive productive capital developed in a mature capitalist economy to bring about such a transformation via the absorption of labor in a Third World country?

Import-substituting industrialization and export-substituting industrialization are two phases in the mature stage of the internationalization of finance capital and productive capital. The former graduates into the latter as a matter of course, when needed to fulfill the process of internationalization of capital and production. The world economy is currently at this state, which has been achieved through comprehensive state intervention in creating the condition for the internationalization of finance capital and import substitution, thereby stimulating industrialization. State intervention took the following forms: social welfarism, the domination of the trade union in the labor market, and expansionary fiscal policy in mature capitalist economies, on the one hand, and on the other, the operation of the state-planning and public sector to boost private sector industrialization in the developing countries. This helped to prepare the following stage of capitalism's internationalization of production, which cannot be served by state intervention but requires complete deregulation of products, labor, and money and foreign exchange markets. The state must be reduced to zero with a budget surplus to reduce cost of production and release money capital for investment in order to make capitalism internationally competitive.

With the internationalization of finance capital, later followed by that of production, the transfer of capital accumulation of mature capitalist economies with little labor content to economies with huge surpluses of laborers eking out a subsistence living in both the urban and rural sectors cannot play the role of development of capitalism in bringing about capitalist transformation. True, the import-substituting industrialization as an inevitable part of the internationalization of finance capital has created and fortified a class of capitalists in all developing countries, but without causing any effects of capitalist transformation. These local capitalist classes now have become the stronger clients of world capitalism in its aim to fulfill its role in the current stage by the internationalization of production (see Chapter 5).

TABLE 4.11 International Investment Position, 1976 and 1987 (billions of $ U.S.)

Type of investment	1976	1987
U.S. assets abroad	347.2	1,167.8
U.S. official reserve assets	18.7	45.8
Nonreserve U.S. government assets	46.0	88.4
U.S. private assets	282.4	1,033.6
Foreign assets in the United States	263.6	1,536.0
Foreign official assets	104.6	283.1
Other foreign assets	159.1	1,252.9

Source: J. Cantwell, *Technological Innovation and Multinational Corporations* (Oxford: Blackwell Publishers, 1989), 98. Used by permission of Blackwell Publishers.

Marx wrote:

The accumulation of capital presupposes surplus value; surplus value presupposes capitalist production; capitalist production presupposes the availability of considerable masses of capital and labour power in the hands of commodity producers . . . which can only get out of by assuming a primitive accumulation which precedes capitalist accumulation; and accumulation, which is not the result of the capitalist mode of production but its point of departure. (1977, 873)

In India, although there exists an unlimited supply of surplus labor in the form of primitive capital accumulation, this has not been transformed into developed capital accumulation as was done in the United Kingdom and later in Continental Europe and the United States. Developed capital that was accumulated in these countries has been transferred to developing countries, which has failed to bring about the capitalist transformation of the economy and therefore made the capitalists of these countries helplessly dependent on the supply of developed capital and its technology. The main reason for the failure of the transfer of capital and technology to bring about changes in economic reorganization and economic structure is that the application of technology in its intensive phase to labor-surplus economies does not bring about such transformation. To develop capital and technology indigenously requires a mobilization of domestic resources which makes it imperative to bring about a reorganization to release resources, as was done in the United Kingdom.

Some Marxist economists have argued that the institution and implementation of the postwar land reform programs have, indeed, deepened the tendency toward proletarianization of the peasantry in developing countries, which in turn resulted in an immense source of surplus labor for the emerging import-substituting industries (Agahia and Bina 1989). In India, land reform policy was introduced

TABLE 4.12 Geographical Distribution of International Production in Manufacturing by Source Country, 1982

Source country	Value of production ($m)	Share of production (%)
U.S.	357,244	42.43
West Germany	89,586	10.64
UK	154,230	18.32
Italy	13,141	1.56
France	45,333	5.38
Japan	41,047	4.87
World Total	842,027	100.00

Source: J. Cantwell, *Technological Innovation and Multinational Corporations* (Oxford: Blackwell Publishers, 1989), 98. Used by permission of Blackwell Publishers.

in 1950s, which produced a huge surplus of labor that, together with the high rate of population growth, has become an unlimited supply of primitive accumulation of the early phase. On the other hand, like many other developing countries, India has been showered with the products of advanced phases of primitive accumulation, that is, with unlimited supplies of developed capital and technology. Therefore, India's huge, primitive accumulation of the early phase is lying unused and keeping the economic structure precapitalist. The Marxists economists completely ignore this effect on the Third World. The early phase of primitive accumulation coincides with the internationalization of commodity capital and the early development of the world market, while the period of advanced primitive accumulation entwines with the internationalization of all circuits of capital and the resultant globalization of production (Bina and Yaghmaian 1990). These authors have not analyzed the effects in terms of capitalist transformation of these societies in this pattern of internationalization of capitalism.

In the Third World, the primitive accumulation of capital consists mainly of huge surplus labor as a result of a high population growth rate and, since 1950, labor released by land reforms. However, the fundamental difference in these two processes lies with the fact that in countries like India, this primitive capital is not being turned into productive capital. Productive capital accumulation is growing fast and at a high rate, but it does not need the primitive accumulation of this sort. In the United Kingdom, the need for surplus labor at the nascent stage of industrial capitalism in the sixteenth and seventeenth centuries led to the completion of enclosures. The two components of early primitive accumulation, money capital and surplus labor, were combined to produce industrial capital and other fundamental reforms to replace the feudal system. However, in the Third World today, productive capital is being created with the help of capital borrowed from overseas, which

TABLE 4.13 Geographical Distribution of International Production and Indigenous Firm Exports in Manufacturing Combined, by Source Country, 1982

Source country	Value of production plus exports ($m)	Share of production plus exports (%)
U.S.	521,269	27.60
West Germany	230,466	12.20
UK	212,816	11.23
Italy	78,434	4.15
France	121,709	6.45
Japan	176,709	9.36
World Total	1,888,357	100.00

Source: J. Cantwell, *Technological Innovation and Multinational Corporations* (Oxford: Blackwell Publishers, 1989), 100. Used by permission of Blackwell Publishers.

does not and cannot use the primitive accumulation that exists in huge quantity in these countries and therefore does not require any fundamental change in socio-economic structure to facilitate its development into productive capital. Society remains feudal in its social mind and economic structure. Land reforms are introduced but this reinforces a small, subsistence peasant economy with surplus labor. Capitalist growth essentially has become superficial, with no root in the history of these economies (see Chapter 2).

INTERNATIONALIZATION OF CAPITALISM AND MASS CONSUMPTION

The internationalization of investment phase of capitalism was accompanied by social welfarism (and military or rightest Keynesism in the United States), with the full employment, high wages, and ever-expanding mass consumption that characterize the stage of consumerism in the center of developed capitalism. This was rendered possible by rapid technological progress and constant innovations stimulated by product cycles according to technology gap trade theories and Hecker-Ohlin's neoclassical trade theory. Great changes in capital accumulation in the form of growth of basic and heavy industries indicate that high productivity must come about before the automobile becomes part of the wage basket (e.g., goods wages are spent on). These changes first reached fruition in the United States in the early 1950s, but, they began in 1920s with Fordism, which allowed higher wages for workers so that demand for automobiles could expand in the local market to help realize economics of scale of production. In those days, the extent of internal markets was limited because of their relatively low level of pro-

TABLE 4.14 National Firms' Shares of International Production by Manufacturing
Sector, 1982 (Percentage)

	United States	West Germany	United Kingdom	Italy	France	Japan
Food products	31.0	2.5	34.7	0.3	1.8	2.4
Chemicals	37.2	27.4	13.4	2.4	4.6	5.8
Metals	34.5	10.3	15.8	0.5	5.5	3.3
Mechanical engineering	38.1	13.9	12.5	0.5	2.4	2.9
Electrical equipment	49.3	13.1	12.5	1.3	6.8	11.0
Motor vehicles	40.5	18.1	8.3	4.7	9.4	8.1
Other transport equipment	25.6	11.1	13.3	0.4	3.5	0.8
Textiles	29.8	15.0	42.7	0.7	4.0	8.0
Rubber products	43.5	7.8	21.9	10.5	9.7	5.9
Non-metallic mineral products	28.6	9.7	22.3	0.1	21.3	6.2
Coal and petroleum products	53.0	0.5	19.6	0.9	5.4	0.3
Other manufacturing	70.7	8.8	7.3	0.1	1.0	14.9
Total	42.4	10.6	18.3	1.6	5.4	4.9

Source: J. Cantwell, *Technological Innovation and Multinational Corporations* (Oxford: Blackwell Publishers, 1989), 105. Used by permission of Blackwell Publishers.

ductivity. Britain's ability was limited by numbers in terms of population as well as relative inequality in incomes. Some mass production and mass consumption began to develop, but the really decisive turning point occurred after World War II, when the automobile became part of the wage basket of the average worker (Albriton 1991). The stage of consumerism is the age of consumer durables, of which the automobile is most prominent.

The automobile is quite different from the preceding sequence of products of cotton, wool, and steel. The automobile introduces the use of a different kind of energy (i.e., a more capital-intensive energy, petroleum) and a much higher level of human capital in the production. Wool and cotton are relatively cheap products with labor-intensive technology and, therefore, low-wage labor feeding the basic necessity of masses, while steel as the basic input of all machinery is a basic need of all industry. In the meantime, higher-level human capital began to be turned out in increasing amounts with the turn of the century (see Chapter 7).

The United States has had slightly higher wages than other capitalist economies, even as far back as 1920s. There are two basic reasons for this. First, America's migrant European economy had to work from the beginning with a relatively limited labor force compared to the vast natural resource of the country and, therefore, had to improve the technology and, thus, productivity of a relatively skilled migrant European labor force. The industrializing economy of the

TABLE 4.15 National Firms' Shares of Exports by Manufacturing Sector, 1974 (Percentages)

	United States	West Germany	United Kingdom	Italy	France	Japan
Food products	32.8	1.1	21.8	0.5	1.2	1.2
Chemicals	52.8	22.1	9.2	3.3	7.8	3.8
Metals	40.4	8.7	23.2	0.2	5.4	1.0
Mechanical engineering	51.1	8.6	10.9	0.3	2.5	1.2
Electrical equipment	65.6	13.2	10.8	1.0	3.8	4.6
Motor vehicles	66.7	11.7	9.3	2.5	6.3	2.6
Other transport equipment	14.4	23.8	36.5	0.3	3.3	0.3
Textiles	40.5	10.3	40.1	0.4	2.4	5.3
Rubber products	55.9	5.6	9.8	12.3	11.3	4.2
Non-metallic mineral products	47.6	5.3	19.9	0.1	11.1	4.2
Coal and petroleum products	66.2	0.3	5.9	0.2	2.9	0.1
Other manufacturing	63.0	7.3	4.7	0.1	0.5	7.3
Total	55.3	6.8	12.4	1.1	3.9	2.1

Source: J. Cantwell, *Technological Innovation and Multinational Corporations* (Oxford: Blackwell Publishers, 1989), 104. Used by permission of Blackwell Publishers.

United States could not use local, preindustrial American Indian labor in modern industrial production.

Second, to attract a labor force with the background of industrial economy of Europe on the one hand, and on the other, to make the jobs attractive to the would-be migrants from these developed industrial economies, paying higher wages was unavoidable. Henry Ford, in the 1920s, introduced automobile technology borrowed from England, where its market was confined to a very limited number of high-income people. Its product quality was also much superior and, hence, the price was prohibitive to mass consumers. Henry Ford began automobile production in the United States with the mass market as the target. Hence, he followed a policy of engaging workers with relatively high wages and, thereby, creating larger markets so that economies of scales of production could be realized.

M. Itoh raises some important points in "The Japanese Model of Post-Fordism," as to the reasons behind the rise of Fordism in America. To summarize his thoughts prior to the 1920s the wages and particularly working conditions in areas were so poor in Ford's factory that the worker turnover became a monumental problem. In 1913, Ford needed approximately 4,000 workers to run his plants at any time and in that year alone 50,000 workers quit working for Ford. Therefore the need for the intensity, continuity and discipline required of assem-

TABLE 4.16   National Shares of Exports by Manufacturing Sector, 1974 (Percentages)

	United States	West Germany	United Kingdom	Italy	France	Japan
Food products	16.7	3.3	2.5	2.5	7.5	0.9
Chemicals	14.7	20.1	8.3	5.2	8.2	6.7
Metals	7.3	17.2	2.8	3.9	7.5	17.1
Mechanical engineering	23.8	23.1	10.7	5.5	6.8	8.1
Electrical equipment	14.1	15.3	5.4	4.2	5.8	12.0
Motor vehicles	17.2	21.7	6.6	5.2	9.1	15.9
Other transport equipment	28.1	7.9	5.4	2.0	5.4	25.9
Textiles	6.1	12.1	8.0	10.9	8.3	9.1
Rubber products	13.4	18.3	7.2	7.4	13.7	9.0
Non-metallic mineral products	8.5	18.8	7.5	11.9	10.4	7.8
Coal and petroleum products	7.9	7.1	4.0	5.4	2.7	0.6
Other manufacturing	13.3	13.6	9.1	4.3	5.8	8.5
Total	14.0	14.0	5.9	4.9	7.1	9.4

Source: J. Cantwell, *Technological Innovation and Multinational Corporations* (Oxford: Blackwell Publishers, 1989), 102. Used by permission of Blackwell Publishers.

bly line production as well as for preparing the work force with specialized skill required for such complex industry which requires continued association with the work and the factory, made Ford realize that labor turnover nearly four times in a year should not be allowed to continue. To alleviate this problem, Ford introduced the Five Dollar Day which effectively doubled his workers' wages. The wage increase was on top of industrial wages that were already approximately twice as high in America as in Europe. The mass automobile market in the 1920s was primarily a middle class market and even that market was artificially expanded by the development of installment selling and buying—a system which may be regarded as the forerunner of the currently universally instituted all over the capitalist countries, the hire purchase system. However, Ford's system of paying wages was substantially above the social average so as to enable his workers to purchase them and also to maintain the necessary number of workers for heavy monotonous work. On a social scale the postwar Ford regime of accumulation, realized both increases in labor productivity and roughly proportional increases in real wages (Itoh 1992, 116–23). However, this became inevitable in a social welfare state where excessive demand for labor strengthened the workers' bargaining power via the trade union and the Keynesian policy of stimulating aggregate demand to equate with the aggregate supply dominated government fiscal policy.

TABLE 4.17 National Shares of Exports by Manufacturing Sector, 1982 (Percentages)

	U.S.	Germany	UK	Italy	France	Japan
Food products	16.4	5.3	4.0	3.2	8.3	0.8
Chemicals	16.3	17.6	8.9	4.4	9.7	5.2
Metals	6.6	14.6	5.3	6.0	7.9	16.4
Mechanical engineering	22.2	19.1	9.3	7.2	6.7	11.8
Electrical equipment	20.1	12.0	6.2	4.2	5.6	22.1
Motor vehicles	11.3	22.4	4.3	3.6	7.7	24.7
Other transport equipment	28.4	13.8	7.5	3.2	8.6	15.4
Textiles	5.2	9.9	4.5	13.4	5.9	6.7
Rubber products	11.1	16.3	7.3	7.3	12.3	11.0
Non-metallic mineral products	7.9	14.4	5.8	13.6	9.3	9.7
Coal and petroleum products	5.6	4.7	3.8	4.4	3.0	0.4
Other manufacturing	14.4	11.6	7.3	6.8	5.5	9.4
Total	14.2	13.2	6.1	5.8	7.0	11.0

Source: J. Cantwell, *Technological Innovation and Multinational Corporations* (Oxford: Blackwell Publishers, 1989), 103. Used by permission of Blackwell Publishers.

Soon, industrializing Europe with its increasing productivity was also able to offer higher wages, at least to more productive workers who could become consumers of automobiles. Therefore, this was followed by trade in this consumer durable and, later, import substitution all over the Western world. Later, in the 1950s, consumerist policies were marked by an extremely large and active welfare state based upon a considerable rate of income tax (which was supposedly progressive) as well as budget deficit policies. As a result, the state sector became an important part of the economy, employing a large number of people with high incomes, which also helped the development of consumerism. However, a more important contribution came from the rapid growth of the foreign trade in capital goods of the capitalist economies. This was caused by the rapid rise in demand for such products (e.g., intermediate and capital goods, knowledge, and technology) in the Third World—the countries that undertook a massive program of planned development with the help of foreign investment (in finance and credit) and foreign aid supplied by developed capitalist economies as part of their internationalization of investment phase. Thus, the demand for physical capital products of Western capitalist economies (particularly the United States, United Kingdom, France, and Italy) stimulated a rapid expansion of these industries, creating a tremendous demand for more labor than could be supplied, on the one hand, and stimulating technological change to substitute more productive capital for labor, on the other. This is one side of the picture; the other side is related to the inevitable relationship of mass production with mass consumption

TABLE 4.18 Sales of U.S. Manufacturing Affiliates in Europe, 1957–1975 (millions of $ U.S.)

		Europe			EEC six			West Germany		
Chemicals	(a)	822	3,417	19,798	275	1,733	12,478	46	464	3,063
and	(b)	353	927	2,666	223	596	1,816	43	121	352
allied	(c)	2.33	3.69	7.43	1.23	2.91	6.87	1.07	3.83	8.7
Primary and	(a)	435	1,619	7,985	145	648	4,458	45	207	2,057
fabricated	(b)	462	497	1,220	214	296	633	70	87	189
metals	(c)	0.94	3.26	6.55	0.68	2.19	7.04	0.64	2.38	10.88
Mechanical	(a)	1,009	4,099	21,235	502	2,431	13,007	228	903	4,571
engineering	(b)	567	1,571	5,451	306	822	2,923	59	238	825
	(c)	1.78	2.61	3.9	1.64	2.96	4.45	3.86	3.79	5.54
Electrical	(a)	678	2,170	11,891	299	1,214	8,463	73	na	3,133
equipment	(b)	114	644	2,179	55	338	1,202	8	100	421
	(c)	5.95	3.37	5.46	5.44	3.59	7.04	9.13	na	7.44
Transportation	(a)	1,700	5,012	16.339	764	2,747	9,822†	na	na	5,917
equipment	(b)	244	647	2,493	130	350	1,152†	14	138	419
	(c)	6.97	7.75	6.55	5.88	7.85	8.53T	na	na	14.12
Rubber	(a)	262	662	2,190	77	276	1,321	na	na	204
products	(b)	97	128	178	60	86	118	19	29	25
	(c)	2.70	5.17	12.30	1.28	3.21	11.19	na	na	8.16
Paper	(a)	34	384	3,221	13	241	1.671‡	6	61	420
and	(b)	91	257	916	44	157	482‡	15	55	195
allied	(c)	0.37	1.49	3.52	0.30	1.54	3.74‡	0.40	1.11	2.15
All Products	(a)	4,490	17,363	82,650	2,074	9,290	52,221	890	3,920	19,365
	(b)	1,928	4,671	15,103	1,032	2,645	8,326	228	768	2,426
	(c)	2.56	3.72	5.47	2.01	3.51	6.27	3.90	5.10	7.98

Source: J. Cantwell, *Technological Innovation and Multinational Corporations* (Oxford: Blackwell Publishers, 1989), 80–81. Used by permission of Blackwell Publishers.
Note: na = not available.
[a]sales of affiliates; [b]U.S. exports; [c]sales/export ratio.
*Excluding paper and allied.
†Excluding the Netherlands transportation equipment.
‡Excluding the Netherlands paper and allied.

(Rostow's mass consumption stage). Keynesian "effective demand" (Keynes 1936) came to dominate economic policy as a crucial and manipulatable economic category and capitalists all over the world, including the Third World, began to occupy themselves equally with the creation of products and the creation of consumers for those products. The welfare states in the West and militarist Keynesianism in the United States offered a strong helping hand to capitalism in this respect, while in the Third World, state economic development planning, led by the public sector and with the help of Western foreign investment and aid, was instituted to prepare the ground for strengthening the weak capitalist sector. This is elaborated further in the section on India (see Chapter 5, "The Mahalanobis Planning Model Revisited"). Wages and consumer credit must rise fast enough to create a mass market for the mass-produced consumer durables. Marketing gradually displaces production as the arena of prime concern. Mass consumption must grow in pace with mass production and in the post–World War II period, a mass market grew that was "far greater than any previously known in history" (Chandler 1977, 407).

This globalization of production has been called by some economists "the stage of consumerism." Rostow used the development of mass consumption to indicate this period, but without any reference to the internationalization of production phase of capitalism. However, the basic features of Rostow's "mass consumption" stage are the same as those of the "stage of consumerism."

It is difficult to demarcate the period of internationalization of production from that of investment. The huge domestic market of the auto industry in the United States, with 76 percent of the total world passenger car registrations in 1950 indicates that the auto industry did not take the lead in the internationalization of production. The period between the 1950s and 1970s is still regarded as the period of internationalization of investment. The income per capita in major Western countries, although rising, still was not sufficient for mass markets for these high-priced products. However, both General Motors and Ford did develop significant international operations (they have operations on all continents). Ford, with the most highly developed international operations, had 38 percent of its total sales from production outside North America in 1979, while GM's share, in that year was only 19 percent. Today, Western Europe and Japan have also entered into this production.

The following sections provide statistics for and discusses the process of internationalization of production. We will attempt to explore here the nature of capitalist development by three stages of the internationalization of goods and commodity capital (see Table 4.2) followed by the globalization of investment (via direct foreign investment; see Tables 4.5 and 4.6), which is expected to help explain the policy dilemma. The dilemma is whether to continue with the policy of state intervention and social welfarism or to introduce the policy of privatization, dismantling of social welfarism, free trade and market, deregulation of labor and money markets, etc. Whether to pursue a policy of developing productive bonus by using market forces or a policy of ensuring economic equality, full employment and maximum social good. Capitalism survives and prospers only when it expands its area of operation and thereby raises its rate of capital accumulation. Thus, capitalism today has reached every corner of the earth in quest of higher rates of profit and capital accumulation. This process began with the internationalization of goods, capital finance, and credit through international trade during the earlier period from the mid-nineteenth century to the mid-twentieth century, which was followed by the internationalization of investment and, later of production (since the 1950s), with the rapid rise of the MNCs (see Table 4.8).

The rate of capital accumulation in most Western capitalist countries during the 1950s–1970s was, on average, 30 to 35 percent of GNP, while in the nineteenth and early twentieth centuries, that rate was between 3 and 10. This huge accumulation of capital resulting from the internationalization of goods and capital in the past needed an expanding scope for investment after the 1950s, the search for which led to the emergence of the internationalization of investment. Fierce monopolistic competition stimulated technological change and innovation and unleashed an unlimited productive capacity, which cannot be supported profitably by the local markets of developed capitalist countries. Hence, the need for internationalization of investment followed by production became inevitable in the 1970s. The features of these stages of capitalist development will explain the factors that have pushed capitalism to its policy dilemma.

INTERNATIONALIZATION OF GOODS AND PRODUCTION

The international mobility of capital goods (construction, capital equipment, and inventories) varies with the nature of the good. It should be made clear that the transfer of capital by a nation does not necessarily take the form of export of capital to another. Instead, capital is transferred by international loans and investments that provide the purchasing power needed to finance either the construction of capital goods in the borrowing country or the importation of capital goods from abroad. The former dominated the policy of transfer of capital since 1950s, to help the Third World to develop import substituting industries, while the latter dominated the period from the late nineteenth century to the 1930s. This explains the criterion for the international mobility of capital is the ease of foreign investment in either or both of these forms. During the nineteenth century and up to the 1930s, most international investment took the form of private lending via subscriptions to foreign bond issues. Although in the 1970s, private lending of this sort and by banks once again became substantial, much private foreign investment today is undertaken by international companies (e.g., MNCs that make direct equity investments in foreign affiliates). The rapid expansion of direct foreign investment by U.S., European, and Japanese companies is a dominant force in the evolution of the contemporary world economy (see Tables 4.5,

TABLE 4.19 Comparison of the Ten Largest Multinational Corporations (MNCs) and Selected Countries According to Size of Annual Gross Domestic Product (GDP), 1990

MNC Rank	Country or Company (Headquarters)	1990 GDP or Gross Sales (billions of dollars)
1	General Motors (U.S.)	125.1
	Indonesia	107.3
2	Royal Dutch/Shell (U.K./Netherlands)	107.2
3	Exxon (U.S.)	105.9
	Norway	105.8
4	Ford Motor (U.S.)	98.3
	Turkey	96.5
	Argentina	93.2
	Thailand	80.1
5	IBM (U.S.)	69.0
6	Toyota (Japan)	64.5
7	IRI (Italy)	61.4
8	British Petroleum (U.K.)	59.5
9	Mobil (U.S.)	58.8
10	General Electric (U.S.)	58.4
	Portugal	56.8
	Venezuela	48.3
	Philippines	43.8
	Malaysia	42.4
	Columba	41.1
	Nigeria	34.7
	Egypt	33.2
	Bangladesh	22.8
	Kenya	7.5

Sources: For MNCs, *Fortune*, July 29, 1991, 245; for GDP, World Bank (1992b), Table 3.

4.6, 4.7, 4.19 and 4.20). Much capital also moves from rich to poor nations through the World Bank and bilateral government and aid programs.

Generally, we are witnessing a process of economic integration on a global scale (particularly among developed countries) that is being carried forward by a complex mix of trade and factor flows. Economists generally agree that factor movements constitute a more powerful instrument for factor price equalization than trade in products. Therefore, unbridled market policy in all areas of economic activity becomes inevitable, so that factor transfers can be expected to attain a higher degree of integration of national economics than goods transfer alone. Thus, the process of the internationalization of capitalist production has culminated with the process of local and regional markets giving way to national markets in the nineteenth century, followed by national markets giving way to international markets, since the mid-twentieth century in particular. In the past, trade in goods and capital created an international economy; presently, factor flows to meet the needs of internationalization of production are creating the world economy.

This process is resulting in fierce competition among MNCs of the developed capitalist countries attempting to avail themselves of expanding market, and to be competitive, these companies, are trying to reduce costs of production via technological competition (which takes the form of newer goods these days, unlike in the earlier days, when technological change involved changes in the production function) and reducing factor prices and budget deficits. The MNCs have become the unique contributors to the internationalization of the innovation process and of the production of newer goods through the transfer of technology and innovations. The MNCs establish operations in the recipient country via direct investment.

The internationalization of investment by developed capitalist economies was accompanied by import substitution of industrialization in the Third World, which was introduced under economic planning in a mixed economy. The model was essentially Keynesian—it was an extension of the ideology of social welfare to ensure full employment in the First World markets via transfer of investment to the Third World. Increasing accumulation of capital in the First World as a result of success of the earlier stages of internationalization of good and capital (through loans, etc.) tended to result in the occurrence of the law of diminishing returns to capital investment in the local market. The way out, according to Keynes, was to look for newer markets for investment to raise the marginal efficiency of capital. Tables 4.6 through 4.12 give us an idea of the trend in foreign investment. The phenomenal growth in the internationalization of investment, followed by the internationalization of production, and the intrinsic need to go beyond the boundaries of nation-states and to relocate production sites in markets across the world, on the one hand, and the Third World struggle to achieve economic development, on the other, gave rise to import substitution industrialization, followed by export substitution industrial growth. These two stages of industrial growth approaches are offshoots of two phases of the internationalization of investment and production supported by a Keynesian state participation policy, with social welfarism and, later, neoclassical privatization and a free market policy.

The phase of internationalization of goods and capital created the potential for import substitution in many Third World economies from the late nineteenth century to the 1950s. With the progress of ISI under state planning, the nascent capitalist class in the Third World became stronger, aided by foreign investment and foreign aid, which was made abundantly available by developed capitalist

TABLE 4.20   The Rise of Multinationals in Continental Europe, Outward FDI from the European Community (EC), the United States and Japan, 1980–1989 (US $ billion)

	Stock of FDI		Outward Flow (annual average)	
	1980	1988	1980–84	1985–89
EC[1]				
Billion dollars	153	332	18	39
% world total	33	34	41	37
USA				
Billion dollars	220	345	14	18
% world total	46	35	31	17
JAPAN				
Billion dollars	20	111	4	24
% world total	4	11	10	23
World[2]				
Billion dollars	474	974	44	105

Source: UNCTC (1991); cited in Jones and Schroter (1993), 4.
[1]The EC figures do not include Ireland, Greece and Luxembourg. They *exclude* intra-EC FDI. Including intra-EC FDI gives an outward stock of U.S. $203 billion (39 percent) in 1980 and U.S. $492 billion in 1988 (44 percent), and raises the flow to U.S. $22 billion (47 percent) in 1980–84 and U.S. $59 billion (47 percent) in 1985–89.
[2]This figure excludes intra-EC FDI.

economies to these Third World economies. Thus, ISI was the early form of the expansion of operations of multinational corporations, which enabled them to exploit new resources on a global scale and to move toward a globally integrated network of capitalist production and exchange. Thus, at a certain historical conjunction, ISI had graduated to export-substituting (or export-promoting) industrialization by the competing forces of local and international capital associated with the developing and advanced capitalist countries, respectively.

By its nature, ISI has been restricted by the size of the domestic market of a prospective developing country due to the fact that it has failed to bring about capitalist transformation of these economies, and therefore their economic structure has remained underdeveloped, with vast masses of the population depending on stagnating agriculture or a labor-surplus urban sector. Being restricted to separate local markets itself posed a constraint to accumulation on a global scale, which has to be overcome by the true unification of the world market. Thus, capital's tendency for global expansion necessitated a future integration of the world market into a unified network of capitalistic production and exchange (Bina and Yaghmaian 1988). In this manner, export-substituting industrialization has been

TABLE 4.21 Foreign Aid Allocations and the Poor

Ten Developing Countries with Greatest Number of Poor	Number of Poor (millions)	Poor as a Percentage of Total World Poor	Official Development Assistance (ODA) per Capita ($)	ODS as a Percentage of Total ODA
India	410	34.2	1.8	3.5
China	120	9.9	1.8	4.7
Bangladesh	99	8.3	18.0	4.7
Indonesia	70	5.8	9.3	3.9
Pakistan	39	3.1	8.8	2.5
Philippines	36	3.0	20.3	2.9
Brazil	33	2.8	1.1	0.4
Ethiopia	30	2.5	17.7	2.0
Myanmar	17	1.4	4.7	0.4
Thailand	17	1.4	14.1	1.8
Total	869	72.4	9.8	26.8

Source: United Nations Development Program 1992, tab. 3.1.

international capital's response to this intrinsic need (see Tables 4.5, 4.6, 4.12–4.19). This is one way of looking at this development. However, there is another and, in my view, more important way to explain it. The explanation lies with the fact that the ISI in the Third World failed to bring about capitalist transformation of these countries but rather resulted in a concentration of capital in the hands of local and collaborating foreign entrepreneurs, the profitable investment of which needed global expansion via export substitution and promotion appraisals.

Global expansion means more severe competition, which necessitates domestic cost cutting, elimination of state participation in savings, dismantling of economic planning, decontrolled market, and rapid privatization of economic activities to stimulate the interests of the MNCs. To be competitive, these economies need a supply of the latest technological research and development, imports of knowledge and information, and updated service sector activities (telecommunications, transport, health, education, etc.). The MNCs are most willing to take the responsibility of making these available, on one hand, while on the other hand, previous ISI helped these economies to advance such infrastructure activities although they were usually limited to urban sectors, which constitute approximately 18 to 20 percent of the total population, including the disguised unemployed (slum dwellers).

The problem inherent in such capitalist development is that severe competition leads to technological sophistication and innovation in the sense of rapid diversi-

TABLE 4.22 Unemployment in OECD Countries, 1985 (Percentage Change at Annual rate)

	Industrial Production		GNP		Retail Sales		Unemployment percentage rate		
	3 mths†	1 year	3 mths†	1 year	3 mths†	1 year	latest	1 year ag
Australia	+1.3	+2.9 (3)	+2.0	-4.4 (3)	+5.0	+3.9 (3)	8.2	(7)	8.
Belguim	+3.0	+3.4 (4)	na	na	-4.5	+3.0 (4)‡	123	(6)*	13.
Canada	-0.9	+3.9 (5)	+3.7	+4.5 (3)	+19.5	+4.9 (4)	10.4	(7)	11.
France	+11.9	nil (5)	nil	+0.7 (3)	-1.5	-2.0 (5)	9.6	(6)*	9.
W. Germany	+6.7	+16.3 (6)	-3.1	+0.4 (3)	-2.8	-1.0 (5)	9.3	(7)	9.
Holland	-6.2	nil (5)	na	na	+9.9	+3.7 (5)‡	15.7	(7)	17.
Italy	+20.0	+2.8 (4)	+2.6	+1.8 (3)	-11.5	-0.1 (4)‡	12.6	(6)*	11.
Japan	+12.5	+5.5 (6)	+0.4	+5.2 (3)	+11.7	+1.6 (4)	2.6	(6)	2.
Sweden	+1.2	-0.7 (5)	-2.8	+1.5 (3)	-3.8	+1.0 (12)‡	2.5	(6)*	2
Switzerland	+13.1	-3.9 (3)	-0.9	+2.0 (3)	+13.0	+3.2 (5)‡	0.9	(6)*	1.
UK	+8.8	+4.7 (6)	+3.4	+2.8 (3)	+8.2	+4.7 (5)	13.1	(7)	12
USA	+2.2	+1.9 (6)	+1.7	+1.9 (6)	+7.0	+4.0 (5)	7.3	(7)	7.

Source: The *Economist*, (1985), August 17, (Economic Financial Indicators. 81.
Note: output, demand and jobs—Britain's industrial production fell by 0.6 percent in June but was still ◄ percent up on a year earlier. The output of Canadian industry was unchanged in May, 3.9 percent higher th◄ a year before. Canada's unemployment rate edged down to 10.4 percent in July from 10.5 percent in June; did West Germany's from 9.4 percent to 9.3 percent; and , more sharply, Australia's—from 8.7 percent to ◄ percent. French retail sales picked up in May, but were still 2 percent below their level 12 months earli◄ West German shoppers are being cautious, with retail sales 1 percent down on May 1984.
‡Value defined by CPL.
†Average of latest 3 months compared with average of previous 3 months, at annual rate.
* Not seasonally adjusted.

fication and differentiation of products, which results in labor shedding. This creates growing problems of unemployment and self-employment, together with employment at lower wages, which means a gradual contraction of local markets. This latter development in turn would require further competition and hence, another round of the same effects, accompanied by a sharp rise in bankruptcies. This trend is evident in both developed and developing countries under an export substitution regime today.

This trend has continued since the 1980s, and if the problems of unemployment and disguised unemployment with the rapid rate of bankruptcies go on unabated, then global accumulation will be severely threatened. This leads to the conclusion that capitalism can generate unlimited capacity to produce but its ability to sell its products becomes increasingly limited under the weight of its system (i.e., production organization and production relation). Global capitalism will increasingly have funding difficulties in meeting the need for a growing market for its expanding productivity growth. In the developed capitalist economies, the growing number of unemployed and self-employed, with a large part of those employed at a relatively low wage in the organized sector, will mean a limited market, while in the Third World, an increasing number of unemployed and disguised unemployed resulting from the use of sophisticated technology used by the MNCs will act as a hindrance to the expansion of markets in these parts of the world. However, MNCs will be happy if they can get hold of a certain percentage of these markets plus the domestic markets of, say, 60 percent or so. However, no economic system can remain dynamic in such a situation. The more the MNCs try to become more competitive, the greater will be the loss of market. The private benefit, with its increasing social cost, cannot last much longer. On the other hand, capitalism today cannot but become more and more private benefit–oriented. In the earlier period, increasing social benefits at private cost helped capitalism to expand and initiate a tremendous growth in productivity.

The internationalization of production is also indicated by the fact that one of the more marked aspects of multinational corporate development over the past 20 years has been the setting up of so-called world market factories in certain selected Third World countries. The locations are called "export-processing zones," or "free-producing zones," or "industrial parks." On these sites, the MNCs have relocated the more labor-intensive parts of their globally fragmented production process in order to benefit from the availability of "free," cheaper, and unorganized labor. One reputed researcher wrote:

> Whereas scarcely any industrial production for the world market existed in Asia [except Japan], Africa and Latin America in the mid 1960s, by the middle of the 1970s world market factories were in operation in seventy-nine free production zones in thirty-nine countries and in many sites outside the zones, employing in all 725,000 workers. (Froebel, Heinrichs, and Keys 1980, 120)

According to recent studies by Magdoff and Sweezy (1987) and Harrison and Bluestone (1988), in the 1980s, as the unemployment rate rose to double digits across Europe and North America while Latin America, Asia, and Africa sank into depression, it seemed plausible that unprecedented capital mobility was leading to the global centralization of control and dispersion of production, increasing proletarization in the periphery and depressing living standards in the core. As speculation displaced production, workers in the older sectors of the manufacturing merger and buyout booms (H. Magdoff and P. Sweezy 1987).

1. Technology has developed in ways that allow spatially decentralized production, while at the same time allowing the management of far-flung production networks from a central place.
2. The falling rate of profit starting in the 1970s encouraged capitalists in the

industrialized nations to look for low-cost offshore production locations. Thus, strategies to raise wages in the developed capitalist countries are self-defeating since they open up unit labor cost differentials and inhibit domestic accumulations (McIntyre 1990).

The following table shows that the rate of growth of U.S. foreign direct investment (FDI) was in most years, greater than its GNP except in the period of 1975 through 1985. Since 1985, it has grown fastest relative to GNP growth. The 1980s, since 1985 especially, have been a period of massive cross-penetration of capital investment across Europe, the United States, and Japan (see also Tables 4.6, 4.7 and 4.10).

Real Growth of U.S. FDI and GNP, 1950-85

Period	FDI	FDI rate	GNP rate
1950–55	7.7	4.2	3.5
1955–60	7.8	2.3	5.5
1960–65	7.5	4.7	2.8
1965–70	4.4	3.2	1.2
1970–75	3.7	2.6	1.1
1975–80	4.6	4.7	−1.0
1980–85	1.5	2.5	−0.1
1985–88	12.3	3.7	8.6

Source: U.S. Department of Commerce, *Survey of Current Business*, 1989.

The process of internationalization of capital and investment can also be traced to the evolution of technological competition between the MNCs of the leading industrial nations. Competition was, at the outset, strongest between the U.S. and the European MNCs, which now has widened to include fast-growing Japanese MNCs. With the formation of the European Economic Community (EEC) in 1958, U.S. manufacturing firms mounted a wave of investment in Europe in order to preserve the strong position in European markets for research-intensive products, which they had held since World War II. By the 1970s, as European firms began a counterinvasion of the United States, Americans themselves became concerned about technological competition and were soon joined by Japanese companies. Technological change predominantly takes the form of innovation of newer and differentiated products. Technological competition between firms in an international industry can be thought of as an evolutionary process in which the most successful companies became MNCs. If new technological developments arise in some foreign country (whose firms will then embark on a course of MNC expansion), home country firms are well placed to catch up and begin to construct networks of international trade, investment, and production of their own and eventually establish foreign production facilities in other countries that are themselves of strong innovative activity. In India, for example, the recent development of technological and innovative activities with an enormous pool of human capital (relative to the level of its economy) available at an incredibly cheap price compared to its counterpart in developed capitalist countries, has attracted MNCs from all over the world, including Japan, at a greater scale than ever before.

The trend toward the internationalization of production became generalized across the firms of all countries. Firms that had previously served international markets, principally from domestic production sites through exports, increasingly attempted to catch up with the global networks of their more mature MNC rivals (see Table 3.5).

It was not only Europe that was catching up with the United States in exports of manufactures but Japan as well. By the late 1970s, there was strong evidence of rapid internationalization on the part of many Japanese companies. Just as innovative U.S. firms moved to international production in other industrialized, and later Third World, countries, in the 1950s through 1980s, so Japanese, West German, Italian, British, and French companies have done likewise in the 1970s and 1980s. Cantwell wrote that as their rate of technological accumulation caught up with, and in some cases surpassed, that of their U.S. rivals, they captured international market shares and realized that such growth was most easily sustained by setting up an international network of productive activity (Cantwell 1989). One important reason is that with the rapid export growth of a group of innovative companies, weaker firms abroad try to persuade governments to erect trade barriers in response, which may have played a role in the promotion of international production by the newer Japanese MNCs. However, this problem of state interference in MNC activities was taken care of in Dunkel's draft text of the Uruguay Round Table (1991).

One factor working toward the rapid internationalization of production has been a continuing fall in transport and communication costs resulting from rapid technological change in this area. However, the initiating factor has been the fact that continuing improvement in higher levels of human capital and resource-intensive technological and innovative activities has resulted in the internationalization of production in order to reach larger and unbridled markets (labor, resource, and products) and, thereby, to reduce costs per unit. The costs of transfer of information and international communication (with electronics playing the leading role in the newly emerging technology paradigm) within the firm have continued to fall. The other reason is that the major technologies of the 1950s and 1960s were essentially scale intensive in their application to chemicals, motor vehicles, aircraft, and other manufacturing industries, but because of the newer electronic technology, the focus today has become much more dependent on economies of scope (Cantwell 1989) and less dependent on economies of scale. The internationalization of the production process creates economies of scale as well as economies of scope, and MNCs are the leaders in this process. Therefore, provisions in the international agreement are being made to allow them to use the economies of scope independent of government control. The economies of scope depend on the levels of State intervention, freedom of market force, trade and movement of foreign investment and also on the level and condition of infrastructure.

Another reason is that firms' motivation to a wider dispersion of production units is that it weakens the bargaining power of trade unions based on the organization of closed shops in large plants. But that problem is already being taken care of by legislation to free the labor market which, again, is being helped by growing and sustained unemployment.

Table 4.7 shows the growing importance of international production over domestic exports of six major industrialized nations. It reveals that the six major industrialized nations had to their credit of 57 percent of world exports of manufactured goods in 1982, as against 83 percent of the sales from international production in manufacturing by their MNCs in the same year. In 1974, the six countries accounted for 55 percent of world exports and their firms for 81.5 percent of international production. This shows that the competitive position of the firms of these countries is somewhat stronger than measures of the competitive position of the countries themselves would indicate. This may be supported by research (Blomstrom, Kravis, and Lipsey 1988) showing that, while U.S.-based production lost market share in the 1980s, U.S. MNCs did not, and that the more a U.S. MNC produces abroad, the higher the skill level of its U.S. employees and the lower its employment per dollar of output.

Tables 4.12 through 4.17 also indicates that firms from the United States and the United Kingdom are substantially more reliant on international production than the average, with 42.4 percent and 18.3 percent, respectively, of international production. In terms of per capita estimates, the U.K. firms have the largest share, its population being much smaller than that of the United States. In terms of share of international production plus exports, they accounted for 27.6 percent and 11 percent respectively. Tables 5.1 and 5.2 testify to the fact that the firms of six industrialized nations accounted for 81.5 percent and 83.2 percent of total world production in manufacturing, in 1974 and 1982, respectively. However, the tables also show the competition between firms of different countries over the period, with the U.S. firms slipping back from 55.3 percent of total international production in manufacturing in 1974 to 42.4 percent in 1984. Firms in the rest of the industrialized nations have bettered their positions significantly between these two periods.

As MNCs are the leader in bringing about the internationalization of capitalist production and investment, one of the basic conditions laid down in the recent Arthur Dankel draft text on the Uruguay Trade Round Table is that sanctions be permitted against those countries, whose national laws serve to limit the growth and profitability of multinationals.

According to Adam Smith, David Ricardo, and Karl Marx, the mainspring of a capitalist economy is the process of capital accumulation. The expansion of the manufacturing industry has been central to capitalist development since the time of the Industrial Revolution. Capital accumulation has been bound up with technological accumulation. The introduction of machinery resulting from the application of scientific advances in production, generated a modern technology which, in turn, unleashed historically unprecedented rates of growth of production. Technological development has been a major force in the critical role played by the manufacturing industry in economic development as a whole, and the manufacturing sector has been the net creator of innovations (i.e., newer and differentiated products). Thus, technological and capital accumulation run alongside each other; if they do not, it results in a serious imbalance. However, in a world of internationalization of production with free movement of factors of production and economic activities, possibilities of such imbalances are rare, except for the fact that increased production must be sold so that capital and technological competition can increase simultaneously and, thereby, produce a higher rate of capital accumulation.

The growth in the internationalization of production has been associated with sustained technological competition between MNCs in the manufacturing industries for two reasons: first, internationalization has supported technological diversification since the form of technological development varies between locations as well as between firms. By increasing the overlap between the technological profile of firms, competition between MNCs is raised in each international industry, as are cooperative agreements as the number of technological spillovers between firms increases as well. Second, today there are a growing number of connections between technologies that formerly were separate. This greater interrelatedness has brought more firms, and especially MNCs, into competition with each other (Cantwell 1989, 13).

THE CAPITALIST CRISIS

This section deals with the crisis of capitalism, which has emerged as a stronger force than ever before. This is evident from sustained problems of unemployment, bankruptcies, a substantial amount of idle capacity, and a continuous low growth rate. Growth rate of late, however, has improved remarkably with increasing problems of unemployment, poverty, and low income employment opportunities. Data for unemployment is shown in Tables 4.21–4.22. This figure would be higher if the number of self-employed, mostly indicating disguised unemployment were included. Besides, the number of unemployed, as shown in the table, does not take into account as official statistics those who have removed themselves from the labor force, having sought work for too long in vain. These people have become homemakers or students at the expense of being breadwinners or started a self-employed business with the prospect of little income. This figure of unemployed of over 10 percent in the Organization for Economic Co-

TABLE 4.23   Unemployment in OECD Countries, 1992 (Percentage Change at Annual Rate)

	Industrial Production		GNP/GDP		Retail Sales (volume)		
	3 mths†	1 year	3 mths†	1 year	3 mths†	1 year	Latest
Australia	+11.3	-0.7 Jan	+1.2**	-0.5** Q4	-3.0	+1.1 Q4	10.5 Mar	9.1
Belgium	- 4.2	-2.4 Nov	na	+1.6 1991	nil	+4.0 Nov	8.8 Mar	8.1
Canada	-7.7	-0.2 Feb	-0.8	-0.2 Q4	+5.1	+2.2 Jan	11.0 Apr	10.2
France	+0.2	+.03 Feb	nil	+1.7 Q4	+1.8	+3.8 Feb	9.9 Mar	9.1
Germany††	+10.2	-1.1 Mar	-1.4	+1.0 Q4	+2.4	-2.3 Feb	6.4 Apr	6.2
Holland	+8.5	+5.2 Feb	+1.3	+1.4 Q4	+3.4	+1.6 Jan‡	4.4 Mar	4.9
Italy	-1.4	-0.3 Feb	+1.2	+1.5 Q4	+44.7	-2.6 Sep‡	10.9 Mar	10.0
Japan	-11.8	-5.3 Mar	+0.1	+3.1 Q4	+0.6	+0.8 Jan	2.1 Mar	2.2
Spain	-6.0	+2.9 Feb	+3.3	+2.7 Q4	+8.4	-2.1 Mar‡	15.0 Apr	15.2
Sweden	+1.4	-6.8 Feb	-1.3	-0.5 Q4	-5.8	-1.8 Jan	4.2 Apr*	2.1
Switzerland	+3.4	+3.5 Q4	+0.3	-0.7 Q4	-9.0	-5.7 Feb ‡	2.6 Apr*	1.1
UK	-3.6	-1.6 Feb	-1.1	-1.7 Q4	nil	-3.0 Mar	9.4 Mar	7.4
USA	-4.1	+2.1 Mar	+2.0	+1.4 Q1	+10.9	+2.3 Mar	7.2 Apr	6.6

Source: "Economic and Financial Indicators." *The Economist* 15 (October 1985).
Notes: Output, demand and jobs—Western Germany's industrial production dropped by 2.8 percent
March, for a year-on-year decline of 1.1 percent. In April America's unemployment rate fell to 72 percent
the workforce, after sticking at a seven-year high of 7.3 percent in both February and March. In April, Can
da's jobless rate fell to 11.0 percent, Spain's edged down to 15.0 percent, West Germany's increased to 6
percent and Sweden's remained at 4.2 percent. Spanish retail sales declined by 7.2 percent in March, leavin
them 2.1 percent down on a year earlier.
†Average of latest 3 months compared with average of previous 3 months, at annual rate.
‡Value index deflated by Customer Price Index (CPI).
*Not seasonally adjusted
††1992.
** New series.

operation and Development (OECD) countries is to be judged against almost full
employment in the 1960s and 1970s.

The number of firms that went bankrupt in the 1980s increased considerably; it
was the highest since the 1930s Depression. Their number increased by 43 percent in 1981 and by 48 percent in 1982, with the losses written off amounting to
nearly $6 billion (Sinai 1990, 12). The number of bankruptcies in West Germany
increased by 27 percent both in 1981 and 1982; it increased in France by 20.3
percent and in Britain by 26.4 percent in the same time period. Several famous
firms (e.g., PanAm airways) went bankrupt (Sinai 1990, 12).

The number of bankruptcies has increased substantially in the recent period. A
report in the *Otago Daily Times* Dunedin, N.Z. dated May 1992 said:

> Reuter writes from Tokyo: Japan's bankruptcy debt rocketed to record heights in
> the year to March 31, 1992. . . . Debt from Japanese corporate bankruptcies in-
> volved 10 million Yen or more and totalled a record 8.14 trillion Yen in 1991–92

when 11,557 corporations failed according to a report issued by Tokyo Commerce and Industry Research. Bad debts in 1991–92 surged 2.5 times from the previous year while the number of bankruptcies rose by 61.4%. There were a record 832 large scale bankruptcies with debt of more than one billion Yen each in 1991–92—far beyond the previous record of 522 set in 1986–87.

Dismayed by sluggish demand and plunging profits, major corporations are hammering out restructuring programs to cut costs and mark up better business results. When this happens, the first to suffer and the last to recover are the major companies' suppliers and subcontractors, according to a Tokyo commerce and industry analyst (*Otago Daily Times*, May 2, 1992). The indicator of success in competition is the growth of monopoly, in other words, the occurrence of bankruptcies or amalgamations at an increasing rate.

The decline and the drop in industrial production assumed even greater proportions despite tremendous technological change, growth in productivity, and internationalization of production and investment in the recent period, as shown in Tables 4.5, 4.6, 4.12 through 4.17. Industrial production of the developed Western countries decreased by about 4 percent between 1981 and 1982. While the gross domestic product fell by 1.8 percent in the United States in 1982, industrial production decreased by 8.2 percent. The decrease went down to 4.9 percent in West Germany, 3.8 percent in France, and 2.9 percent in Italy. The growth in output and industrial output in the Third World fell and the underutilization of industrial capacity reached 80 percent in some of the Third World countries. In the developed Western countries, unused capacity accounted for over 33 percent in 1982, while in the United States, the industrial production capacity was used only to 68 percent even as late as February 1983. A recent report says the U.S. government reported sharply lower factory orders in December 1991 (*Otago Daily Times*, May 5, 1992). The U.S. Commerce Department reported that orders for durable and nondurable goods plunged nearly 4 percent in December 1991. It also said that factory orders were slashed by 2.6 percent last year, to $3 trillion. This was the largest drop since a 3.5 percent plunge in the recession year of 1982 and the first decrease since a 0.3 percent loss in 1986. The drop in orders for both durable and nondurable goods was the steepest since orders sank 6.2 percent in November, 1990 (*Otago Daily Times*, Dunedin N.Z., May 5, 1992).

This is a brief account of the continued downward trend in all aspects of economic activities that is happening despite the rapid growth of productivity and internationalization of production. If this trend cannot be stemmed, then capitalism will die under the weight of its huge and unlimited ability to produce, improve, diversity, and differentiate output.

A BRIEF REFERENCE TO THE THIRD WORLD

In the context of internationalization of the production stage of capitalism, it is not difficult to see that the main target of globalization of production today is the

Third World, that is, a market consisting of over 70 percent of a world market of over 5 billion people. All efforts are being made to make it easy for the entry and operation of multinationals in this part of the world.

The International Monetary Fund Stabilization program, the leasee components of which are given in the next paragraph; demands from the Third World the same policy of dismantling of state influence, rapid reduction in the government budget deficit, wage reduction and control, free trade, and an appropriate monetary policy to reduce the rate of interest and inflation. The world follows the process of world capitalism in 1960s and 1970s. This was a period of internationalization of investment that needed the same policy to be applied to all countries.

The four basic components to the IMF stabilization program are

1. Abolition or liberalization of foreign exchange and import controls.
2. Devaluation of the official exchange rate.
3. A stringent, domestic antiinflation program consisting of (a) control of bank credit to raise interest rates and reserve requirements; (b) control of the government deficit through curbs on spending, especially in the areas of social services for the poor and staple food subsidies, along with increases in taxes and in public enterprise prices; (c) control of wage increases, in particular insuring that such increases are at rates less than the inflation rate (i.e., abolishing wage indexing); and (d) dismantling of various forms of price controls.
4. Greater hospitality to foreign investment and a general opening up of the economy to international commerce.

Arthur Dunkell's draft text for the Uruguay Round has also laid down conditions for making MNC activities in the Third World unrestricted.

The negative effects of such policies have been the same as in the developed capitalist economies—growing unemployment problems of all sorts and a rising number of bankruptcies, on the one hand, and on the other, increasing surpluses of sophisticated technology and products which we never imagined would be available to an economy with a per capita income of $250 to $300. That is, the foreign market has been made the target of achieving "self-sustained" development with the help of increasing amounts of foreign capital, technology, and skill.

The adverse effects of these policies are crippling the capitalist economies. These effects on world capitalism have alarmed the IMF and World Bank, as a recent newspaper report (*Otago Daily Times*, September 9, 1993) shows: "Governments of the West are being urged to boost economic demand to rescue the world from recession." However, the call in the 1993 report of the United Nations Conference on Trade and Development (UNCTAD) is a direct challenge to the existing policies of Western governments (The Main Issues for the UNCTAD in 1980s, UNCTAD Seminar Reports July 4, 1981). Until late 1992, there was widespread optimism about global recovery, but the economic situation in Japan and Western Europe has deteriorated sharply that year, while recovery in North America remained subdued. Because the projected recovery has failed to materialize, "commodity prices are falling, intensifying poverty in the South, and the unemployed are multiplying, intensifying poverty in the North" (UNCTAD) Secretary General K. Dadrie (1978). In the South, unemployment is a luxury that they cannot afford.

Has capitalism any other policy options left today that will not affect its profit, capital accumulation, and its unending capacity to produce, improve, and diversify products and, at the same time, bring about social justice, greater economic equality, and full employment? (See Chapter 5, "The Mahalanobis Planning Model Revisited," on import-substituting industrialization, economic planning, and the development of the capitalist sector in India.)

INTERNATIONALIZATION OF PRODUCTION AND THE NATURE OF CAPITALIST GROWTH

In this section I discuss the nature of capitalist growth and policy implications. To illustrate the relationship between government policy and consumerism I would like to mention that the major economic thrusts of consumerist policies of the government are counter cyclical demand management, investment in infrastructure, and investment in an expanding military establishment. These are the major components in the United States, and investment in welfare of all sorts is the major component in Western Europe. The very weight of the consumerist state in the economy enables it to manage demand by active fiscal policies (by taxation, debt, and spending policies and by passive monetary policies). Prior to World War II, state spending in advanced capitalist countries was less than 10 percent of GNP, while in the 1950s to 1970s, it was typically 30 to 40 percent of GNP. With the progress of internationalization of production process, state spending has began to drop sharply since about the 1980s, in order to reduce the rate of interest, rate of inflation, and wage rates and, thereby, to make products internationally competitive. "Cost-cutting" competition between developed capitalist countries has become their main policy exercise.

Capitalism's problems and crises paradoxically arise from its very source in the accumulation of capital. In this process, the more the productive forces are developed, the greater become the problems for further accumulation. The competitive drive of capitalists among themselves results in a massive scale of new investment, which cannot be sustained by the rate of profit. To maintain or raise the rate of profit under the circumstances, capitalists vigorously attempt to constantly push technological change to reduce labor costs per unit of output, and thereby reducing prices, they attempt to capture the competitors' market. Second, by bringing about continuous technological innovations, product diversification and consumerism are constantly stimulated. The product cycle and technology gap trade theories explain this feature of capitalism at its internationalization of production phase. In the quest for higher rates of profit, capitalism encourages technological change and innovations by product diversification to stimulate consumerism and while it tries to spread its tentacles to every nook and corner of the earth. However, some successful capitalists attempt to make an adequate profit, which can only be made at the cost of some other capitalists being driven out of business by competition. Thus, the drive to accumulate leads inevitably to crisis, and the greater the scale of past accumulation, the deeper the crisis will be. The more important reason is that in the capitalist system, technological change and capital accumulation, causing the increased productivity of labor, result in the cutting of costs of providing workers with a livelihood. With the increase in the productivity of the labor force due to technological progress, there is a continual fall in the amount of labor time and, therefore, of value needed to produce each unit of plant, equipment, raw materials, and consumer goods.

Harman's work (1993, 1) shows that the period known for social welfarism had a high profit rate at the beginning but that during the later period, the rate of profit began to decline, one important cause of which was the high bargaining power of the workers in an economy with full employment (defined as 96–97 percent employment). "The wage bargaining is the crucial dynamic element" in the rapid growth in productivity and expansion of domestic markets and consumerism (Glynn and Sutcliffe 1972). In the British economy, the decline in the profit rate was caused by the increase in the amount of wages as a proportion of the total national income. This happened to all developed capitalist economics of the West. This explains the change in policy since 1980s to dismantle state intervention and social welfarism in order to reduce the budget deficit, which reduced the rates of interest and inflation drastically to one digit (in other words, raising the rate of profit rapidly). During this period, capital accumulation as a proportion of total GNP rose from nearly 20 percent in the 1950s to 35 percent in the mid-1970s. This happened during the second phase of the internationalization of investment in capitalism (see Section 3, Chapter 5 of this book). At the start of the first phase in the nineteenth century, the rate was as low as 3 to 5 percent of the GNP and, for good reasons; that is, in those days capital and, therefore, the workforce were much less productive. In those days, capital mainly consisted of working capital, for obvious reasons. Since 1980–1985, vigorous attempts have been made to globalize production via the strong policy of rapid introduction of free markets, reduction of state participation to a minimum to reduce budget deficits and secure budget surplus, and deregulation of money and the labor markets.

Social welfarism, known as leftist Keynesianism in Western Europe, as opposed to the rightist Keynesianism or military Keynesianism as in the United

States, was capitalism's ploy to increase the domestic market and raise profit and accumulation rates so that consumerism can prosper. Social welfarism and consumerism stimulated technological change, innovation, and productivity and created the need and scope for more productive energy (first oil and later nuclear power), followed by the possible development of other fuels. Technological progress obviously needed this improvement in energy resources, but the more immediate reason at the time was to reduce the expensive labor content in production and, thereby, the cost of production. Energy is a substitute for labor. A fully employed, high-income, domestic economy of the West in those days, was the condition that capitalism needed to survive and prosper after the 1930s Depression. However, in due course, the rise in the labor cost of production and welfare costs began to cut into the profitability of investment and production, on the one hand, and on the other hand, rapid technological change (known as the Technological Revolution) during this period since World War II made it imperative for capitalism to undertake direct production overseas, particularly in the Third World (which has 70 percent of the world population). It was inevitable that this policy of dismantling social welfare and the deregulation of the money, product, and labor markets would result in a rapid rise in unemployment, income inequality, and bankruptcies in the domestic economy, as well as hurt consumerism and limit markets for (capitalists') products. However, the phase of internationalization of production via the free market and the policy of deregulation of the economy produces no concern for a domestic market stricken with unsoluble unemployment and low-paid employment. MNCs now have more than a 5 billion population market in which to compete, and if they could muster 10 to 15 percent of that market plus some share of the domestic market they would have much larger market than a fully employed and costly domestic market.

Unemployment and the Internationalization of Production

The nature of the unemployment problem in this phase of the globalization of capitalism should be briefly noted here. In all developed capitalist economies, employment in large-scale organized sectors is dropping at an alarming rate, while productivity growth, technological progress, and innovations are rising at a remarkable rate. An increasing number of the workforce is trying to survive with employment in small family business shops, takeout foodshops, street vending, domestic help, and all sorts of low-skilled employment. Part-time employment opportunities are flourishing, with an income devoid of medical benefits. The dismantling of intervention and social welfarism and the deregulation of markets—money, product, and labor markets, which are considered a necessary condition for the internationalization of production phase of capitalism—have resulted in high unemployment and disguised unemployment (see Tables 4.21 and 4.22). The deregulation of the labor market with reduced employment opportunities due to technological change to make products more competitive reduces the resistance of workers and their unions to management's cost-cutting programs involved in deregulation. The most vivid examples were in the United States, where the threat of the closure of the third largest auto manufacturer, Chrysler, in 1980, led the United Auto Workers' union to agree to concessions that cut wages and health benefits.

The more progress continues in production and management technology, the more a firm reduces its costs (which directly and indirectly involves employment reduction). The workers who are fortunate to get jobs have to remain satisfied with whatever poor conditions offered by employers. Medical benefits, medical insurance, leave with pay, and overtime are becoming matters of the past. Obviously, cost-cutting programs like this will result in an increasing rate of profit.

There is another distinctive feature of unemployment that seems to be inevitable in the circumstances. That is, in an organized sector, income gaps between executives and high officials and the average workers are increasingly widening beyond recognition. In 1980s, the chief executive officers of the 300 largest American companies had incomes 29 times higher than those of the average manufacturing workers. Ten years later, the incomes of the top executives were 93 times greater (Galbraith 1992, 126). In Britain, "the rate of growth of company directors' incomes was 20 percent a year throughout the 1980s; the dividend payment of the largest 1,400 companies rose 20.4 percent in 1988, 33 percent in 1989, and 20.3 percent in 1990; real manufacturing dividends were 73 percent higher in 1989 than 10 years earlier, while the total real wage bill was 5 percent lower" (cited in Harman's paper Where is capitalism going? p. 26, International socialism, Spring, 1993).

Real weekly wages of workers are 19.1 percent lower in 1991 than in 1973. As a result, all members of the family, irrespective of age and education, to run small business, street vending, small shops, and so forth, which require small amounts of capital, low education (even people with high education are getting involved in such ventures with poor returns), and low establishment costs (a large number of them are being run from the home). Consequently, average real incomes have declined for all but the top one-fifth of families. The average decline of the lowest income of these people was sometimes over 5 percent (Hilbroner 1991). In a recent study, it has been stated that the rate of exploitation has increased by 25 percent between 1977 and 1988 (Moseley, 1991).

In OECD countries, income from capital in 1975–1979 was 31 percent of total income, which went up to 34 percent in 1990, despite continuous growth in unemployment and recession. In a study on the United Kingdom, it was stated that the average real disposal income from employment rose in the years 1987–1989 by a total of 11.7 percent. However, a shrinkage in the total workforce turned this into a rise of only 0.2 percent a year in total disposable income from wages and salaries and a fall in their share of GNP of 3 percent (Glynn 1989, 67–69). The *New York Times* (September 2, 1993, D3) reported:

Manufacturing in August [1993] slumped for the third straight month, with factory employment falling sharply. . . . The rate of job cutting was the highest in more than two years. A survey of corporate purchasing executives reports manufacturing job loses were worst in the aerospace and defense industries which have been hurt by airline and government military cutbacks.

The gradual dismantling of military Keynesism in the United States is to account for this loss of employment. It is also happening in the United Kingdom, Germany, and France due to a decline in state welfarism. In the United States, according to the American Defense Secretary; "We have already lost hundreds of jobs and there are that many more ahead of us to lose. . . . We clearly expect many more to go out of business. And we will stand by and see that happen" (*Los Angeles Times*, September 2, 1993).

An unrestricted market system at the present stage of capitalism results in the crisis that involves the opting out of some individual capitalists. Thus, over time, the system comes to be dominated by an even smaller number of ever larger funds of capital (Harman 1993). With the internationalization of the production process, accompanied by the national policy of deregulation, in full swing in capitalist countries, there were more outright bankruptcies in the early 1990s than there were in the recessions of the mid-1970s or the early 1980s, especially in the United States and Britain. According to the Bank of England *Quarterly Bulletin* (August 1992), in Britain the total number of insolvencies in 1990 was double that of the 1980.

Internationalization of Production and Capitalism's Dilemma

Capitalism today is on the horns of a dilemma. Rather than standing on the threshold of a second great capitalist age, it has to seek a new way in which to develop. It cannot go back to the social welfare policies of John Maynard Keynes or return to unbridled privatization and a free market policy without risking self-destruction. During the interwar period, the state in capitalist societies had learned that the crises in capitalist economies could be averted by undertaking large-scale public expenditures. Later, Keynes (1936) made a theoretical summary of what the capitalist state had already learned from its practical experience. He showed that in a market economy, there is an inbuilt trend toward stagnation, that is, the effective demand tends to be less than what is required for full utilization of productive capacity and, as a consequence, the sources of capital accumulation tend to dry up. To counteract the falling demand, Keynes advocated increasingly large-scale government expenditure on public works, especially on roads, power projects, schools, and hospitals, because it is in capital goods industries that the fluctuations in employment tend to be greatest during booms and slumps. Thus, Keynesian economics has provided the ideological basis for the postwar growth of the welfare state, comprising the provision of social services like education, health, housing, transport, and other measures to maintain full employment. Capitalist production benefited for 40 years from consumption in home markets brought about by full employment and social welfare policies. However, these policies created an increasing demand for labor, which raised wage rates in a market regulated by trade unions. The answer was to use more productive energy (oil) and fewer, more productive workers to reduce the cost per unit of output. Oil-based technology has developed enormously since then, creating conditions of affluence but reemphasizing the need for a lower cost per unit. High productive capacity made it imperative to look to the international market. Until 1975, trade between developed countries contributed on average 15 percent of gross national product, with the Third World contributing less than 5 percent. However in the past 16 years, the international (Third World) proportion of a developed country's trade has risen rapidly, to nearly 25 percent. Union power and social welfarism exerted pressure on inflation and this was enhanced by the sharp rise in oil prices in 1973 (Harman 1993, 43). The result was recession in most developed economies. Companies sought a solution in a larger slice of the international market, but to be competitive, capitalism must lower the cost of production by lowering wage costs, inflation, interest rates, and taxes.

The welfare state is the greatest hindrance because it supports costly wage rates, even in a recession with high unemployment. It requires a higher and progressive tax system and an increasing budget deficit, the consequences of which are higher inflation and higher interest rates. The consequences of a weak welfare state, however, are rising unemployment, poverty, and crime. Unfortunately, an internationally oriented economy does not need to depend on local demand, much of which is created by full employment. One solution to this dilemma is for the unemployed to become self-employed, and this is already evident in all developed economies. Self-employment activities require a low level of human capital and provide a low wage and little health care. Attendance at work is one's own affair, and unpunctuality does not matter much in terms of production loss. Therefore, the welfare state's role in supplying free or subsidized education and health is not needed.

In sum, over the years, capitalism has achieved an unlimited capacity to produce, improve, and diversify output at a declining cost per unit of output but paradoxically has also created an increasing problem in marketing its ever-expanding output. Thus, the twenty-first century signals a critical period for capitalism.

True, during the early phase of the Industrial Revolution, the classical school advocated an almost identical approach, and it worked. Traditional technology was improved to serve modern uses and changes such as the conversion of artisan workshops to large factories boosted economic growth and produced many employment opportunities. However, the change was both uncomplicated and far-reaching in that the population was exposed to previously unheard-of opportunities in employment. It also provided a template for the distribution of population growth.

The 1990s situation requires improvements to technology within a restrictive framework that cannot create employment opportunities, let alone provide the conditions for full employment. The present phase of intensive technology is an answer to the growing expense of labor as the slow rise in real wages over the decades has made producers' profits untenable without increased mechanization. That position has been further intensified by the growing competitive environment. With more skilled labor available, unskilled workers are the first to be unemployed. The trend in most developed economies is that this section of the population turns to small self-employed businesses, household workshops, and service activities to survive. Thus, the growing problems of open unemployment and disguised unemployment will be inevitable in a market economy using technological sophistication to increase productivity. The race to improve technology can be justified only when existing resources are fully employed. Paradoxically, while all developed economies, including New Zealand, feverishly search for more sophisticated technology just to be more competitive, they leave behind another valuable resource, underutilized labor.

In the Marxian view, the primary objective of state in a capitalist society is the suppression of contradictions inherent in capitalism. One such fundamental capitalist contradiction is the separation of the means of production from the producers of surplus value. During the free competitive stage in capitalist development, the state followed a laissez-faire economic policy, confining its economic role mainly to the protection of private property relation, and the creation and maintenance of a stable currency. However, the transformation of competitive capitalism into its monopoly stage and the intensification of capitalist contradictions has resulted in an increasingly large role for the capitalist state. To cope with the intensification of the profit realization crisis under monopoly capitalism, the state started undertaking large-scale spending on various public services to delink the level of effective demand from the incomes of people in market economies. The breakdown of laissez-faire and the growth of state intervention is therefore structurally rooted in the changing nature of capitalism.

In general, accumulation and legitimization are the two basic functions of the state in a capitalist society. Accumulation refers to the economic function of creating and maintaining profitable investment opportunities for private capital, while legitimization is a social function of maintaining peace and political stability in a class. Unrestrained capital accumulation and technological changes create sectoral, regional, and social imbalances, resulting in the pauperization of increasingly large numbers of people. Characteristically, the growth under monopoly capitalism is achieved by the substitution of labor-saving techniques in production, creating surplus population with no purchasing power. Public expenditures on social welfare measures have the twofold objective of maintaining effective demand and social harmony in a class-divided society.

With this background of various facets of the globalization of capitalism, a more detailed discussion of a Third World country would complete the picture as to how the globalization worked in the rest of the world. We have selected India as a candidate for this study.

5

THE INDIAN ECONOMY

MUGHAL PERIOD—PRECAPITALIST PHASE

Introduction

We will begin with the well-known concept of the Asiatic mode of production, which Marx and Engels developed to show its divergence from that of Western feudalism. However, F. Moulder pointed out, Marx and Engels never fully integrated this concept into a systematic statement on comparative history. We summarize here five characteristics of "Asiatic" societies that Marx and Engels developed to distinguish them from feudal Europe and to give an idea of the basic features of the industrial economy of India.

1. Marx wrote in 1853:

> Climate and territorial conditions, especially the vast tracts of desert extending from Sahara, through Arabia, Persia, India, and Tartary, to the most elevated Asiatic highlands, constituted artificial irrigation by canals and water works, the basis of Oriental agriculture. . . . The prime necessity of an economical and common use of water, which in the Occident drove private enterprise to voluntary association, as in Flanders and Italy, necessitated in the orient where civilisation was too low and the territorial extent too vast to call into life voluntary association, the interference of the centralising power of government. (Marx 1968, 85).

However, we could look at the question from another angle, that is, because of the vastness of the territorial extent and relatively small population, it was the greater paternalistic sense of feudal rulers toward their subjects, which was ultimately more beneficial to them, that led to the use of the governmental power in these kinds of projects. A more rational explanation is that under these circumstances, government power and resources were considered more effective than those of individuals. This may be taken to mean that the rulers were conscious of the needs of the people. It also means that these projects would be more helpful to the rulers by bringing more revenue as the land, and those projects all belonged to them.

2. Unlike feudal Europe, property was undeveloped in Asia. There was no nobility and no bourgeoisie. On the one hand, the state was the "real landlord," that is, all property was legally owned by the state; village communities possessed land only as a grant from the state. This constituted the rationale for tribune or labor services extracted from the villagers by the state. On the other hand, land was in fact the communal or common property of the villagers who tilled it (Hobsbawm 1964, 69–70).

3. Unlike feudal Europe, the division of labor was little developed in Asia. Production was organized through a multitude of tiny, similar, self-sufficient village communities. Cities were not autonomous centers of industry and commerce but administrative outposts of the state, which were superimposed on the fundamental, village economic structure.

The village communities united agriculture and domestic manufacturing, "that peculiar combination of hand weaving, hand spinning and hand tilling agriculture which gave them self-supporting power" (Marx 1968, 88). That is, the villagers owned the means of production and produced for their own use; thus, both the market and the laborers for capitalist production were lacking (Marx cited in Moulder 1977, 15). Accounts of Hobson (1926), Dobb (1947), and Mandel (1968) of European village economies in the medieval period hardly differ from this. The only difference that is discernable is in degree, and not in kind.

4. The combination of centralized control of the water supply and the isolation of peasants within self-sufficient villages provided a solid foundation for a highly despotic form of government, known as "Asiatic despotism" or "Oriental despotism."

5. Finally, as a result, society was stagnant or "stationary." However, this concept of Asia's stationary state contradicts what Marx wrote about the causes of the rise of the dynamic industrial capital in the temperate West zone. Marx commented on India: "India has no history at all, at least no known history. What we call its history, is but the history of successive intruders who founded their empires on the passive basis of unresisting and unchanging society" (Marx 1968, 89). It was only with the extension of capitalism to Asia, by the British and others, that real social and economic change began to work.

I will now try to analyze the real nature of economic and social change that the "extension of capitalism" to India by the British has contributed. In my view, if

India's mature rural and mercantile economy were allowed to reach a stage when its population growth rate would have been sufficiently high and sustained, then its huge accumulation of mercantile capital would have, of necessity because of the changed conditions, entered into the production of industrial capital. The frequent intrusion of foreign feudal powers and, later, Western mercantile and industrial capitalism and colonial rule aborted India's industrial development. In this section, I present a brief outline of the nature of mercantile capitalism in India. This will be followed by an analysis of the colonial and postcolonial period of growth of industrial capitalism in India which proceeded without the capitalist transformation of the economy, unlike the United Kingdom or Continental Europe. India was forced by the colonial power to skip the extensive phase of technological change and thereby to leave its vast masses of population underdeveloped. The introduced intensive technological change has little use for these huge underdeveloped numbers. In sum, the basic features of the mode of production emphasize the lack of growth of a property-owning class in Asia which, unlike in Europe, acted as a hindrance to the economic transformation. The rise of property owning class in those days was essentially a function of the growth of population vis-à-vis land and other resources. The following sections discuss the nature of India's development process, beginning with a brief reference to the level of precapitalist economy during the Mughal period (i.e., just on the eve of British colonization of the Indian economy).

India's Population—Pre-British Period (A Brief Note)

It is well known that India was one of the few countries that was rich in prototechnology and in the accumulation of mercantile capital in the past. On this basis, we will examine the process of India's failed case of development of an industrial capitalism of its own, which also explains India's failure to bring about the capitalist transformation of its society and economy. We will begin with a very brief account of the level of India's mercantile capitalism. I shall draw substantially from the works of Irfan Habib (1963), an internationally recognized authority on Indian economic history, to give an account of the state of India's mercantile economy during the late Mughal period. Habib's work shows how rich was India's period of mercantile capitalism during the pre-British days. He, like other economic historians mentioned later in the following section, wondered why India's rich mercantile capitalism could not progress toward industrial capitalism, as it had done in the United Kingdom with the Industrial Revolution. Like many others, he too failed to take into account the positive effects that a high rate of population growth, together with the increasing supply of surplus labor, had on technological and organizational changes from the period of prototechnology of the mercantile period to the industrial technology and capitalism of the industrial revolution in the United Kingdom. This positive factor was missing at this critical juncture of India's history. If we look at the trends in population growth in India at that time, we will find that it exerted no pressure on existing technology and resources. Habib wrote: "A study of the official Mughal area statistics and other geographical information indicates that the extent of cultivation then was about half of what it was at the beginning of this century in the middle Gangetic basin and Central India, and from two-thirds of one-fifth in other regions" (1963, 20). He concluded that it may reasonably be inferred that "compared to the conditions around the year 1900, cultivation was confined to the more fertile land in 1600; that owing to larger wastes and pastures more cattle could be kept indicating not only a larger output of pastoral products per capita, but also a greater use of cattle power in agriculture" (Habib 1963, 35). He also pointed out that the productivity per capita in agriculture was not in any way inferior, even to the West. Slicher Van Bath, in a noted work (Van Bath 1963), concluded that agricultural technology was superior to that of Europe. Assuming that the total food consumption in Emperor Akbar's time was one-fifth that of the 1960s and that cultivation was then concentrated on the areas with highest yields, Desai's study (1972) shows that productivity per unit of area should have been 25 to 30 percent higher in 1595 than in 1961. This in turn means, according to him, that the productivity per worker in agriculture was twice as high in 1595 as in 1961.

Population growth has been regarded as an indicator of efficiency of the precapitalist and early capitalist periods, because population growth then was caused by a fall in death rate due to availability of sufficient food, a sign of good agriculture. On this ground, we may conclude that the Mughal economy could not be regarded as absolutely static or stagnant when the population tended to grow at the rate of between 3.6 and 4.4 percent in 200 years (Moosvi 1987). Table 5.1 gives data on India's population for 1600–1800, which shows an annual growth rate of 0.28 percent. This trend would suggest an economy in which there was some room for national savings and a net increase in food production, although the growth on balance was slow. Besides, this so-called savings must have been spent on conspicuous consumption by land-owning classes, as they normally did instead of investing it for further production.

Another point to note is that in a country of India's size, which is rich with lush vegetation and a congenial climate compared to Britain, this growth rate of population, even though not a sustained one, was not expected to create a condition

TABLE 5.1   Population of Undivided India, 1600–1800

Year	Millions of Inhabitants
1600	125.0
1700	153.0
1800	186.0

Source: Davis (1951), 26–27.

forcing the changes in feudal land tenure to release surplus labor to induce development of industrial capital, as it did in the United Kingdom. Britain's population growth rate in the eighteenth century was a sustained one and at a much higher rate. Moreover, we will see later in this chapter how oppressive was the institutional framework of India's feudal system, leading to poverty, malnutrition, and a very low life expectancy for the vast masses of the population.

It would be interesting to compare here the rate of India's population growth with those of some European countries including Great Britain (see Table 5.2). We noted earlier that a sustained high rate of growth of population since the mid-eighteenth century marked the beginning of the Industrial Revolution.

Habib's account showed that the pressure of population in India was light. In the United Kingdom, a high and sustained growth of population pressure on agriculture and prototechnology confined to household industry, at a time when mercantile capitalism was rich and booming, led to the transformation of commercial capital into industrial capital. With this brief note on the trend in population growth, it is time to discuss the nature and level of mercantile capitalism on the eve of the colonial period in India.

Merchant Capital in Mughal India (A Brief Note)

Mughal India had an urban population of a considerable size, probably amounting to about 20 percent of the total population, which was much higher than the urban India of the 1950s and 1960s and clearly that of today's urban India. The urban India of today is largely composed of slum dwellers, the disguised unemployed. Towards the beginning of the seventeenth century, the largest town of Mughal India appears to have been much larger than the largest European town of that period. A high proportion of urban population in India was employed in industrial crafts. There was plenty of evidence to show that in those days, there was a large urban market for nonagricultural goods and a division of labor based on skilled specialization. Urban artisans as commodity producers were also operating in those days. The putting-out system was widely in use, and both cash ad-

TABLE 5.2 Population Growth Rates in European Countries

Countries	1500–1600	1600–1700	1500–1700
Britain	0.43	0.31	0.37
France	0.12	0.08	0.09
Germany	0.25	0.00	0.11
Spain and Portugal	0.19	0.12	0.03
Russia	0.54	0.11	0.33

Source: S. Moosvi, The Economy of Mughal Empire, C1595 (Delhi: Oxford University Press, 1987), 406.

vances and the giving out of the raw material were established practices (Habib 1963, 69), indicating that mercantile capitalism was in an advanced stage. However, the *Karkhanas* (workshops) of the emperor and the nobles in Mughal India were regarded by some as the real counterparts of European manufactories (Smith 1976, 258–59). Bernier reported (1916), in his "Travels," that large halls were seen in many places, called *Kauri-Karkanas*, meaning workshops for the artisans. In one hall embroiderers were busily employed, superintended by a master. In another, you see the goldsmiths; in a third, painters; in a fourth, varnishers in lacquer work; in a fifth, joiners, turners, tailors, and shoe makers; in a sixth, many ventures of silk, brocade, and those fine muslins. The artisans reappear every morning to their respective Karkanas, where they remain the whole day; and in the evening return to their homes. In this quiet and regular manner their time slides away. The Karkhanas thus converted the previously independent artisan or contract producer into a wage laborer. Thus, the development of the practice of broad division of labor under one roof was evident, but it was rather different from the more minute and detailed division of labor that characterized the process of European manufactory production. One fundamental point of difference to be made from the European manufactory was that these Karkhanas of the emperor or nobles did not undertake commodity production but rather production of luxury articles for direct use and not for the market (cited in Habib 1963, 36).

Irfan Habib in his research also noted that merchant capital was considerable in size and that an efficient system of credit not only enlarged it but also gave it great mobility. However, most evidence shows that there was little improvement in the tools and the technical principles. "The tools of Indian crafts had been the extremely sparing use of metal, wood often serving where iron might be expected" (Habib 1963, 63). Similarly, the ordinary spinning wheel included in it two important mechanical drives, namely, belt transmission of power and the flywheel principle, though it was entirely made of wood (Habib 1963, 64).

Irfan Habib gave a detailed account of urban market and artisan production which reflects the level of preindustrial economy of India. He showed in his analysis the existence of a large urban market for nonagricultural production and a division of labor based on skilled specialization. According to his account, there developed the practice of expanding their production by no longer confining it to the household but engaging apprentices and servants. Habib commented that this should have been an important development, possibly representing a step in the evolution of capitalism "from below in a really revolutionary way" according to Marx (1959, 329–90; see also Sweezy, Dobb, and Takahshi 1976). However, it should be mentioned here that imported capitalism in India in later days was introduced from above and thus not rooted in the society, and so it failed to revolutionize the mode of production of the day.

Mughal India had extensive commodity production and sufficient development of merchant capital. The following accounts of the merchant capital based on Irfan Habib's study will give an idea of the extent of the merchant capital in Mughal India. The system of credit and banking that prevailed in India should be a matter of great pride to any Indian according to Travenier's account. He wrote, "in India a village must be very small indeed if it has not a money changer, called Shroff (sarraf) who acts as a banker to make remittances of money and issue letter of exchange" (1963, 31). The *shroffs* also discounted *Hundis* (hand notes used in the transaction of money) and finance commerce, particularly long-distance trade and international trade, to a very large extent. So brisk was the use of these bills that in the Ahmedabad market, merchants made their payments or adjusted their obligations almost entirely through the transfer of paper. Moreover, the *insurance* (Bima) business carried on by Shroffs involved well-developed; *Hundis*, goods in transit, and cargo could all be insured. Shroffs accepted deposits while they advanced loans and then acted as deposit bankers. Owing to the ability of Shroffs to advance large loans to merchants, some of the capital was mopped up through deposits, which the shroffs did turn into merchant capital (Habib 1963, 74). Habib quoted a well-traveled European visitor who said that of the three great surprises at Agra, one was "the immense wealth or fortune of the merchants" (Habib 1963, 79). We cannot produce reliable statistical data, but facts as reported by various scholars abound to indicate the immensity of merchant capital in Mughal India. For example, it was written about a merchant, Abdul Gaffar, that he possessed 20 ships of between 300 and 800 tons each. He alone conducted trade equal to that of the whole English East India Company (Das 1959, 224; Habib 1963). It was also stated that Surat merchants were very rich, some of them worth more than 5 or 6 million rupees. They had 50 ships trading with overseas countries. The richest of them Viji Vora, who was said to have an estate of 8 million rupees. Thus, despite the development of agricultural and nonagricultural production for market, cultivations based on hired labor, considerable development of merchant capital, a putting-out system, extensive credit, and banking, industrial capital failed to emerge in the Indian economy. The manufactory that was in operation in those days was outside the sphere of commodity production. In other words, despite the development of all these preconditions, industrial capitalism failed to appear. The most important precondition of sustained growth of population at a high rate was absent, as was surplus labor arising from land reforms, the need for which did not occur because of the vast amount of land compared to population. Land reforms in the United Kingdom were needed to make cheaper labor available to be combined with money capital in the process of turning out industrial capital. A high population growth rate supplied both the factor labor and a market. Industrial production needs an increased division of labor and involves long-term investment, which requires large and expanding markets in a capitalist system. Lack of population growth, therefore, acted as a hindrance to transformation of commercial capital into the industrial capital. Irfan Habib and other economists completely ignored this condition.

India's underdevelopment, in the sense we understand it today, began with its colonization and domination by the British capitalist economy. This capitalist colonization resulted in a distortion of the course of India's economic life, culminating in underdevelopment. India had been colonized before by many foreign feudal powers, which plundered its massive wealth. However, these feudal colonizations had left India's own feudal economy and prosperous commerce little affected, for obvious reasons. The exploitation of one feudal economy by another cannot bring about any fundamental change in the mode and method of economic production and economic structure. The only result is that the exploited country becomes impoverished. However, when an industrial economy dominates a feudal economy to serve its own economic interests, it invariably introduces new products and new methods and modes of production that destroy the historical course of indigenous economic development, destabilize factor endowments, divert the social mind from its historical course, and thus inhibit the development of the country's own technology, which would form the basis of the relationship between production and society. When a new but alien technology (with a fundamentally different objective of production developed in different historical circumstances) is introduced into another country with the help of political power, it gradually destroys the potential indigenous force of social and economic development of the latter. In such a situation, introduced production becomes divorced from the society.

Many other authors praised the high level of human resources of pre-British India: "The great mass of the Indian people possess a great industrial energy, is well fitted to accumulate capital and remarkable for a mathematical clearness of head, and talent for figures and exact sciences" (Marx 1953, 390). However, the society's need for harnessing these resources in production is conditioned by its own historical force, that is, only when the pressure of population on existing resources, technology, and economic organization reaches a critical point does change become inevitable in a human society. In those days, the pressure of population on existing resources could have brought about these changes, as the Industrial Revolution in England has shown. In spite of the development of modern science in Europe long before the Industrial Revolution, it was not used in economic production until the historical condition of growing population pressure prepared the ground for it and supplied the resources for its use in technological and economic change.

Plundering resources from a country, whether done by a foreign feudal or capitalist country, does not make the country underdeveloped but undoubtedly makes it poorer. However, a poorer economy meant in those days low population growth and poorer health, which retarded technological change. Underdevelopment is caused and perpetuated by the destruction of the productivity of indigenous technology even if, in its place, a much higher level of productivity through the transfer of capital, skill, education, and technology is introduced from outside, thereby enhancing the growth, but not the development, of the country. Vera Anstey wrote about the pre-British Indian economy:

> Up to the eighteenth century, the economic condition of India was relatively advanced, and Indian methods of production and of industrial and commercial organisation could stand comparison with those in vogue in any part in the world. A country which has manufactured and exported the finest muslins and other luxurious fabrics and articles, at a time when the ancestors of the British were living an extremely primitive life, has failed to take part in the economic revolution initiated by the descendants of those same wild barbarians. (Anstey 1952, 5)

Paul Baran (1957, 277) also quoted Anstey in his work to support his arguments for India's failure to initiate its own industrial revolution being due to exploitation by Britain and not due to lack of sufficient surplus labor. Angus Maddison's study (1971, 69) showed that 18 percent of total population in India was living in a nonvillage economy, with merchants, bankers, petty traders and entrepreneurs, urban artisans, and construction workers constituting a large part of these population, which gives a rough indication of the social structure of the Mughal Empire based largely on nonquantitative evidence. Habib's study shows that in this period, a market mechanism was in operation even in agricultural production. A large part of rural surplus was not used for self-consumption but was put on the market, and this should be regarded as commodity production. This rural surplus took the form of land revenue. However, the market mechanism, once established, must have reacted with the mode of agricultural production. Thus money relations emerged in a system of natural economy, and the cultivation of high-grade and cash crops (e.g., sugar cane, grapes, wheat, indigo, cotton, tobacco, etc.) began (Moreland 1919a). During the Mughal period, the main market for the urban cottage industry products was domestic, but a significant portion of luxury textiles was exported to Europe and Southeast Asia. Europeans in those days had great difficulties in finding products to exchange for these Indian textiles. The same was true of China, whose emperor wrote to George III of England: "The celestial Empire possesses all things in prolific abundance and lacks no products within its borders. Therefore, there is no need to import the manufactures of outside barbarians in exchange for our own products" (Bland 1914, 326; cf. Maddison 1971, 16).

India, therefore, at that time, was happy to get precious metals in exchange. There was a constant flow of silver and gold to India which absorbed a good deal of the bullion produced by the Spaniards in the New World. European travelers of the time mentioned in their accounts that urban centers of India were bigger than the biggest cities in Europe in the same period. For example, Clive considered that Murshidabad was more prosperous than London (c.f. A. Maddison,

1971, who quoted from Jahar lal Nehru, *Glimpses of World History*). Habib wrote: "Agra was the biggest seventeenth century town with a population of 500,000 to 600,000" (Habib, 1963, 76).

Most of the luxury handicraft trades were located in cities, and there was also a well-established banking system for the transfer of funds from one part of India to another. Maddison wrote:

> The luxury of court life, the international trade in silks, and muslins, the large size and splendour of Indian cities, the disdain for European products these were the reason for which Moghul India was regarded as wealthy by some European travellers. The standard of living of the upper class was certainly high and therefore, had bigger hoards of gold and precious stones than in Europe (Maddison, 1971, 18).

However, on the other hand, there is substantial evidence that the mass of the population was worse off than in Europe.

Francisco Pelsaert, in a report to the Dutch East India Company (1620–1627), described conditions in early seventeenth-century India:

> The rich in their great superfuity and absolute power, and the utter subjection and poverty of the common people—poverty so great and miserable that the life of the people can be depicted or accurately described only as the home of stark want and the dwelling place of bitter woe. . . . A workman's children can follow no occupation other than that of their father, nor can they inter-marry with any other caste. . . . They know little of the taste of meat. For their monotonous daily food they have nothing but a little "khichri," made of green pulse mixed with rice, which is cooked with water over a little fire until the moisture has evaporated, and eaten hot with butter in the evening; in the day time they munch a little parched pulse or other gain, which they say suffices for their lean stomachs.
>
> Their houses are built of mud with thatched roofs. Furniture there is little or none. . . . Bed clothes are scanty, merely a sheet or perhaps two, serving as under- and over sheet; this is sufficient in the hot weather, but the bitter cold nights are miserable indeed. (Moreland and Geyl 1925, 60–61)

E. L. Jones and S. J. Woolf (1969, 1) wrote in their book, *The Historical Role of Agrarian Change in Economic Development*:

> Technically their [East, Middle East, etc.] farming organisation was superb, especially in the wet-rice areas where extensive irrigation net works were by "covers" so large and well drilled as to make the problems of labour management in the early factory system look trifling. Equally, the physical volume of grain they produced was impressive. Yet their social histories were appalling tales of population cycles without a lasting rise in real incomes of the mass of the people on either the upswings or downswings. Their political histories are cycles of Cathay, the saga of dynasty after dynasty interrupted only by conquests or palace revolution which resulted in the retirement of one ruling clique by another.

It is evident from the history of these empires with immense state power that their great agricultural works, which were undertaken to add new cultivatable land by the construction of irrigation canals, did not fundamentally change the system. We may also mention the cases of Chinese Great Wall, which was 24 feet high, studded by watch towers 500 yards apart at the most, and so long that it would enclose large parts of France, Italy, Austria, Switzerland, Hungary, Rumania, Bulgaria, Poland, and a segment of Russia, or the magnificent construction of palaces and tombs to glorify their rulers, such as the Pyramids or the Taj Mahal, where enormous resources of surveying and engineering skills, construction materials, labor and footware were expended. The mass of the people, the agricultural peasantry, supplied the resources in the form of taxes and labor for public works, which were unproductive in economic terms. These huge resources were used not to raise productivity but to satisfy the consumer demand of the aristocracy. Therefore, these highly impressive archaeological constructions did not lead to commercialism or industrialization and, therefore, these agrarian empires remained essentially ·sterile. The changes that the peasantry might raise their standard of living significantly and thus provide a broadly based market were severely circumscribed. Tax burdens were so onerous and collection was so efficient that local consumption was kept at a low, often subsistence, level and might be further depressed in times of stress. Any significant rise in the surplus of food produced above the subsistence level could be skimmed off by the state. Consumer goods of any variety were inevitably only available as luxury items. On the other hand, labor for food production on the family holding and to meet obligations to the state was a real asset. Probably, this situation encouraged population growth to meet whatever level of food supplies could be produced and retained by the bulk of the people (Jones and Woolf 1969, 2).

However, this kind of oppressive feudal rule and extreme economic inequality, with only 1 percent of total population (consisting of feudal landowning classes) enjoyed 15 percent of the national income after tax, according to Maddison's (1971, 69) rough estimate, was able to continue for a long period because of two important basic factors: (1) tropical countries with their lush vegetation and congenial weather enabled vast masses of the poor people to survive with few resources, which required little effort under these circumstances. They took available resources as a gift of God through nature. In the West, with their then-untamed and unfriendly nature and weather, to survive, the people needed much greater efforts and income. The kind of oppression that characterized the lives of the masses of the population of tropical countries, which they did survive, would have wiped out large numbers of those in the West, which would have been severely harmful to the owners of wealth. Marx's views on the rise of the industrial capital in the tropical countries are very relevant and objective in this respect.

Moreover, (2) because of severe oppression, vast masses of the population had a very poor level of living, which caused malnutrition and high death rates.

TABLE 5.3 Social Structure of the Mughal Empire

	Percentage of labor force	Percentage of national income after tax
NONVILLAGE ECONOMY	18	52
Moghul emperor and court	1	15
Mansabdars		
Jagirdars		
Native princes		
Appointed zamindars		
Hereditary zamindars		
Merchants and bankers	17	37
Traditional professionals		
Petty traders and entrepreneurs		
Soldiers and petty bureaucracy		
Urban artisans and construction workers		
Servants		
Sweepers		
Scavengers		
VILLAGE ECONOMY	72	45
Dominant castes		
Cultivators and rural artisans		
Landless laborers		
Servants		
Sweepers		
Scavengers		
TRIBAL ECONOMY	10	3

Source: A. Maddison. (1971) *Class Structure and Economic Growth: India and Pakistan since the Moghals.* London: Unwin. Used by permission of Oxford University Press.

Famine visited these people quite often, and hence, the population growth rate was very small in those days. Therefore, a small population compared to vast land rich with gifts of nature proved to be too small and required little effort to manipulate it and thereby develop greater productivity and capital. In the West, the need to manipulate nature just to survive in those days was a necessary condition for survival.

Nature of India's Capitalist Development during the Colonial and Post–World War Periods

Mandel wrote: "While capitalism has spread all over the world, the greater part of the world has experienced only its disintegrating effects, without benefiting from its creative side" (Mandel 1968, 441). The Indian economy, since the introduction of capitalist production in the nineteenth century, bears a testimony to this. An introduced capitalism in its intensive phase cannot play a creative role in regenerating a feudal or semifeudal economy like that of India because at this phase, capitalism accumulates capital by dispensing labor and, therefore, its introduction to an economy like that of India does not lead to the absorption of huge surplus labor in the process of production, thereby developing its creative potential as capitalism did at the early stage of its rise in the West. It does not bring about capitalist transformation of the economy and society in terms of (1) economic structural change, (2) creating social conditions leading to the demographic change suitable for a society advancing from a preindustrial one, and (3) a social consciousness of secularism and humanism that the use of science and reason in the process of industrial production is expected to bring about. Mandel, like most Marxist economists, regarded the Western exploitation as the cause of such maldevelopment of developing countries. However, exploitation is inherent in capitalism; in other words deprivation of the producer of ownership of the product of its labor is the substance of capitalism. However, in the country where capitalism originated, it made a creative contribution. Why would it fail to do so when introduced to another country at its mature phase? Mandel has not addressed this question. Another point must be made here; industrial capitalism, which evolved originally in Britain, eventually penetrated into Continental Europe via trade in goods and commodity capital. These countries benefited from capitalism's "creative effects." The reason for this lies with capitalism's three creative contributions mentioned earlier, resulting from technology transferred to these countries from the United Kingdom, because at that stage of capitalism, it created opportunities for the productive absorption of labor in the process of production based on science (see Maitra 1980, 1988b).

The transfer of capitalist production in the latter period, particularly since World War II when its technology became capital-biased (supplied by developed countries) and, therefore, labor dispensing, has failed to produce the creative effects of capitalism. That is why the United Nations admitted that despite the huge transfer of technology, capital skill, human capital, and the consequent rapid growth of the capitalist sector and high rate of capital accumulation, the poor countries are becoming poorer and the rich ones, richer (Myrdal 1971). The condition of existence of natural resources in a country is not a guarantee that the country will undergo successful industrial development. True, England, France, Belgium, and Germany had substantial deposits of coal; so, too, do India, China, and many other Third World countries. Besides coal, India has the largest share of (21 percent) total iron ores in the world, followed by Brazil (15 percent). The density of population does not matter, but the rate of sustained growth of population and the causes of such growth matter in dynamic changes such as industrial development. For example, population growth due to a high birthrate, as in the early period of the development of industrial capital in the United Kingdom (in the eighteenth and nineteenth centuries), the phenomenon known as "population take-off," and the high population growth due, mainly, to the fall in death rate in

India and other Third World countries mean fundamentally two different things in terms of their role in economic development; the phenomena, therefore, may be called population inflation (Maitra 1980, 1986; see, for a detailed study, Chapter 6). Mandel summed up the factors responsible for the rise of industrial capitalism as in Europe as follows: the prehistory of capitalism, the extent of accumulation of commercial capital, the degree of penetration of money into agriculture, and the totality of socioeconomic conditions favorable or unfavorable for the application of scientific techniques to production (Mandel 1968, 442). In explaining why the development of capitalism has not been so successful in the Third World, Mandel said, "The catastrophic aspect of underdevelopment was due first and foremost to the particular way, that is, a violent and plundering way, in which contact was made between the two worlds (Mandel 1068, 442).

The preindustrial condition of India has been described by Helen Lamb of Massachusetts Institute of Technology:

> By the eighteenth century India had attained a high degree of development in pre-industrial terms. Agriculture was sufficiently developed to support a relatively large number of non-agricultural workers; There were highly skilled craftsmen, in iron, steel, textiles, ship building, and metal work. India produced manufactured goods not only for home consumption but also for export. India's economic wealth for centuries had been controlled by merchants bankers and princes who siphoned off the surplus of production over consumption in the form of idle hoards of gold and bullion; hence this wealth was sufficiently concentrated to represent a potential source of investment funds. India's resources of good quality coal and iron ore were located in convenient proximity to each other. (1955, 464–65)

However, while explaining the reasons for India's failure to develop industrial capitalism of its own despite the presence of favorable conditions, Lamb said that the colonial relationship inhibited such development; it stimulated India's development in some ways and inhibited it in others. Marx also came to the same conclusion. He wrote:

> The railway system . . . allowed, and even forced states where capitalism was confined to a few summits of society, to suddenly create and enlarge their capitalistic superstructure in dimensions altogether disproportionate to the bulk of the social body; carrying on the great work of production in transitional modes. . . . The railways gave of course an immense impulse to the development of foreign commerce, but the commerce in countries which export principally raw produce increased the misery of the masses. . . . All the changes were very useful indeed for the great landed proprietor, the usurer, the merchant, the railways, the bankers and so forth, but very dismal for contradiction in these societies. (Marx 1975, 298–99)

In the present work I have attempted to probe further the causes of persistence of India's underdevelopment. The next section of this chapter includes a further discussion on the accumulation of merchant capital in India, which will show that

India had a sufficient accumulation of merchant capital, which needed to be combined with cheaper supply of labor. India's population growth rate was very low and not sustained at that point in history. On the other hand, the loot in precious metal constituted an important source of money capital in the United Kingdom, which at that time had a sustained and relatively high population growth, led to the development of industrial capital and the Industrial Revolution. Mandel and most other Marxist economists have ignored this aspect.

We will keep our analysis on India confined to the following three aspects:

1. accumulation of merchant capital
2. population growth as a source of surplus labor and the lack of it in India on both counts because of the absence of land reforms, which was due to the low rate of growth of population compared to the vast amount of fertile land
3. a brief outline of India's socioeconomic condition

We can guess the vast amount of accumulation of merchant capital from a brief statement by Sir Percival Griffiths (1952, 374–75, 402–3) that the £100 to £150 million was the outcome of the British plundering in India between 1750 and 1800: "The total amount comes to over a billion pounds sterling, or more than the capital of all the industrial enterprises operated by steam which existed in Europe around 1800" (Mandel 1968, 442). Around 1770 the British national income was only £125 million. The whole of Britain's modern metallurgical industry (including steel) around 1790 had cost only an investment of £650 (Hoslitz 1968, cited in Mandel 1970, 443).

Brook Adams, referred to the direct relationship between the plundering of India by the East India Company and the beginning of the Industrial Revolution. The plundering of India helped the process of the development of industrial capitalism by providing merchant capital, but did not cause the Industrial Revolution, which I must emphasize here.

> Very soon after Plassey the Bengal plunder began to arrive in London, and the effect appears to have been instantaneous for all the authorities agree that the "industrial revolution" the event which has divided the nineteenth century from all antecedent time, began with the year 1760 (the battle of Plassy occurred in 1757). At once in 1759, the Bank of England issued £10 and £15 notes for the first time (Adams, 313, 319, cited in Mandel 1968).

Edmund Burkes's estimate of the British extortions in India between 1757 and 1780 was put at £40 million.

All these accounts plus the huge sums of money that the Indian merchant class lent to the East India Company for their business in India (Dutt 1971) point to the fact that India had a vast accumulation of merchant capital which could have been transformed into industrial capital if the vital condition of supply of sufficient surplus labor was fulfilled. We have referred to a study of Helen Lamb (1955) that sums up the puzzle of India's failure to stage an industrial revolution of its own. Many economic historians, both Marxists and non-Marxists, consider the British plundering of India as responsible for the failure to bring about industrialization in India in the past. True, the plundering made India poorer but could not keep it underdeveloped (Maitra 1991b).

There is no doubt about the fact that the British exploitation and plundering of India have impoverished India, but this surely has not kept it underdeveloped. Underdevelopment results from the lack of growth of reproducible capital (i.e., industrial capital). The industrial capital results from the combination of two factors (a) the static factor of sufficient accumulation of merchant capital and, more importantly, (b) the dynamic factor of sufficient surplus labor. The existence of these two factors in combination creates the favorable condition conducive to the development of industrial capital. The existence of these two conditions presuppose the rise of risk-taking owners of the capital or entreprenuing class from rich landowning and merchant classes and an increasing population as the source of inputs (i.e., labor and wage goods (i.e., food and raw materials and shelters), as well as an expanding markets for manufacturing products.

Despite the rich precapitalist accumulation of merchant capital and the agricultural economy, Indian could not graduate into an industrial economy. Industrial growth was later, as in all latecomer countries, introduced from overseas, first to feed the interest of the colonial power, and then to aid the local merchant capitalist class, which was propped up by foreign investment for nearly the past 200 years. This pattern of industrial growth has resulted in the rapid growth in the rate of capital accumulation, from about 5 percent of the GNP in 1950s to over 20 percent today. Nonetheless, India's economy has shown no sign of having undergone capitalist transformation in terms of economic structural change, the demographic transition (see Chapter 6), and human resource development (see Chapter 7).

Trade in India began with exports of finished manufactured goods and some capital goods from the West to build the infrastructure to facilitate transportation of goods to and from the country. However, the export of productive capital was limited in the nineteenth century because of a limited market, while that of manufactured products became the principal means of capturing the Indian market, which was mainly made up of rich people; that is, less than 2 to 3 percent of the total population or about 4 to 6 million. This size at the initial stage was considered to be very large, considering the low level of organic composition of capital or capital intensity of production of manufactured goods in those days in the United Kingdom. The bulk of export of capital from England, that is, the foreign capital, was invested in trading and financial companies servicing the import trade of industrial goods from England and export of agricultural products and raw materials from India, as well as financing the plantation and mineral industries. The development of railways in India as part of infrastructure development was expected, according to Marx, to regenerate the Indian economy. However, this kind of investment of foreign capital did not lead to the dynamic development of capitalism in India and thereby capitalist transformation of the economy. India remained underdeveloped, with over 70 percent of the population eking out a subsistence living, even after more than 100 years of penetration of Western capital into the economy.

Non-Marxists economists tried to explain this failure in terms of India's traditional social life and strong religious influence as the great retarding factor. Nationalists and some Marxists (Paul Baran, for example) made political dependency the cause of the failure of introduced capitalism to become a dynamic force. The Japanese case is advanced in support of this argument. Japan was not a colony and therefore escaped the characteristic features of foreign investment of a colonial economy. The Japanese government planned the investment of foreign resources and economic development in such a way that the capitalist transformation of the economy advanced, though slowly compared to Britain as well as France and Germany. It took a much longer time in Japan than it did in France or Germany (see Maitra 1980, 1986). In India, it has not materialized even today, despite a very rapid growth of industries, rise in the ratio of capital formation since 1950s. One Marxist economist explained it as follows: foreign investments

were mainly concentrated in those spheres of production which supplied the metropolitan country with mineral raw materials, and cash crops and also infrastructure to the extent it was necessary for foreign trade interests of metropolitan capital and its enterprises in the colony itself. The linkages of the foreign enterprises with indigenous capital as well as with other sectors and formations within the colonial economy were extremely limited. (Malyarov 1992, 2–3)

Capitalism, when it evolves from below, that is, from agriculture in the form of agricultural surplus as it did in the United Kingdom, automatically brings about the capitalist transformation of the entire economy. When it is superimposed on an economy, it may also bring about this transformation by absorbing agricultural surplus labor and thereby bring about the capitalist transformation of agriculture, the demographic transition, and the gradual development of human resources into human capital, commensurate with the growth of industrial capital (as it did in France, Germany, Holland, Japan, etc.). However, in Japan, it took a longer time to bring about the effects due to changes in the level of capitalist technology borrowed from overseas (see Maitra 1980). The link between agriculture and industry via the supply of labor to the latter and supply of its products, physical capital, to the farmer took over 80 years (1868–1950) to forge. In the case of India, there is little prospect of this linkage to materialize because of the policy of dependence on Western capitalism for capital and technology and the level of technological change. Capitalist production has reached today its globalization phase, and therefore, the future of this linkage is doomed forever.

During the colonial period, foreign enterprises in India were engaged in economic activities that were dependent on overseas industrial, technical, and scientific bases (i.e., imported plants and machinery). They were largely oriented toward rich overseas markets rather than engaged in manufactures for the domestic market. The domestic market was extremely limited due to preponderance of poor subsistence agriculture, which absorbed more than 80 percent of the total population, and economic activities were mostly nonmonetized. Foreign investment had created little linkage with the agriculture.

Marx wrote, "With the development of the capitalist mode of production, there is an increase in the minimum amount of individual capital" (1978, 142). This results from economic structural change that constantly reorganizes economic resources between sectors and activities so that the capital accumulation rate rises. In India, this minimum was not provided by increased productivity of the workforce or indigenous capital, but it was determined and supplied by overseas enterprises. A higher stage of development of the capitalist mode of production (i.e., capital intensive), and therefore of concentration and centralization, on the one hand, and on the other, devoid of domestic resources as this capital is imported, could not have any linkage effects in India. Imported foreign capital of even a middle-sized factory retarded the development of industrial capital from below, that is, from India's rich cottage and small-scale industries, unlike in the United Kingdom (see Chapter 3). Rather, it ruined many artisan industries and impoverished artisans in the remaining industries. It thus destroyed the possibility of accumulating the necessary minimum capital for developing into industrial capital with a growth in labor surplus caused by population growth and land reforms.

The development of India's rich prototechnology into industrial technology was blocked with the transfer of technology from the industrialized West. The foreign capital and competition also blocked the transition of merchant capital and household industry into industrial capital. However, the population has been growing at fast rate in recent times, not due to better living condition effects of land reforms, but as a result of a massive injection of medical technology and health services from overseas, leading to a sharp fall in the mortality rate.

The inhibition of industrial growth, retardation of the transition of merchant capital into industrial capital, and consequent stagnation of cottage and small-scale industry and conservation of feudal agriculture, which became the source of livelihood of a growing pool of rural surplus labor, along with the grip of imported manufactured goods and commodity capital in the limited monetized economy of India and the rise of local big business, caused the growth of comprador and merchant-cum-moneylender capital, which in turn has become one of the main hindrances to the development of Industrial capitalism and capitalist transformation of the Indian economy (Malyarov 1982). Malyarov's account did not take into consideration the other vital force, that is, of availability of surplus labor in the development of industrial capitalism from merchant capitalism. India's big merchant capital was invested in the export-import business, in collaboration with foreign business, and not in India's small-scale industries because of lack of market for products of these industries, as well as due to the fact that the import of finished light consumer goods from overseas was more attractive to those limited numbers who could afford to buy them.

In India during the colonial period, factories were established from the United Kingdom and did not evolve from India's prototechnology-based household industries. India's is a case of transplanted industrial capitalism. Capitalist factories owed their existence to the accumulation of capital that took place in the sphere of the comprador-merchant in combination with foreign capital, equipment, and technology. Foreign enterprises in India relied mainly on the external capital market via British managing agency houses, which functioned as trading agents of the industrial capital of the metropolis. Growing Indian money or merchant capital out of the export-import business partly remained confined to trading-cum-mercantile activities, due to the fewer risks involved and higher returns, and partly invested in foreign enterprises engaged in cash crop production for exports and a limited number of industrial enterprises. In this way, a comprador merchant and trader-cum-moneylending class emerged.

Whereas industrial capitalism historically should evolve from the use of merchant capital in combination with surplus labor, in the case of India, it was transplanted, which obviously did not result from the use of India's primitive accumulation of capital in terms of surplus labor. That is, India's industrial capitalism did not evolve from the extensive phase of technology of using surplus labor. Consequently, a growing population remained dependent on underdeveloped feudal agriculture. This pattern of transplanted industrial capitalism did not induce land reforms to bring about capitalist transformation of agriculture. Even after independence, when the transformation of industrial capitalism under the state leadership in a mixed economy continued, growing surplus labor still remained outside the capitalist sector. The capitalist sector, after nearly 40 years of operation, still absorbs only about 20 percent of the labor force, including the capitalist service sector, which is developing fast today under the impact of internationalization of production phase of Western capitalism (see Chapter 4).

The dualistic economy thus emerged with little linkage between indigenous capitalist formations and transplanted industrial capitalist formations, which had strong outward linkages that grew stronger in India's colonial economy. "Industrial capital of the metropolitan country was represented in the colonial market mainly by imported goods and commodity capital together with a high share of trading and financial companies (accounting for about 45% of the total private foreign investment on the eve of independence) and enterprises producing raw materials and tropical goods for exports (e.g., tea, jute, manganese and other minerals etc.), constituting nearly half of the foreign investment in the production sphere" (Government of India 1950). Foreign and Indian monopolies dominated the industrial capitalist sector, with 40 percent of total paid-up capital controlled by the 20 biggest industrial groups, while the tradition of the household with unorganized type of small-scale enterprise dominated the rest of the economy. Economists, including Marxists, thought that under the general laws of social development, this process would inevitably evolve toward capitalism (Malyarov 1992, 9). There is no doubt about the fact that there has been a substantial growth of capitalist industries in India; particularly since independence, the proportion of GDP contributed by large-scale industries in India has gone up. Production is as diversified as it is in most developed countries. India's dependence on imported capital also has been reduced. However, foreign investment is expanding in leaps and bounds. Capital formation as proportion of total GNP since the 1950s, also increased over the period. However, there has been no sign of capitalist transformation of the economy. The capitalist formation process is confined to a small percentage of population (about 6 percent in factory production) and has been coexisting with precapitalist formations involving an overwhelming proportion of the population and economic activities. There has been change, not in kind, but in degree. India's Industrial capitalist development, as in the other Third World countries, has not evolved from below. It has been imposed from overseas and from above as a result of growth of industrial capital as an offshoot of the internationalization of capitalism. I discuss in the next section the nature of capitalist development in India after independence under the state participation in the economy (i.e., during the phases of internationalization of capitalism via financial investment and production in the recent period). It will be evident from these discussions that there has been no capitalist transformation of the Indian economy if we measure it by Lewis's (1954) "criterion" or the criteria of the demographic transition and development of education as an integral part of the transformation, and we will find a paradoxical development when compared with Britain (see Chapters 6 and 7).

The next section will highlight some important changes accompanying the growth of Industrial capitalism in India (see Maitra 1988, 14–31; 1991, ch. 4). In the third section, the Mahalanobis Planning Model will be revisited, followed by a brief review of current changes.

RECENT CHANGES IN THE INDIAN ECONOMY

The Pre-British Structure was extremely complex with a hierarchy of land rights and also at least to some extent identifiable class relationships. There was considerable monetisation and commodity production with the consequent tendency towards differential among the peasantry and the emergence of trade as a two way process between country and town. Manufacturing was quite developed. It was, however, non-mechanised but catering for international market (Patrick, 1972, 26).

During the internationalization of investment period, when planned import-substituting industrialization was undertaken in India's mixed economy, the protectection, combined with large government expenditure, created extremely profitable markets for a whole range of commodities. To exploit this market, Indian capital had necessarily to turn overseas for technology. Foreign finance capital poured in to take advantage of the expanding market and escape tariff barriers. The joint venture emerged as a marriage of convenience.

The foreign capital this time differed from the old one in three main respects. First, it was interested in the modern, technologically advanced sectors of industry, which were most dynamic areas of the economy. Foreign financial investment in these areas necessarily was prompted by the interest of the lending countries, the technology of which was undergoing rapid development. Therefore, the foreign loans were meant to enable India to pursue technology and capital goods; thus, the foreign collaboration practice appeared in a new form. Between 1948 and 1955, only 284 collaboration agreements (i.e., about 40 a year) were approved by the government, but in 1956, there were 86; with 103 in 1958; 150 in 1959; and 380 in 1960. Since then, there have been around 300 to 400 a year. According to a study of the Reserve Bank of India, of a total of 1867, such agreements, manufacturing accounted for 1,056, 115 were for transport equipment, 250 for machinery and machine tools, 107 for metals, 162 for electrical goods, and 177 for chemicals. Second, there was an increasing trend to rely on the participation of Indian capital. The form of investment was no longer in branches of a European company but in local subsidiaries, or more frequently, in ventures involving a minority participation. Even in subsidiaries there was a fall in the parent companies' share (Reserve Bank of India 1968, 4, 102, 14; c.f. Patnaik 1972).

Out of 2,000 pure technical collaborations before 1963, 1,750 were purely technical agreements. However, in 1967, out of 341 of these agreements, 211 involved financial participation (Hazari 1968, 140). This suited the governments as well as the foreign partner, which got a foothold in the Indian market. In its total operation, the Indian partner was extremely small by comparison, particularly since it was the smaller monopoly houses that displayed the greatest enthusiasm for teaming up. For example, the Mafatal Group increased its total assets by 176 percent between 1963–1964 and 1966–1967, largely by expanding its interests in chemicals with foreign collaboration (Government of India 1969; c.f. Patnaik 1968).

Indian authors like Patnaik took the view of this development that "if the Indian capital was not to be swamped, it needed state backing, and in the first phase of development, the state retained a curtain autonomy in relation to foreign capital and foreign assets" (Patnaik 1972, 219), but state backing and government economic planning were inevitable processes of the globalization of investment phase of world capitalism. It benefited both foreign and rising Indian capitalist groups and helped lay the groundwork for the next phase (i.e., globalization of production).

The public sector has been responsible for the development of infrastructure and basic and heavy industries. It has been successful in this respect, as is indicated by the growth of this sector. The public sectors' share in the production of reproducible capital increased from 15 percent in 1950–1951 to 40 percent in 1976–1977, while the share of the state enterprises in the net domestic product grew from 3 percent in 1950–1951 to 16 percent in 1984–1985 (Malyarov 1991, 12). The infrastructure and basic industries have been built up, providing a great incentive to the rapid growth of the private sector, particularly in the production of consumer durables. The objective of the Keynesian policy of state intervention was to stimulate the private sector, and this was fulfilled.

The public sector, needless to say, is not an independent socioeconomic formation. Foreign investment and foreign aid via the supply of finance and credit helped the public sector promote the growth of the private capitalist sector. Thus, the sphere of the public sector was limited to industrial (basic and heavy), social (educational and health), and financial (banking to financial institutions to supply the private sector with cheap loans) infrastructures, as well as to the production of the most important fuel and industrial raw materials for the development of the private sector. The private sector did not make much contribution to the financing of public sector activities. The share of the direct taxes in the GNP remained virtually unchanged, at a very low level of 3 percent, while in the budget revenue, its share diminished from 28 percent in 1950–1951 to 10 percent in 1986–1987 and tax revenue, from 40 percent in 1948–1949 to 14 percent in 1986–1987 (Government of India 1985, 29; 75h Five Year Plan, Government of India, 1955c, 5).

This has been accompanied by an increase in the share of subsidies and current transfers to other sectors in current budget expenditures from 16 percent in 1961–1962 to 1965–1966 to 26 percent in the period between 1980–1981 and 1983–1984. The policy of low, often subsidized, prices of the public sector stimulated the private sector but limited the former's profitability and the ability to self-finance. The dividends and profits of the public sector enterprises constituted 5 percent of the current budget revenue in 1950–1951, 6 percent in 1960–1961, and only 1 percent in 1983–1984; while in 1980–1981 and 1984–1985, central public enterprises financed only 28 percent of their outlay from their own internal resources and enterprises at the state government at levels of only 3.5 percent, paradoxically (Government of India 1985b, 5). This declining ability of the public and state-level public enterprises is now being used by the private sector in its argument for dismantling the public sector. The public sector enjoyed greater independence at the earlier stage of capitalist development starting in the 1950s, when the private sector was small and weak.

With the growth and strengthening of the private sector in this process of planned development of infrastructure and basic industries, the relative independence and importance of the role of the public sector in developing the private sector tend to diminish. The rate of growth of capital formation in the public sector also consequently began to decline. The sharp fall in the annual rate of growth of capital formation in the public sector (as shown in Table 5.13) was followed by a decrease in its share in total capital formation. According to the source in Table 5.13, the public sector's share in the value-added in manufacturing has stagnated at 15 percent, and within the factory sector, at about 25 percent.

In the joint sector (public and private), the share partners of the state are usually of the highest strata of private capital—foreign capital and Indian big business. The number of joint companies with participation of the central government increased from 2 to 3 in 1966–1967 to 40 in 1980–1984, and their share of capital from 935 rubles to 6,310 rubles. Moreover, the number of joint companies with the participation of financial institutions of the state governments constituting 26 to 50 percent of their share capital increased from 18 in 1970 to 481 in 1986 (though their size was generally much smaller) (Murthy 1988; cited in Malyarov 1992, 15). These changes indicate the gradual rise of the internationalization of production phase which supports a free market policy. Import substitution industrialization in the 1950s and 1960s, supported by foreign investment in terms of credit and loans protected by protectionist policy, meant safer and enlarging market for investment from overseas. Expansion of Indian market as a result of protected import-substituting industrialization meant increased demand for inputs of the countries helping India with foreign loans, credit, investment, and aid. This, on the other hand, stimulated economic activities of the western countries, leading to full employment and unprecedented affluence for the masses.

However, one point needs to be mentioned here: after independence, the Indian government's policy toward colonial-type foreign investment changed. The Indian government had sought to prevent the separate functioning of foreign capital and utilize it as a catalyst for the formation and growth of Indian capital. This was a source of technology, equipment, and foreign exchange that precisely covered the role of the internationalization of investment phase of world capitalism. India government's new policy (after the 1950s) led to the demise of the branch form of foreign investment. Statistics show that the number of branches of foreign companies decreased from 842 in 1955–1956 to 217 in 1983–1984, and their share in foreign business investments decreased from 52 percent in 1947–1948 to 6 percent in 1979–1980. The number of subsidiaries of foreign companies decreased from 150 in 1947–1948 to 80 in 1983–1984, with a concurrent increase in average Indian shareholding in them from 5 percent in 1947–1948 to 40 percent in 1980–1981. The present policy provides for the effective participation of Indian partners in management and control. The typical form of foreign investment is now a company with foreign shareholdings ranging from 30 to 40 percent. In 1970, the colonial form of joint functioning of foreign and Indian capital as the managing agency system was abolished. Instead, a government policy of encouraging collaboration between foreign and Indian capital has led to an increase in the growth of the average annual number of foreign collaboration agreements from 36 in 1948–1950 to 659 in 1980–85 (Reserve Bank of India 1950, 1968; Government of India 1950).

The Indian big business is the greatest beneficiary of this change, which makes it the most preferred and typical partner of foreign capital. This was the objective of state participation—to boost the growth of Indian big business, which would act as a facilitator of internationalization of direct foreign investment and production in India. The Tables (5.6, 5.7, and 5.12) on the "Mahalanobis Planning Model Revisited" show spectacular rises of some big business houses. Foreign collaboration provide the big business sector with more advanced foreign technology, much needed foreign exchange, and equipment. This new arrangement also has helped it to extend its hold over markets by using foreign, well-known trademarks and to enhance the popularity of its companies in the Indian capital market and their capacity to draw the flow of financial resources to it. There is no doubt about the fact that the new foreign investment policy and the policy of protection helped the growth of Indian monopoly capital. Other benefits in the form of the provision of developed infrastructure services, cheaper capital goods, and a supply of subsidized energy input and the long-term industrial finance provided by the government helped the growth of financial institutions and, thereby, the growth of monopoly capital and development of the Indian capital market. It is well known that Indian stock markets in the past provided little resources for investment. Only about 1 percent of the Indian population actively participated there, and the investments in company securities constituting only 6 to 7 percent of the savings of the average Indian family (Goyale 1979, 52). The underwriting and investment activities of the state financial institutions compensated significantly for the deficiency of individual investors but also contributed to the popularity of the state financial corporations, and thereby increased the number of investors.

The number of investors in industrial securities jumped up from hardly .5 million in the 1950s, and about 3 million at the end of the 1970s to 15 to 20 million in the late 1980s, and the average amount of capital raised from the primary market increased from Rs. 40 crore in the 1950s, about Rs. 70 crore in the 1960s, Rs. 90 crore in the 1970s, and about Rs. 3,0000 crore in the 1980s. However, all the time, from the colonial period onward, the lion's share of the financial resources coming to the stock market was attracted by the large companies belonging to foreign capital and a handful of large Indian houses. The growth of the stock market was, therefore, contributing largely to the centralization of capital under the control of monopoly groups. The assets of the 20 largest industrial houses in India increased from about Rs. 500 crore in 1951, Rs. 1,800 crore in 1964, Rs. 4,500 crore in 1975, and Rs. 7,500 crore in 1980 to Rs. 23,200 crore in 1986, constituting about one-third of the total assets of the private corporate sector. Similarly, assets of the 75 largest industrial houses increased from Rs. 2,600 crore in 1964 to Rs. .7,400 crore in 1975, and their share increased from 47 percent to 56 percent during that period (Goyale 1979, 52).

In the 1950s, government policy was also geared to stimulate rural and cottage household industries which mainly constituted the precapitalist sector of small industry. It implies that a dual policy of stimulating the rapid growth of large-scale industrialization and big business with foreign capital and technology as the dominant part of the policy, on one hand, and on the other, bolstering the growth of small-scale precapitalist industries, has been followed. Obviously, in effect the latter will have little impact in an economy now led by big industries conditioned by the prospect of international market and limited by a small domestic market. This was evident from the fact that since 1960s, state support to small industries was shifted to a modernized, mechanized, capitalist system essentially based on foreign capital and highly capital-intensive technology. The inability of the whole policy to bring about economic development and a consequent capitalist transformation of Indian economy is evident from the stagnant economic structural change in the economy. The basic fault of this approach can easily be detected by examining the natural process of industrial growth and capitalist formation that took place in the United Kingdom. True, India cannot avoid adopting this since its development has become part and parcel of the development of world capitalism.

However, this policy helped spur tremendous growth in Indian capitalism, (see Table 5.11) as well as industrial growth, as indicated by the fact that the share of imported equipment in the total investment in equipment decreased from 60 percent in 1950–1951 to 15 percent in 1977–1978. The import of paper, metal, engineering, and chemical products as a percentage of gross output of the factory industry decreased from 83 percent in 1960–1961 to 49 percent in 1977–78. In other words, the import substitution policy is largely successful in this respect. However, economic structural change effects of import-substituting industrialization, led by the state in collaboration with foreign capital and India's private sector, completely failed, with over 70 percent of the workforce still eking out a living from agriculture.

A land reform policy was adopted long after the industrialization was underway and was based on foreign capital, skill, and technology. Therefore, a huge amount of surplus labor, which was released by the land reform and also contributed to by high population growth was never able to be utilized in the process of industrial growth. Large numbers remained tied to underdeveloped agriculture or became self-employed or employed in petty distributive activities in urban areas, such as street vendors, hawkers, railway porters, domestic servants, and numerous other low-income family businesses and shops. They formed between 30 and 40 percent of the urban disguised unemployed, with close to subsistence income living in sprawling slums in the big cities in India. The following section discusses the Mahalanobis planning model, which has been the main policy frame in India's economic development in the postindependence period. Land reform policy has been given importance during this period as a means to prepare the agricultural sector for industrial growth. We will also briefly examine the implications of land reform for the economic development of India. Land reform policy as a precondition to industrial development is expected to play an impor-

TABLE 5.4 Social Structure at the End of British Rule

	Percentage of labor force	Percentage of national income
NONVILLAGE ECONOMY	18	44
British officials and military, British capitalists, plantation owners, traders, bankers, and managers	0.06	5
Native princes, big zamindars and jagirdars		3
Indian capitalists, merchants, and managers	0.94	3
Petty traders, small entrepreneurs, traditional professionals, clerical and manual workers in government, soldiers, railway workers, industrial workers, urban artisans, servants, sweepers, and scavengers	17	30
VILLAGE ECONOMY	75	54
Village rentiers, rural moneylenders, small zamindars, and tenants-in-chief	9	20
Working proprietors and protected tenants	20	18
Tenants-at-will, sharecroppers, village artisans, and servants	29	12
Landless laborers and scavengers	17	4
TRIBAL ECONOMY	7	2

Source: A. Maddison. (1971). *Class Structure and Economic Growth: India and Pakistan since the Moghals*. London: Unwin. Used by permission of Oxford University Press.

tant role in bringing about the capitalist transformation of an economy by introducing mobility of the labor force between sectors, promoting freedom of occupation, and creating conditions conducive to the supply of capital and labor to and from agriculture and industry at the initial stage.

THE MAHALANOBIS PLANNING MODEL REVISITED (A HISTORICAL APPROACH)

It is well known that the classical years of Keynesianism and consumerism are from 1950 to 1970, although the basic elements of consumerism were beginning to emerge, in the United States in particular, as early as the 1920s. The imperialist mode of capital accumulation more or less ended with World War I. Many people believed that imperialism was the last stage of capitalism. After that, there was a transition away from free market capitalism.[1] However, extensive state intervention or Keynesianism during the post–World War II period was intended to stimulate capital accumulation, which gave vigour to capitalism. Thus, state intervention became the policy to prop up capitalism after the serious depression it suffered in the 1930s. Capitalism was later stimulated by World War II (in Keynesian analysis, MPI for marginal propensity to invest needs, such as defense expenditures when excess capital accumulation cannot be profitably put to investment). The United States followed this policy of Keynesianism to bolster investment in defense goods production, even in peacetime in order to create the conditions for fuller employment opportunities and expanding aggregate demand so that private sector activities could be stimulated and the rate of capital accumulation increased.

TABLE 5.5   Wealth in the Private Sector between 1956–1964 (in Crores of Rupees)

Capitalist Groups	Wealth in Crores of Rupees	
	1956	1964
Tata	116	418
Birla	104	299
Mafatlah	13	46
J.K. Singhania	29	59
Thapar	15	72
Bangur	17	104
Sindhia	25	47
A.C.C.	22	77
Kirloskar	2	19
Walchand	13	55
Kasturbhai Lallbhai	13	34
Mahindra	1	20
Khatau	3	14
Bird Co	34	60
Sahu Jaén	59	68
Martin Burns	41	150
Andrew Yule	28	42

Source: Ashim Chaudhuri, *Private Economic Power in India* (New Delhi: The Peoples Publishing House, 1985), 32.
Note: The above table indicates how rapidly Indian Capital Classes amassed wealth under a planned economy with public sector as the leading sector.

Many economists, including the Marxists, termed this state intervention variously as state capitalism, monopoly state capitalism, welfare state capitalism, military capitalism, or rightist Keynesianism, as in United States. However, this stage of capitalism was the product of a new mode of capital accumulation. At the first or early stage, the internationalization of goods and commodity capital through trade and colonialism had widened capitalism's market beyond the border of each capitalist country (Chapter 4). This mode of capital accumulation resulted in an unprecedented growth of finance in the center of world capitalism, which was earned through the export of commodity capital and goods. (The internationalization of investment was the natural outcome of capital to expand for further profit and accumulation.) The period between 1950 and 1970 may be termed the period of internationalization of investment. (Foreign investment through loans and capital was the principal investment in this phase). This was the period when all Third World countries, including India, undertook initiatives to bring about economic development, with the public sector as the leading sector and having responsibility for the development of infrastructure (including education, communication, and transport) and heavy industries.

This policy was the offshoot of Keynesian state social welfarism in a mixed economy, which was to create opportunities for full employment, stimulate sagging aggregate demand, and create conditions for the development of consumerist industries, which, in turn, would serve as a market for the products of developed capitalist economies. This policy was highly successful, as judged by the full employment conditions, affluence, and consumerist life-style of the masses in the capitalist West, on the one hand, and some high level of employment opportunities, some affluence, and a consumerist life-style for a handful of people in the Third World, who were expected to benefit from such development. However, most important of all in India and other Third World countries is the growth of a stronger and more organized industrial capitalist groups. However, these remained basically merchant capitalist, as they did not have roots in their respective societies (see Maitra 1992a).

However, neither Keynesianism as a theory nor the Mahalanobis plan as an embodiment of the basics of Keynesianism as applied to the Indian situation of underdevelopment were an independent approach. One instrument for developed economies and another for the Third World were needed by the aggressive second stage of expansion of world capitalism, which is known as the internationalization of investment. The need for a second phase became unavoidable as the growth of capital accumulation resulting from the effects of the first phase of the internationalization of goods and commodity capital of the 100 years needed larger markets for profitable investment.

It is well known today that world industrial capitalism originated in the United Kingdom with the Industrial Revolution and then expanded all over the world in three major phases:

1. Internationalization of goods and capital, covering the period of the late nineteenth to mid-twentieth centuries. This was the main instrument of expansion of capitalism from the center of world capitalism, the United Kingdom (see Chapter 4);

2. The post–World War II period (1950–1970): known as the internationalization of investment phase (via a supply of loans, credit, and investments), this was the leading factor, with the first phase operating side by side in a supporting role (Maitra 1993). This was the period when Keynesian social welfarism in a mixed economy system became the policy in the developed economies and also for planned development in a mixed economy in the Third World;

3. The third phase of expansion began in the late 1970s when the second phase, having fulfilled its role and becoming a drag on Western capitalism,

TABLE 5.6 Wealth in Crores of Rupees 1964–1980

Capitalist Groups/Companies	1964	1980
Tata	417.72	1538.97
Birla	292.72	437.99
Mafatlah	45.91	427.54
J.K. Singhania	59.20	412.72
Thapar	71.90	348.00
I.C.I.	36.89	343.01
Sarabhai	43.20	327.94
A.C.C.	77.36	274.51
Bangur	77.91	264.33
Larsen and Turbo	10.00	246.48
Sri Ram	54.68	241.00
Kirloskar	29.20	220.39
Hindusthan Lever	19.92	219.30
Sindhia	46.96	212.80
Oil India	89.73	205.88
Modi Group	11.30	198.82
TVS Iyenger	21.90	188.64
Mahindra	20.12	186.03
Chongule		184.68
Bajaj	2.10	179.26

Source: Ashim Chaudhuri, *Private Economic Power in India* (New Delhi: The Peoples Publishing House, 1985), 32.

proved to be the greatest hindrance to the efficient working of world capitalism. This phase is known as the globalization of production (Cantwell 1989; Maitra 1993). The second phase of internationalization of investment, via instruments of loan and credit, created a tremendous demand for capital goods from the Western world. Keynesian state welfarism, together with the expansion of the West's investment in the Third World, including India, in the name of aiding economic development, created an unprecedented demand for labor in the West, resulting in full employment and conditions that were highly favorable to the rapid growth of consumerist industries and consumerism. In this third phase, the dismantling of planning, privatization, and the free market become the dominant policy instruments.

Development of the Planning Model

The Mahalanobis planning model was the first serious attempt to apply the logic of quantitative economic policy making to an underdeveloped economy with its characteristic limitations of statistical data and the economic structure itself. This planning model provided, for the first time, the basis of actual calculations of investment, its allocation, and other details of the five-year plans, setting the prospective framework of long-term planning (see Tables 5.8 and 5.9). Under the plan, the economy was divided into two sectors producing, respectively, consumer and capital goods, from which further divisions into different types of consumer goods could be extended. It was believed that additional investments had differing productivity-creating effects in the consumption goods and capital goods sectors; greater stress was given to the allocation of resources to the investment goods sector so that productivity of the economy may be raised faster. The public sector undertook the major responsibilities of investment goods production, and the consumption goods production was left to the private sector. Increased investment in the public sector created a market for the consumption goods sector, which was designed to boost private sector investment (Bhattacharyya 1976; Sengupta and Sengupta 1961).

The Mahalanobis plan was introduced to bring about rapid industrial growth with increasing employment opportunities. The Mahalanobis plan for the growth of industrial capitalist industries consisted of two broad programs:

TABLE 5.7   Growth of Wealth in the Private Sector, 1969–1980 (Percentages)

1969–72	1972–76	1976–80	1969–80
15.09	12.303	11.77	12.427

Source: Rangnekar (1982) 8.

1. rapid industrialization, with particular emphasis on the development of basic and heavy industries;
2. a large expansion of employment opportunities, "a large increase in employment opportunities must be regarded as the principal objective—the Kingpin of the Plan" (Government of India 1956, 39). The development of basic industries should not result in the destruction of the small-scale industries, which provide opportunities for employment and reduction in income inequalities (Bhattacharyya 1976; see also Bettelheim 1959).

The above objectives may also be looked at from a technology policy point of view. That is, the Mahalanobis plan, by implication, suggested a concurrent application of the extensive and intensive phases of the technological change for India's industrial development. The extensive phase was meant for the small-scale cottage industries sector so it would absorb labor, while the intensive one was meant for the basic and machine-making industrial sectors, which would not have much employment effect. A much larger proportion of total investment was allocated to the producer goods industries under the public sector. These investment resources were mainly available through foreign aid and foreign investment, loans, and credit.

The approach to industrialization was an import substitution one. The import-substituting industrialization policy advocated during this period created a tremendous demand for goods—sophisticated consumer durables and producers' goods. The type of industrial growth that took place, for obvious reasons, resulted in increased income inequality and a demand for consumer durables, which is termed "U" sector growth.

Professor Mahalanobis has been regarded as a pioneer in economic planning in the Third World. His economic planning never meant socialism, as many people tried to argue. It was undertaken in a mixed economy system as the basic condition. It was meant to act as a boost to a nascent and weak private sector mainly composed of merchant capital engaged in the import-export business, and small groups of light consumer goods industries, and one or two basic industries.

This planning model was intended to lay down the foundation of capitalist industrial growth under state direction, with the private sector as the main beneficiary (see Tables 5.8 and 5.9). The plan in a mixed economy has fulfilled the role it was intended to play. Otherwise, the private sector in India today would not have the strength to oppose the operation of the public sector and demand its dismantling so that resources—domestic and foreign—can be channeled to it unhindered. After about two and a half decades of its operation under planning, the private sector in India has become strong enough to stand on its own feet and so consider the existence of the public sector (causing budget deficits, high inflation, high interest rate, high wages, etc.) as the greatest hindrance to its rapid and profitable expansion. The same sort of IMF and World Bank arguments as advocated today in developed capitalist economies in support of dismantling their Keynesian social welfare systems to make the market economy operate unhindered are being orchestrated in the Third World, too.

The process and pace of growth in developing economies in the 1960s and 1970s reveal a tremendous demand for goods—consumer, consumer durables, and producers goods; in other words, "U" sector growth (see *Economic Weekly*, 1960s issues). However, few economists took note of the fact that this pattern of growth was inevitable and was intended to meet the needs of world capitalism which was at the stage of internationalization of investment. At the center of world capitalism (i.e., in the West), this phase of capitalism helped create the conditions for an unprecedented affluence for vast masses of the population and full employment. In India and other Third World economies, this planned development of import-substituting industrialization with foreign capital created a limited opportunity for employment in the productive sectors and a negligible demand for cottage industry products among people with rising incomes. The demand for economic durables flourished among the beneficiaries of such development. This group consisted of about 5 to 8 percent of the total population, which constituted nearly 25–30 million (based on the total population of India at that time). This was a considerable market of more than half the British market (Britain's population was just over 50 million in the 1960s). Obviously, those products became the hot target for substitution by domestic production with, again, very little employment effects. Because of this approach, the economic structures basically remained undeveloped, with over 70 percent of the population eking out their living from subsistence agriculture and contributing about 40 percent of GNP. This indicates the low productivity of the labor force. In other words, there were little economic structural effects from the approach of import-substituting industrial development. This trend is continuing, and will continue with a vengeance under the export-substituting industrialization policy of the free market economy today, because of fast technological change and acute competitiveness in the international market. It will be increasingly difficult to bring about economic structural change and capitalist transformation today, compared to the opportunities of the past. However, opportunities for low-income jobs and

TABLE 5.8 Public and Private Sector Investment in the First, Second, and Third Plans (Crores of Rubles)

Period	Public Sector Investment	Private Sector Investment
1951–56	1,560 (40.4)	1,800 (53.6)
1956–61	3,731 (54.6)	3,100 (45.4)
1960–66	6,300* (60.6)	4,100 (39.4)

Note: *Excludes funds transferred to the private sector.
Figures in brackets indicate percentages of total investment.

TABLE 5.9   Allocation of Public Sector Plan Outlays, 1974–1979 (based on December 1973 Draft; in Crores of Rubles)

Head of Outlay	Amount	Percentage of Total Outlay
Agriculture and Allied Sectors	4,730	13
Irrigation and Power	8,871	24
Industry and Minerals	8,939	24
Transport and Communications	7,115	19
Social Services	7,309	20
Others	418	neg
	3,7382*	100.0

*Though the sectoral outlays aggregate to Rs. 37,382 crores, the public sector outlay in the Plan is taken as Rs. 37,250 crores. The difference is to be made up either by economy in expenditure or by additional resource mobilization.

self-employment will be growing in plenty, maintaining the nation's preindustrial character.

Under the Mahalanobis plan, India attempted rapid industrial growth so that the problems of population growth, unemployment and disguised unemployment, and the low standard of living could be solved. However, the kind of industrial growth that took place, aggravated all these problems. It failed to reduce population growth because industrial growth created little demand for labor and capitalist transformation effects. When industrial growth creates sufficient demand for labor, it simultaneously creates the condition for family planning, which leads to a fall in the birthrate (see Chapter 4). A stagnating economic structure is another indicator of failure by the import-substituting industrialization approach, which is based on a combination of intensive and extensive technological change. However, Japan was successful in bringing about economic structural change with the help of imported technology, capital, and skills, although it took a much longer time than latecomers in the West in the nineteenth century (Maitra 1980).

The Case of Japan—A Brief Reference

Japan's technology policy was also a combination of the two phases from the very beginning of its modernization. Japan had several advantages. First, when Japan started its vigorous industrialization program in the late nineteenth century, technology borrowed from the West was at its late extensive and early intensive phase and, therefore, was more employment effective, which helped bring about economic structural change and capitalist transformation of the economy. Second, population growth was around 1 to 1.2 percent, compared with India's 3 percent in the 1950s. Japan at that time did not have to face the impact of imported medical technology effects. The widespread use of modern medicine, medical and health technology, and health services had not evolved in the West at that time. Third, Japan's literacy rate at that time was comparable to that of mid-nineteenth-century Britain, which helped the former country absorb modern technology effectively and created the necessary skilled labor force for both "modern" and traditional, small-scale sectors. On the contrary, India had a much higher literacy rate (Dharmapal 1971) before the British came than in 1947 (about 10 percent), when the British left. This also helped Japan undertake the extensive phase of technological change, absorbing labor relatively productively in agriculture, small-scale factory, and artisans' industries. The latter played a very important role as a source of cheaper spare parts and accessories to the large scale manufacturing sector and, thus, to Japan's international trade. Thus, a process, although a weak one, of integration between the two sectors began in Japan in the early stage of its modern development. The state played a dominant role in the entire process.

Last, Japan seldom indulged in importing finished consumer goods, let alone consumer durables (which, however, were nonexistent in the West at that phase of its industrial growth) and thus, import substitution was essentially limited to producer goods industries, unlike in India.

The Positive Contribution of the Mahalanobis Plan

Having said all these things, I must point out that no economist—Indian or non-Indian—can deny the fact that the tremendous growth of heavy and producer goods industries in India under the Mahalanobis' plan has made India one of the largest industrial capitalist economies of the world (although, paradoxically, with an underdeveloped economic structure and little capitalist transformation) ready for playing a vital role at the present internationalization of the production stage of world capitalism (Maitra 1993). Those who criticize today the mixed economy approach of India to industrial development (with the public sector playing the leading role during the 1950s to 1970s) ignore the economic history of the development of world capitalism in particular. India's transplanted capitalist sector evolved as part and parcel of world capitalism. Therefore, India has to follow the dictates of the needs of world capitalism. Had India not followed a mixed economy policy, with the public sector leading the basic industry sector, it would have missed its place as one of the largest industrial countries of the world today in terms of its infrastructure, including high levels of education, research and development sectors, and the fundamental basis of industrial growth (i.e., basic and producer goods industries). Without this development, economists who condemn the Mahalanobis plan would not have any economic foundation on which to stand and propagate free market policy.

As an example, Japan in general, since the beginning of its modernization and particularly since the 1950s, laid the principal stress on the development of heavy and producer goods industries and thoroughly prepared itself as a leading capitalist economy in the era of the internationalization of production stage of world capitalism, in the late 1960s. American foreign aid had prepared it for the earlier stage of the internationalization of investment. All developed industrial capitalist countries before that time had a developed infrastructure, high levels of human capital, and R and D sectors—the essential inputs for this stage of internationalization of production. However, many of the basic and light consumer goods industries from these developed economies, including Japan, have been transplanted to cheap labor economies in recent times with the start of globalization of production.

If India had not had a planned development of basic industries and industrial development had been left to market forces in the 1950s and 1960s, its economy would have remained very weak and confined to mainly light consumer goods at the most. A market economy approach in those days would have meant an interplay of market forces consisting of merchant capital and small-scale industries. Sufficient and necessary foreign capital with the high productivity needed to develop a productive industrial sector could not have been attracted without the guarantee of government control and direction of the economy in a planned way, and without the government's policy of mobilization of resources required for such investment. Under a weak capitalist regime, India, with very little industrial growth (mainly confined to light consumer goods production) and per capita income below $100 dollars at that time, would have failed, without a strong public sector, to attract foreign loans and capital as well as domestic resources for investment, and therefore would never have reached the present position of a major industrialized nation. What I am trying to point out here is that had there been no Mahalanobis industrial development plan during the 1950s to 1970s, India would have been very ill prepared for the current stage of internationalization of production of world capitalism and would have had the fate of an economy comparable to that of many African countries.

We will understand the value of the Mahalanobis planning model and the historical role it played in the design of world capitalist development if we take a brief look at the process of internationalization of goods, commodity capital, investment, and production discussed briefly in the fourth section of Chapter 4 (see also Maitra 1993).

However, if we believe that world capitalism in its new phase of internationalization of production based on free market policies can solve its rising unemployment problems, growing poverty, and social tensions, then we are living in a fool's paradise. The following brief analysis of capitalism's present policy dilemma will help clarify this (see Maitra 1993, for a detailed discussion).

The Post–World War II Period

Import substitution followed by the current export substitution industrialization strategies are both part and parcel of the internationalization of world capitalism that began with trade in goods and commodity capital in late nineteenth

TABLE 5.10 Foreign Aid Utilized in the Periods 1951–1956, 1956–1961, and 1961–1966 (Crores of Rubles)

Period	Foreign Aid Utilized
1951–1956	201.67
1956–1961	1,430.19
1961–1966	2,867.72

Source: Bhattacharyya (1976).

TABLE 5.11 Import Availability Ratios by Industry Groups (Indicates Growth of Import Substituting Industrialization)

	Value of imports as percentage of total availability		
Industry group	1959–60	1965–66	1978–79
Food except beverages	4.2	2.9	9.4
Beverages	15.8	7.5	0.9
Tobacco	1.5	0.9	
Textiles	2.9	1.3	1.6
Footwear, etc.	-	-	-
Wood and cork	22.1	4.5	2.2
Furniture and fixtures	0.9	0.4	0.4
Paper and paper products	23.4	17.1	18.8
Printing and publishing	-	-	-
Leather and fur products	5.4	4.6	0.1
Rubber products	11.5	3.5	5.5
Chemical and Chemical products	30.2	17.2	18.2
Petroleum products	43.9	27.8	32.5
Non-metallic mineral products	6.5	2.2	29.3
Basic metals	32.3	22.2	18.9
Metal products	23.4	6.8	6.1
Non-electrical machinery	65.8	56.3	31.4
Electrical machinery	38.1	27.7	9.7
Transport equipment	25.7	15.8	11.6
Miscellaneous	18.8	15.6	16.4

Source: Ahluwalia (1983). Cited in P. Bardhan, *The Political Economy of Development in India* (Calcutta: Oxford University Press, 1984): 94. Used by permission of Oxford University Press.

TABLE 5.12   Sales of Top 20 Industrial Houses

		No. of companies		Sales (Rs billions)	
Industrial House		1972	1981	1972	1981
1	Tata	32	38	6.93	23.90
2	Birla	70	77	5.90	21.62
3	Mafatlal	14	13	1.91	7.98
4	Hindusthan Lever	8	6	1.88	6.10
5	Thapar	35	31	1.55	5.90
6	J.K.Singhania	28	27	1.04	5.52
7	Shri Ram	14	14	1.76	5.31
8	Bangur	44	51	1.43	4.46
9	Kirloskar	15	15	0.71	4.29
10	Modi Group	9	9	0.94	4.25
11	ICI	7	7	1.49	4.17
12	Sarabhai	11	11	0.96	4.06
13	Mahindra & Mahindra	13	13	0.74	3.45
14	Ashok Leyland	2	2	0.35	3.23
15	Bajaj	29	29	0.83	3.18
16	Reliance Textiles	-	12	-	3.15
17	TVS Iyenger	19	24	0.82	3.09
18	A.C.C.	5	5	0.94	2.70
19	Larsen and Toubro	10	9	0.56	1.80
20	Sindhia	3	3	0.51	1.16
Total of these 20 houses				31.25	119.32
Total sales as a percentage of net domestic product in private organized sector at current prices.				61	87
Wholesale price Index with 1970–71 as base				113.0	270.6

Source: These estimates are based on CMIE (1983). For computing the figures of total sales as a percentage of net domestic product in private organized sector, the figures for the latter have been taken for 1971–72 and 1980–81. Cited in Bardhan, *The Political Economy of Development in India* (Calcutta: Oxford University Press, 1984): 105. Used by permission of Oxford University Press.

century. Planned import-substituting industrialization in the Third World was the outcome of the internationalization of investment via credit and loans. Import-substituting industrialization (ISI) was undertaken in most countries in a mixed economy framework, with the public sector as the dominant partner. This stage was essential to create the condition for the subsequent development of world capitalism into the present internationalization of production phase. The main strategy of this phase is export substitution with minimal public sector in-

TABLE 5.13 Annual Rate of Growth of Capital Formation in
India's Public Sector (Per Year)

Year	Rate
1950–51—1965–66	12.2
1966–67—1978–79	4.3
1981–82—1983–84	2.8

Source: National Accounts Statistics, C.S.O., New Delhi, 1985

tervention[2] and unrestricted entry for multinationals, which will act as the leading force instead of the state, as in the past two to three decades. The internationalization of the production phase of capitalism does not need to depend on economies of scale of production because the unrestricted world economy is market (and no longer the national economy). It rather depends on the economics of scope indicated by factor price, availability of high-level human capital, more efficient communication and transport systems, availability of resources, a free trade and market economy, unrestricted entry of foreign capital, low wages, and similar factor. These were created in India during the planned economy period, which was followed by a recent privatization policy.

The Mahalanobis planning model was meant to fulfill the aim of internationalization of investment in the Third World and, simultaneously but indirectly, in the developed capitalist economies of the West. The growth of ISI needed industrial imports to be bought against the loans and credit granted under this process and created tremendous demand for the products of developed economies (imports, consumer durables, etc.). The consequence was rampant consumerism, affluence, and full employment in all developed capitalist economies, with state welfare policy as the instrument. However, in the process, the demand for labor that exceeded supply resulted in a need for rapid technological change and growth of human capital in these economies (see Maitra 1991).

Economic planning in India in the mixed economy set up stimulated "U" sector and consumerist industries and thereby created tremendous opportunity for the investment of foreign capital in the form of loans, credit, and aid. On the other hand, consumerist policies were also dominant in the developed capitalist economies, which were supported by large and active welfare states. The welfare state was based on a progressive income tax policy and full employment policies in the West during the period 1950 to 1980. Thus, the state sector became the dominant sector of the total economy. Not only did the state take considerable responsibility for maintaining basic social welfare and health and extending education, it also actively managed the economy to prevent serious depressions or runaway inflation.

TABLE 5.14 Savings and Investment Ratios (Three-Year Moving Averages)

	Gross domestic savings as percentage of gross domestic product at current market prices	Gross fixed capital formation as percentage of gross domestic product at 1970–71 market prices	Gross fixed capital formation in the public sector as percentage of gross domestic product at 1970–71 market prices
1951–52	9.5	12.2	3.3
1952–53	9.0	11.1	3.5
1953–54	9.0	10.5	3.7
1954–55	11.2	11.2	4.4
1955–56	12.8	12.8	5.0
1956–57	12.9	14.7	5.8
1957–58	11.8	14.7	5.7
1958–59	11.5	14.2	6.0
1959–60	12.3	13.5	6.2
1960–61	13.1	14.0	6.6
1961–62	13.8	14.5	7.0
1962–63	14.0	15.1	7.3
1963–64	14.2	15.8	7.8
1964–65	14.6	16.8	8.3
1965–66	15.2	17.5	8.4
1966–67	15.3	17.7	7.9
1967–68	14.8	17.3	7.1
1968–69	14.8	16.8	6.5
1969–70	15.8	16.3	6.2
1970–71	16.8	16.1	6.2
1971–72	16.8	16.3	6.8
1972–73	17.6	16.7	7.3
1973–74	17.9	16.7	7.2
1974–75	19.2	16.3	6.9
1975–76	20.2	16.8	7.2
1976–77	21.4	17.5	7.9
1977–78	22.8	17.9	8.2
1978–79	22.9	17.7	8.2
1979–80	22.9	17.3	8.1
1980–81	22.8	17.5	8.3
1981–82	22.7	17.4	8.5

Source: Cited in, Bardhan, *The Political Economy of Development in India* (Calcutta: Oxford University Press, 1984): 97–98. Used by permission of Oxford University Press.
Note:These estimates are from national accounts statistics. The data are not adjusted for what are called "errors and omissions" or net purchase of second–hand physical assets. The 1982–83 figures used for calculating the three–year moving average for 1981–82 are based on"quick estimates" by the Central Statistical Organization released in 1984. The same price deflator has been used for both public and total gross fixed capital formation.

Conclusion

The implications of India's present unrestricted market policy, which is an inevitable follow-up of the policy of planned industrial growth led by the state were discussed (see also Chapter 4). The Mahalanobish planning model has been highly successful in India in building an industrial capitalist sector and preparing this sector for the third stage of the internationalization of production phase of world capitalism.

However, it has failed to bring about the capitalist transformation of the economy as defined in terms of economic structural change and, thereby, create the conditions conducive to the demographic transition and the transformation of a feudal social mind into the humanist social consciousness of a successful industrial capitalist society. The fly in the ointment of the Mahalanobis planning model lies with the fact that it attempted to develop industrial capitalism with the help of foreign capital and technology during the mid-twentieth century, when the introduction of these resources from overseas at this stage of world capitalism had been divested of any role to play in bringing about the capitalist transformation of Third World countries and, thereby, their development, unlike its introduction in the nineteenth and early twentieth centuries (Maitra 1981, 1986).

Implications of India's present policy of dismantling planning, and privatization with unrestricted market economy, which is an inevitable follow-up of the previous globalization of investment phase of capitalism, will be presented, in brief, in the following section.

THE DEREGULATION PROCESS AND THE INDIAN ECONOMY—(A BRIEF REVIEW)

We should examine here a brief account of the Indian economy under the impact of new policy introduced to meet the need of being a part of internationalization of production. All governments that followed state intervention policy to maintain full employment in the developed capitalist economies and state planning to achieve rapid industrial growth in the Third World borrowed huge sums of capital from the world market. All these governments faced acute budget deficits. (The previous policy under the globalization of investment phase of capitalism was expected to produce these two effects.) All these countries began to face high inflation rates, interest rates, and wage costs. Thus, a new policy of "liberalizing the Economy" was felt necessary.

The government of India had, in fact, found in early January 1991, that India was "close to technical default" on its foreign debts and that foreign exchange reserves had dropped to the equivalent of two weeks of imports. The government's budget deficit grew from 6.4 percent of GNP in 1980 to 8.9 percent in 1990, leading to an annual rate of inflation rate of close to 10 percent (Harman

1994). By 1991, the government's domestic debt had risen to 56 percent of GDP.

The foreign exchange crisis of 1991 forced the government to undertake the IMF's "structural adjustment program" (see Chapter 4). This program combined short-term measures to improve the balance of payments with long-term "liberalization" reforms which the finance ministry claimed, would put the economy on the path of high and sustained growth . . . by 1993." The first part of the program seemed to have had some effect as far as the aim was concerned. A sharp recession and emergency import controls in 1991 led to a limited improvement in the balance of payments and a fall in inflation from about 17 percent in August 1991 to about 12 percent in March 1992, while cuts in government expenditures reduced the budget deficit to about 5 percent of GDP. However, the second part, that is, liberalization policy intended to return the country to "sustained growth," appeared to have been much more problematic. The liberalization included the easing of restrictions on imports and foreign investment and making rupee convertible, as well as cuts in sugar and fertilizer subsidies, the deregulation of steel distribution, and a reduction in the top rate of the personal income tax. Although growth returned, that is not difficult to achieve under this policy, and particularly, the open door policy to foreign investment under multinational corporations. A recent figure shows that $42 billion dollars of foreign investment entered into India in 1993 alone (*The Statesman* May 20, 1994). Obviously, these foreign investments are highly productive. Therefore, the growth rate cannot but be expected to rise. However, the concomitant problems of such a policy also cannot be avoided. These are the rapid growth of unemployment and disguised unemployment and also of low-income self-employment. These are mostly redistributive by nature, with little return, and therefore cannot serve as sufficient markets for the products of foreign investments.

Industrial output in India shows strong growth rate, rising from 5.2 percent in 1973–1980 to 6.3 percent in 1980–1981. IMF and the World Bank felt greatly enthused about the effects of their prescription to liberalize the economy, especially in 1981 and 1985 (World Bank 1991, 38; 1992, 262). However, they deliberately ignored the other side of the coin. "The mounting burden of borrowings both domestic and overseas, brought the economy to the brink of insolvency" (Datta 1992, 1018). It became clear that for at least five years of the liberalization, the high growth rate in industry had been a result of the boost to consumption of upper-income groups, who constitute about 90 to 100 million population (considered a sufficiently large market to foreign investors as a tiny part of their total, global market). This level of consumption was brought about by the government's loose macroeconomic policy of excess spending over taxation. The government's budget deficit grew from 6.4 percent of GNP to 8.9 percent in 1990, raising the inflation rate to 10 percent. Moreover, exports grew much more slowly than imports, especially those of sophisticated consumer durables, including electronic products. Imports of other goods grew tenfold between 1980 and

1990, until they were roughly at the same level as imports of capital goods intended to modernize Indian industry (World Bank 1992, 266). By 1991, the government's domestic debt had risen to 56 percent of GDP (World Bank 1992, 262–63). These developments will lead to further and heavier doses of liberalization, as is happening elsewhere in the world.

We discussed earlier in Chapter 4, the role of the state in spreading consumerism during the period of social welfarism in the developed countries and of state planning for development in India and the Third World. Now, with the liberalization policy, the same policy of pushing consumerism continues to supply the market for these products.

It may be pointed out here that the growth of consumerism and investment in industry geared to feed consumerism was taking place at the expense of investment in agriculture. Fixed capital formation in agriculture at 8 percent of GDP in the sixth plan (1980–1985) was lower than in the fifth plan and declined further in the seventh. We should remember that even in 1980s, 70 percent of India's population lived on agriculture, most of whom were at a subsistence level of living as indicated by their contribution of less than 40 percent of GDP (World Development Report 1987). For obvious reasons, they do not matter to foreign investors or the government's export-oriented industrial growth policy.

The other side of the coin has been stagnation, or even a deterioration, of the conditions of the mass of the population, a trend that further liberalization is likely to aggravate. The government's measures for controlling the budget deficit involve cutting food subsidies and making welfare cost-effective, on the one hand, and on the other, enacting a substantial reduction in tax on high-income groups.

The average Bombay textile worker earned 39.77 rupees (about 2.5 dollars) a day in 1986 and the average coal miner, 30.42 rupees ($1.10). However, these groups of workers are still better off than the great masses of the population. Wage rates in the unorganized sectors, which constitute 75 percent of the total manufacturing workforce, are a quarter of these figures. The 75.6 million agricultural laborers earn one-tenth of what an organized sector worker earns. Agricultural incomes as a proportion of GDP have declined, and there is no evidence of a significant and declining trend in the incidence of rural poverty.

India's unemployment situation is deteriorating fast, which anybody can see by examining the nature of investment and economic activities. In the 1980s, the number of persons registering at employment exchanges in India doubled, until it had reached 34 million or 10 percent of the total active population. This number of registered unemployed says nothing about the actual situation if we take into consideration the fact that only about 40 percent of the population are literate and that this figure does not include urban disguised unemployed such as pavement vendors, domestic servants, railporters, and street hawkers. In the countryside, the supply of labor has been growing much more quickly than the demands for agricultural workers, leading to unemployment and migration to the towns, which will swell the numbers of urban disguised shanty dwellers. Already, this group constitutes over 25 percent of the population of these cities. In the urban centers, jobs in the organized sector only grew by 15.2 percent (i.e., by less than 2 percent on average per annum) and the traditional sector is stagnating to take up the slack. Therefore, the total manufacturing employment of 25 million is less than the total registered at the employment exchanges, which was 30 million in 1988 (i.e., only 3.3 percent of total labor force). Half the registered unemployed come from the small proportion of the population of qualified secondary school graduates. A research study stated: "The towns provide many more graduates than the local economy is able to assimilate; 60 percent registered at the government employment exchange are termed as educated."

In India, despite the abundance of labor the tendency is for investment to be capital intensive: there has been a 30-fold increase in investment in the main export industry, textiles, in 17 years. The secondary sector, and manufacturing in particular, cannot make much contribution to employment creating due to technology constraints. Imported technology with little labor content, which is suitable for the labor-short Western economies, is responsible for this failure. Moreover, as this kind of technology creates little demand for labor, the growth of industrial capitalism has not produced the demographic transition effects; hence, the population and unemployment problems (for further discussion see Chapter 6). On the other hand, the traditional sector employs only 18 million workers and capital investment is very low. Even in the towns, 66 percent of units belonging to this sector do not use any power other than the human hand; therefore, output is low and so are their incomes.

It is difficult to ignore the fact that whatever is happening elsewhere is also happening in India under the impact of globalization of production, this is inevitable.

NOTES

1. According to the Mahalanobis Committee report, "The growth of the private sector in industry and specially of the big companies has been facilitated by the financial assistance rendered by the public institutions like the Industrial Finanace Corporation (IFC), The National Industrial Development Corporation (NIDC), etc"(Mahalanobis Committee 1984, 3).

The then Trade and Industry Minister, Lal Bahadur Sastry, in a speech in Parliament (reported in the *Hindu Journal* 1961), commented: "If there was any reason for the Government to undertake production at all, it was beacause the investment was too large or complex for the private sector or because the Goverment were able to get more reasonable terms than the private sector could manage." Even the leading Indian industrialist, G. D.

Birla, commented in support of the public sector (*Capital,* April 9, 1989): "the public sector is even worse now, helping to give a tremendous push to th private sector."

2. Moreover, "across Asia the public sector is in decisive retreat" and the countries in Asia, among them India, are "actively privatising state owned enterprises and giving private business a larger role than before in the National Development plans" (*Economic and Political Weekly* (Bombay), March 11, 1984).

6

THE DEMOGRAPHIC TRANSITION, TECHNOLOGICAL CHANGE, AND CAPITALIST TRANSFORMATION

CAPITALIST TRANSFORMATION AND POPULATION GROWTH

In the conventional theory and practice of economic development, population policy involving family planning to induce population growth, on the one hand, and technology transfer as a means to raise productivity, on the other, has been vigorously advocated by economists, demographers, and planners since the beginning of the "development decade—1960s." Population growth of late has shown noticeable signs of a declining trend and there has also been a rapid growth in productivity and diversification of output as a result of these two policies, but with little effects of capitalist transformation and economic development.

In this section, we will try to find out what has gone wrong with these two policies using (1) Britain as a case where population growth and technological change have functionally influenced each other since the rise of industrial capitalism and the capitalist transformation of the British economy; and (2) India as a failed case in this respect. India has faithfully followed these economic theories and the approaches advocated by economists of developed and successful capitalist countries, and it has achieved tremendous growth of the capitalist sector, rapid and diversified industrial growth, and a high level human capital. However, it has an acute problem in the poverty of the vast masses of population, an under-developed economic structure dominated by feudal social consciousness, and a parliamentary democracy that is being increasingly dominated by religious fundamentalist parties. All these indicators of the capitalist transformation of the Indian economy cannot be ignored by socially conscious economists and policy makers.

In this chapter, we will examine the causes behind the failure of technological change and rapid capitalist accumulation to bring about capitalist transformation of the Indian economy, contrary to what happened in Britain at the comparable period. Therefore, I have had to repeat some of the terms and concepts discussed earlier to help in the present analysis. There is also a close interlinkage in the main theme of this book. In the analysis of the various parts of the theme, I cannot avoid some repetitions of terms and concepts dealing with the demographic effects and the development of education and energy use patterns vis-à-vis the capitalist transformation of an economy. These analyses are offshoots of the first five chapters.

Introduction

This chapter will examine the process of capitalist transformation and its effects on population growth using the cases of the United Kingdom and India. The nature and source of technological change play the vital role in the process of economic structural change, which is the most important indicator of capitalist transformation. In this context, the two phases of technological change—extensive and intensive—will be briefly analyzed along with their effects on the demand for labor and the consequent effects on the fertility rate. This will be studied using the cases of:

1. the United Kingdom, where the technological change has *evolved* from the extensive phase to the intensive phase, influencing the demographic change patterns;

2. India, where technological change has been *introduced* from the United Kingdom and other developed economies at their mature phase of intensive technological change. In this connection, the relationship between the technological change and demographic and capitalist transformation of an economy will also be examined, using the United Kingdom and India as case studies.

An attempt will be made to reinterpret the demographic transition theory in terms of effects of (a) capitalist transformation of an economy and (b) two phases of technological change. These two are functionally related, as experienced in developed economics. The theory in its original form ignored these two factors, which had serious effects on demographic change; consequently, policy implications of the theory for demographic policy in the Third World have been impaired. Two cases have been chosen in this study: first, the case of the British economy as the pioneer economy, which underwent capitalist transformation and generated modern technological change in two phases, with consequent demographic effects. The cases of France, Germany, and some other European countries may also be mentioned in this group, but with some qualifications. Second is the case of India in the mid-twentieth century. It has achieved substantial industrial growth with the policy of introduced technological change but has failed to achieve a sufficient capitalist transformation of its economy and thereby solve its enormous demographic problem.

The indicators of capitalist transformation of an economy, together with definitions of extensive and intensive phases of technological change vis-à-vis demographic transition and economic growth, will be presented in the following section. This will be followed by a study of the interrelationship between demographic transition, capitalist transformation, and technological change using the two contrasting cases of the United Kingdom and India.

This chapter attempts to examine whether the demographic effects depend on (a) the extent of capitalist transformation of an economy and the (b) nature and level of imported technological change. The well known demographic transition theory of W. S. Thompson (1929) and Notestein (1945, 1948, 1950, 1953) and subsequent discussions of the theory have ignored these two aspects (for example, Thirewall, 1982, and Todaro, 1989).

We shall begin first with a brief outline of indicators of the capitalist transformation of an economy. The demographic effects of an economy depend on the nature of capitalist transformation of the society, which in turn is determined by the nature and sources of technological change, that is, first, whether it has been introduced, as occurred in latecomer countries, as a result of technology transfer in the nineteenth and twentieth centuries or whether it evolved indigenously, organizing its surplus labor and prototechnology into large scale production, as was the case in the United Kingdom, the only country of the Industrial Revolution (Maitra 1980, 14–69, 70–90; 1986, 16–45; Henderson 1953).

Second, in the cases of introduced capitalism that resulted from a technology transfer from the already developed capitalist countries, the question remains whether the transfer took place when the technology was at its extensive or intensive phase. The phase of relatively large-scale organization based on an increasing division of labor intended to use labor and prototechnology more productively was the first phase (1760s–1860s) of the Industrial Revolution (Hobsbawm 1969, 29; Boulding 1983, 3). France and Germany, for example, borrowed technology from the United Kingdom at the later part of this phase. Rapid capitalist transformation (relative to the present-day cases of introduced capitalism via technology transfer from mature capitalist economies) marked the process of development of these countries with concomitant demographic effects (Maitra 1986, 30–65).

In the cases of capitalism introduced in the later period via technology transfer from the mature capitalist economies of today, technology has already reached its intensive phase, particularly since the 1950s. The capitalist transformation effects of technology transfer, in terms of economic structural change and, consequently, of demographic and social changes, will be basically different from the cases of the Industrial Revolution and those of earlier technology transfer (see Tables 6.3, 6.4 & 7.6). A discussion on these effects will follow in the next section, which is on indicators.

Indicators of Capitalist Transformation of an Economy

The capitalist transformation of a society is indicated by the following changes:

1. Dynamic changes in the sectoral distribution of the labor force with labor gradually moving out of the primary sector to the secondary or industrial sector, and then to the tertiary sector (Clark 1957; and Kuznets 1957). These changes are functionally related to technological changes from the extensive to the intensive phases. However, in some Third World countries, the labor force dependence on agriculture has declined, at the cost of disguised unemployment in the urban sector in service and family enterprise activities.

2. With the capitalist transformation of an economy, the disguised unemployment of surplus labor, which is characteristic of a precapitalist economy, is replaced by a cyclical open unemployment. The factor price (e.g., wage payment) system, based on the average product of labor (i.e., sharing of the output of labor in small-scale and family enterprises) of the past is replaced by the marginal product (Lewis 1957; Fei and Ranis 1963).

3. The capitalist transformation of an economy should have significant demographic effects. That is, with the capitalist transformation, population growth tends to rise at the initial stage, when technological change at its extensive phase creates an increased demand for labor, and begins to decline with the rise and expansion of the intensive phase of technological change. Both these trends are affected by changes in birthrates; unlike the Third World, population growth in the partly developed capitalist economies of today is caused by rapidly falling mortality rates. (See Figures 6.1 & 6.2).

Rate per thousand

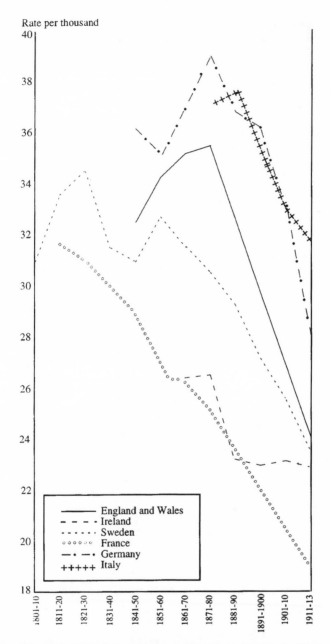

Figure 6.1 Birth-rate in Several European Countries in the Nineteenth Century

*Source:*Andre Armengaud. (1973). "Population in Europe 1700–1914," in C. M. Cipolla (ed.). *The Industrial Revolution.*

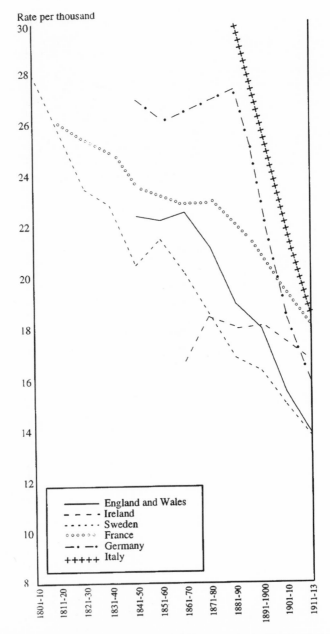

Rate per thousand

Figure 6.2 Death-rate in Several European Countries in the Nineteenth Century

*Source:*Andre Armengaud. (1973). "Population in Europe 1700–1914," in C. M. Cipolla (ed.). *The Industrial Revolution.*

These changes in economic structure, demography, and the factor pricing system must take place simultaneously because of the nature of their interrelatedness in a society that is undergoing capitalist transformation.

Unfortunately, Third World countries have hardly shown any sign of these changes, despite the rapid growth of modern capitalist enterprises (see Tables. which show the structural changes in different periods with India as an example). The studies in the following discussion also show the nature of capitalist transformation in India and other Asian countries, despite the rapid growth of modern capitalist industries.

The reference to *Asian Drama*, a basic, social study on the continent by Gunnar Myrdal (1968), however, offers a proper starting point for the discussion on the informal (i.e., noncapitalist) sector in Asia. The informal sector characterizes preindustrial and precapitalist economic activities.

> In South Asia's urban areas . . . economic activities are to be found, which are sometimes labelled "informally organized" although they are actually unorganized or very loosely organized. This category embraces a wide range of heterogeneous activities that have only one attribute in common: a set of institutional properties differing from those observed in either the more formally structured westernized units of production or the traditional rural crafts. These "informally organized" activities have in many ways been shaped by Western intervention and the increase in monetized economic activity accompanying it. Some are geared to serve modern demands—at least for those types of goods and services increasingly sought as a result of the expansion of monetized economic activity and import restrictions. Most, however, have tended to perpetuate traditional patterns, such as an emphasis on the family as the central unit of productive organization.
>
> The services sector contains perhaps the most conspicuous and pervasive example of the loosely organized—if not totally unorganized—type of economic activity. In South Asia service occupations typically account for a far larger proportion of the urban labour force than do all varieties of urban manufacturing . . . .
>
> The crowded field of retail trade accounts for a substantial share of the tertiary sector's claim on the labor force. Much retail trade is conducted on a petty basis by itinerant hawkers and peddlers. (248)

An economist, Dasgupta (1982, 23–24), presented a very illuminating account of India's unorganized sector based on his research:

> The presence of a large, elastic informal sector in the bigger urban centres is an important feature of urban life in India. According to various estimates, the informal sector accounts for between two-fifth and half of the earners in the major industrial centres of the country. Compared with the size of this sector, its contribution to the national product is marginal; the vast majority of coolies, domestic servants, street peddlers and trades, magicians, car-minders and so on are undertaking those activities, not because they are remunerative, but because that alternatives to these are unemployment and no income. The informal sector is usually dominated by mi-

grants, especially the more recent ones who do not see any immediate prospect of a regular job, and who, for various reasons, are unwilling to return to their villages. The ease of entry, small need of capital and skill, and the flexibility of operation attract them to a wide range of informal activities.

Limited capitalist transformation effects can be assessed also from the following research studies. The conditions described here are getting worse as the days go by because of the failure of industrial growth to create a sufficient demand for labor in organized productive activities. Technological change is becoming increasingly human capital–intensive, requiring a higher level of human capital. Quality labor is replacing quantity labor and, therefore, the number of disguised unemployed in all unorganized and family labor based activities—agricultural service, transport, and small industries—is growing.

According to V. M. Dandekar (1978), "It is only monopoly capital, whether state or private, and monopoly labour, that is organised, which can combine and share common gains. This organised sector comprising about 20 million workers constitutes only one-ninth of the total working population" (170).

A recent study based on the 1981 Census of Population (Government of India 1981) shows the following distribution of workers (Table 6.1).

According to Dandekar and many others, the process of capitalist transformation in India has been checked "because of the rise of the state and private monopoly capital and monopoly of the organised labour." Perfect competition prevailed when technology was simple, requiring a relatively small amount of resources and a small market. With the development of intensive technology, perfect competition has been transformed into a monopoly and subsequently monopolistic competition has become the basic condition because a large market and an increasingly sophisticated resource (human capital and more productive energy) requires a concentration of resources, markets, and a decision making process in a few monopolistic but competitive organizations to make the technology nationally and, gradually, internationally competitive. India's industrial

TABLE 6.1   Distribution of Workers in India, 1981

Precapitalist Class	
Cultivator class, agricultural laborers, and household industry	73.5%
Independent workers in the capitalist sector	8.9%
Employees	1.2%
White-collar employees	6.8%
Blue-collar workers	9.8%

Note: Due to rounding, figures do not exactly total 100%.

growth is based on imported technology from the West at a time when its technology has reached the mature intensive phase. Therefore, a monopolistic concentration of resources and control of the market resulted long before India traversed the perfect competition stage of early capitalist development. Trade union monopoly is also an inevitable development in the Western labor-short economies, and India has imported this trade union practice, with technology as a part of the package of the technology transfer. In the nineteenth century, the situation was different (see Maitra 1980, 1986, 1991). Dandekar and most other economists consider technology as "neutral" to history, factor endowments, the economic system, and its aims of production; hence this confusion.

The Demographic Transition Theory

With this background of knowledge of limited effects of capitalist transformation based on imported technology when it is at its intensive phase, we should examine the demographic transition theory. The demographic transition theory can be traced to works of W. S. Thompson (1929) and of F. W. Notestein (1945, 1948, 1950, 1953). The Thomson-Notestein theory seeks to explain the causes of the modern rise of population via the effects of modernization.

Notestein's 1945 article is important in the sense that it outlines the mechanism by which the demographic transition occurred and could take place in the future, together with the causes of the inferred changes. According to Notestein, "The growth of population came from the decline of mortality" and "so far we can tell from the available evidence, no substantial part of the modern population growth has come from a rise in fertility" (Notestein 1945, 39). The fertility rate in all preindustrial societies was already high and, therefore, further substantial acceleration could not occur. The death rate was equally high, and occasionally in those days it rose further. However, with the onset of the agricultural and industrial revolutions, which increased the availability of better food, shelter, sanitation, and clothing, the death rate began to decline slowly, and later, with the development of modern medical technology and health services, it started falling sharply. The birthrate remained high but began to decline with the increasing demand for labor in excess of its supply.

Notestein's theory can be summarized here in the form of four propositions:

1. The demographic revolution is initiated by the secular decline of mortality.
2. A mortality decline is caused by the cumulative influences of the agricultural, industrial, and sanitary revolutions which, respectively, lead to better food supplies, an improvement in the factors of production and the standard of living in general, and improvements in public health.
3. Rapid population growth is the result of the temporal lag between the decline of mortality and that of fertility.

4. Fertility decline eventually occurs because the social and economic supports to high fertility are removed. The materialism and individualism associated with the urban way of life give impetus to the rational control of fertility by means of contraceptive practices.

In Notestein's theory of demographic transition, three stages are involved: high mortality and high fertility; low mortality and high fertility; low mortality and low fertility.

The analysis of demographic effects of technological change and the capitalist transformation of an economy requires a reinterpretation of the demographic transition theory. The theory has ignored these basic factors in influencing the demographic change. An analysis of these two factors will help in understanding the difficulties in applying this model to explain the demographic trends in the Third World and also the basic factors that brought about the demographic transition in the developed capitalist economics and have been left out of the original model. The present analysis has serious policy implications.

Several authors have evaluated Thompson-Notestein's theory of the demographic transition in the light of European and the Third World demographic changes. One school argues that the theory's inability to adequately describe and explain the European experience make it of little use in predicting transition related demographic change, either in Euro-American countries or in the Third World (Mayer 1969; van de Walle and Knodel 1967; Gold 1971). Another school contends that the theory offers a reasonably accurate description, if not interpretation, of past demographic change and has at least, limited predictive ability (Cowgill 1962; Satin 1969; Coale 1973; Beaver 1975). According to some of these authors, the theory is a viable descriptive tool but is short as an explanatory model.

Coale (1973) and Caldwell (1976) take an in-between view. According to Coale, whereas the strength of the transition concept resides in the undeniable fact that with sufficient modernization, fertility and mortality change in a particular manner, its weakness lies with the difficulty of defining a precise threshold of modernization that will identify a population in which fertility is about to fall. In a more recent paper, Caldwell (1976) argued that in general, in societies of every type and stage of development, fertility behaviour is rational and fertility is either high or low as a result of the economic benefit to individuals, couples, or families.

Interestingly, in none of these discussions have the demographic effects of the changing combination of factors of production (i.e., technological change) and the changing pattern of demand for labor (first for quantity and then for quality of labor) with a capitalist transformation of the society and economic growth been taken into account. In the present chapter, the demographic effects of technological change and the capitalist transformation with economic growth have been taken into account to reinterpret the theory in the context of demographic changes in the Third World.

A New Interpretation of the Demographic Transition Theory Using Technological Change and the Capitalist Transformation as Explanatory Factors

This chapter attempts to reinterpret the demographic transition model and explain the limitations of its applicability to the Third World. When the technological change evolves within an economy from the stage of prototechnology through the extensive and then to the intensive phases, consequent changes in the economic structure in terms of dynamic changes in the sectoral distribution of the labor force reflect the process of the capitalist transformation of the economy, as was the case with the United Kingdom first, followed by latecomers of the nineteenth century (see Tables 3.2, 6.1 & 6.4). This process of transformation creates, first, a demand for labor in excess of its supply, which then promotes conditions conducive to the decline in population growth. This happens when the need for the intensive phase of technological change emerges after modern science begins to be used in production (1860s). In the Third World, these conditions, which are favorable to a decline in population growth, do not arise because of the faulty technology approach. The demographic transition theory can be traced to the works of W. S. Thompson (1929) and F. W. Notestein (1945, 1948, 1950, 1953). Recent developments in this theory can be summed up as follows.

The first stage is marked by high birthrates and death rates. The preindustrial period in most economies has this demographic characteristic. The beginning of the second stage of demographic transition was initiated during the first quarter of the nineteenth century, when the Industrial Revolution in the United Kingdom was at the extensive phase of technological change. This second stage of demographic transition is characterized by slowly falling death rates and the continuation of high birthrates. It is mainly caused by a relatively high demand for labors thereby making child labor an important labor source, which had the effect of maintaining the previous trend of a high birthrate. This period was also accompanied by slowly falling death rates due to better economic conditions and improvements in medical and sanitation services.

The third stage of declining birthrates did not really begin until the intensive phase of technological change had progressed substantially (i.e., until the late nineteenth century). The intensive phase of technological change was accompanied by the rapid expansion of literacy, primary and secondary education, and, soon, higher education. Obviously, this had an effect on the fertility of the population. The third stage was also gradually accompanied by a mass consumption stage, which also affected fertility rates. The neoclassical model of family fertility has tended to explain this in its familiar market mechanism model, while the technological explanation was advanced above. The economic structure at this stage becomes dominated by the tertiary sector, in which research and development activities in technology, education, information, and communication infrastructure play the dominant role. In the early phase of modern technological change (i.e., from the beginning of the extensive phase until the early intensive phase), when demand for labor gradually begins to exceed its supply, economic structural change is indicated by the movement of labor out of agriculture to the manufacturing sector. Primary or agricultural sectors by then begin to shed labor for industry, which in turn starts supplying productive inputs for agriculture (see Tables 3.1, 3.2 & 6.2).

The model of microeconomic determinants of family fertility, which was advanced in recent times to explain the rapidly falling birthrates in developed economies today, is shown in the third stage of the demographic transition model (Wrigley 1969). This model is based on the traditional neoclassical framework of household and consumer behavior in the mass consumption stage of development of a society and uses the principles of economy and optimization to explain family size decisions. According to this model, the demand for children is determined by the level of income. The costs of having a child are mostly the opportunity cost of a mother's time and benefits, potential child income and old age support, prices of all other goods, and the desire for goods relative to that for children. Some economists and demographers regard the time element as the most important factor in influencing technological change and, thus, demographic trends. The technological change from the extensive to intensive phase is a result, first, of an increasing demand for "quantity" labor, followed by demand for "quality" labor when science began to be introduced in production (to substitute for the former) and the need to be competitive in national and international markets. These changes are intended to use time more productively.

1. The extensive phase period of technological change (Maitra 1986, 1991): in this stage, the demand for quantity labor is high, which stimulated the fertility rate. Therefore, this period is marked by a high birthrate (see Table). This was reflected in the movement of the labor force away from the agricultural to the industrial sector (see Table 6.4).

2. The intensive phase period of technological change (Maitra 1986, 1991): this is the period when the demand for labor exceeded its supply, necessitating the introduction of science (i.e., modern technology) in production to substitute more productive labor for quantity labor. A period of a declining birthrate ensued (see Figure 6.1 and Tables 6.1, 6.2, and 6.3).

These changes had effects, first, on the structure of the economy, which were marked by an increasing proportion of the labor force being absorbed in manufacturing activities in the place of agriculture (which then began to bear the burden of increasingly smaller population) and in the development of education from primary to secondary and, later, higher education. With the emergence of the intensive phase, the tertiary sector began to absorb the larger proportion of skilled labor and the secondary sector's share declined (Tables 6.1, 6.2, and 6.3 and the Figure 6.2).

The first phase of technological change (i.e., the extensive phase) failed to emerge in the Third World societies. The birthrate remained high until the 1960s, when there was a slight fall due to the modern sector effects on a limited section of the population. With industrialization based on the intensive phase, with its consequent little demand for labor, the effects on fertility have been little, on the one hand, but on the other, the use of imported medical technology has caused the death rate to decline very fast.

Technological Change and Demographic Effects

It would be helpful to refer to the nature of technological change that took place during the Industrial Revolution, which will clarify the factors behind the changes in the demand for labor that influenced the demographic changes of the period (see Table 3.2). When population growth is high and economic structural change is stagnant, the demand for labor in production will be very low.

In the United Kingdom, the demand for labor at the early phase of technological change acted as the main stimulus to a continuation of the high birthrate which, together with a decline in the death rate resulting from better food, shelter, sanitation, and clothing (as economic development effects), led to the rise in population growth. The latter was the consequence of the Industrial Revolution generated by technological change (from the prototechnology to the extensive phase) and organizational changes (from household enterprise to large-scale manufactories) resulting in higher output. In those days, technological change was essentially labor using. The technological change that took place with the Industrial Revolution evolved from Britain's own prototechnology through the extensive phase to the intensive phase (for a detailed discussion, see Maitra 1980, 1986, 1988).

K. E. Boulding (1983, 7) wrote:

> In a certain sense, technology begins with the first human artefact, whatever it was. On the other hand, there is a certain break between pre-scientific artefacts, which come out of folk knowledge and often almost unconscious skill, and science based artefacts, which come out of the extraordinary expansion of human knowledge which has been the result of the development of the scientific sub-culture in the last five hundred years or so. One can argue that science-based technology was not very important before 1860: . . . the so-called "Industrial Revolution" in England in the eighteenth century was built largely on the development from medieval technology, even the steam engine owed nothing to thermodynamics, nor did the railway. From about 1860, however, we do detect an almost exponential explosion of science based technology, beginning perhaps with the chemical industry.

According to Landes (1969), before 1880, most technological innovations were craft based and were made not, by people of learning but by craftsmen. A growing labor force organized on a large scale was using prototechnology (i.e., the process of substitution for the domestic system and manufacture then the factory, which was the consequence of mechanical devices of the time). Hobsbawm wrote about the nature of technological change:

> The technological problems of the early Industrial Revolution were fairly simple. They required no class of men with specialised scientific qualifications but merely a sufficiency of men with ordinary literacy, familiar with simple mechanical devices and the working of metals, practical experience and initiative. The centuries since 1500 has certainly provided such a supply. Most of the new technical inventions and productive establishments could be started economically on a small scale and expanded piecemeal by successive addition. That is to say, they required little initial investment, and their expansion could be financed out of accumulated profits. Industrial development was only within the capacity of multiplicity of small entrepreneurs and skilled traditional artisans. (Hobsbawm 1969, 39)

That technological change in the Industrial Revolution was made possible by a high rate of growth of population in England, which in turn created a demand for labor, can be supported by the works of P. Deane (1965), E. Boserup (1981), and others. The persistence of "child labor" up until the 1860s also supports the case for the demand for labor.

Phyllis Deane observed: "It is difficult to conceive of a way of enlarging the natural resource endowments or of adding to the national capital which did not involve an increase in the labour supply to the sector affected. . . . Even where technical change in the industrial revolution was labour saving in its effects, the immense impetus that it gave to the expansion of invested capital promoted a considerable net increase in the demand for labour" (1965, 137).

Deane also wrote: "Domestic industry found work for children almost as soon as they could crawl and the early textile factories were taking batches of pauper children from the age of five upwards" (1965, 138). Thus, the burden of dependents so often created by a growing population tended to fall less heavily on the British economy of the late eighteenth and early nineteenth centuries, which, in its turn, helped the further development of the economy by providing expanding demand.

Deane observed (1965), while writing about the growing population at the time of the rise of the Industrial Revolution, that there is no doubt that as more people abandoned the kind of domestic industry that was a subsidiary activity of agriculturists and went into full-time manufacturing in the factory and workshop, the effective input of labor per member of the labor force rose. This happened not only in the manufacturing industry but also in farming. As yields per acre rose and animal husbandry became more sophisticated, the average agricultural laborer of the late eighteenth century to mid-nineteenth centuries found himself spending more hours of each day and more days of each year in active, gainful employment than had his predecessors. During the extensive phase of technological change, quantity labor organized in large-scale production that was based on an increasing division of labor was used more productively. Hence, an increased demand for quantity labor characterized the period. This is reflected in the structural change of the economy.

According to Mendels (1972), "The earlier industrialising countries (Britain, France, etc.) have begun their industrialisation through labour-using industrial techniques" (261). The whole extensive growth phase and the early parts of the intensive growth phase of the Industrial Revolution were labor absorbing, as revealed in the pattern of sectoral distribution of the labor force of the period. Hobsbawm (1969) called this intensive growth phase the second phase (1840–1995) of industrial growth, a time when there was a remarkable improvement in employment all round and a large-scale transfer of labor from worse- to better-paid jobs. This phase is characterized by the rise of capital goods, which provided a comparable stimulus to the employment of skilled labor in the vast expansion of engineering and the building of machines, ships, and so on (118).

The complex process of economic change known as the Industrial Revolution called for a massive increase in the input of labor, especially at the initial stage of technological change, and itself provided part of the occasion for that increase. The factories gave full-time, gainful employment, not only to men but also to women and children, groups that had rarely enjoyed more than seasonal or part-time work for pay in the domestic industry era (Deane 1965, 151).

It should, however, be noted here that during the first stage of the Industrial Revolution (i.e., approximately 1780 to 1830), despite the increase in demand for labor, daily wage rates showed little evidence of marked or sustained improvement that could be advanced as a support to the claim that the elastic labor supply constituted one of the main reasons for the enormous and unprecedented expansion of the British economy over the period. Hicks wrote (1969, 165): "The whole Industrial Revolution of the last 200 years has been nothing else but a vast secular boom, largely induced by the unparalleled rise in population."

After 1860s, the demand for labor in excess of its supply necessitated the emergence of intensive technological change; the use of science in production made this possible. The increased demand for labor resulted in a dynamic structural change of the economy from agriculture through industry to the tertiary sector. (The Tables 3.2 and 6.4 on structural change in the United Kingdom show how dynamic was this change caused by technological and demographic change.) This dynamic change resulted from technological change, which evolved from prototechnology through the extensive phase and to the intensive phase.

In this process, increased production and capital formation led to further demand for labor and the improvement of prototechnology, which finally resulted in the development of the intensive phase of technology, based on modern science and substituting for quantity labor scientific technology to solve the problems of scarcity of quantity labor and, therefore, the prospect of the higher wage costs of quality labor. The birthrate began to decline starting in the late nineteenth century and population growth has declined since the early twentieth century. The increasing demand for labor in excess of its supply as a result of economic development, growing competition, and expanding foreign trade in manufactures since the late nineteenth century needed the substitution for quantity labor of quality labor to make use of science in production and result in the intensive phase of production, which is imperative for the free enterprise, capitalist economies. This change in demand from quantity labor to quality labor, in turn, produced a demographic effect of sharply declining fertility rates.

These changes in technology have been reflected in structural change and demographic changes (see Tables 6.2B & 6.2C on the United Kingdom). In England and Wales, the birthrate had reached a peak of more than 35 per 1,000 from 1862–1878, a marked decline began in 1879, and from 1896 on, the average birthrate was less·than 30 per 1000 (Mathias and Davis 1989, 142). This may be compared with the situation in India, where technological change introduced from overseas began in its mature intensive phase, with a minimal demand for labor, thus skipping over the extensive phase of using quantity labor more productively. The effects of such changes are amply reflected in India's stagnant structural change and high population growth, with a high birthrate and falling death rate that are not due to endogenous economic development effects (see Table 6.2 on India).

According to Armengaud (1973, 43), the mortality rate in England started to fall after 1740, dropping from 35–36 percent in 1740 to 26–27 percent in 1791–1800. This long period of declining mortality was a new and even revolutionary fact in the history of European demography, the more so as it occurred well after famine had been reduced or eliminated. Did this decline become even more pronounced during the first 20 years of the nineteenth century, as used to be generally believed? Probably it did not, but it does seem likely that the English mortality rate continued its slow decline until 1850 (except, perhaps during 1820–1840), despite several epidemics. That the decline was slow was because it was due to better food, shelter, and sanitation. A relatively rapid fall since the late nineteenth century onward was caused by improved medical technology and medical service on the top of better food and so forth.

In the case of the United Kingdom, when the birthrate declined to 32.8 in 1900, the capitalist transformation indicator showed that only 11 percent of the workforce was engaged in agriculture, while in the case of India at the comparable period, the rate of decline in birth rate was 32, as evident in 1987 (see Table 6.2). Moreover, the capitalist transformation indicator shows that over 70 percent of the labor force was dependent on agriculture, revealing a stagnant economic structure. From the point of view of any development implications of demographic analysis, the Indian economy has shown over this period a little demand

TABLE 6.2 Population Change in India and the United Kingdom: Crude Birthrate and Crude Death Rate (per 1,000)

A.

India	CBR	CDR	PGR
1965	45	21	24
1979	34	14	20
1985	33	12	21
1987	32	11	21

Source: World Bank World Development Report (1987, 1989).

B.

United Kingdom	CBR	CDR	PGR
1776–1800	35.5	26.4	9.1
1826–1850	36.0	22.5	13.5
1851–1875	35.8	22.2	13.6
1876–1900	32.8	19.2	13.0
1901–1925	24.2	14.2	10.0
1926–1950	16.6	12.2	3.9
1951–1975	16.7	11.7	5.0

Source: Robert Woods. (1989) *Population Growth and Economic Change in the Eighteenth and Nineteenth Centuries*, cited in P. Mathias and J. A. Davis.

C.

United Kingdom	Birth Rate	Death Rate
1965	18	12
1987	13	12

Source: World Bank Development Report (1989).

for labor because of the nature of technological change. Therefore, the environment conducive to an automatic decline in the birthrate via family planning has never evolved except in limited urban centers, and there only in a negligible way. This has been happening mainly among upper-income groups (comprising about 10 percent of total population) for more or less the same reasons as in the United Kingdom. Industrialization using imported technology (when this technology has reached its intensive phase requiring quality and not quantity labor) results in a dualistic economic structure with limited urban centers and an enormous sector of traditional activities both in urban and rural areas, which absorb over 85 percent of the population including people depending on noncapitalist, labor-intensive, family enterprise activities. On the other hand, industrial activities in the modern sector have been growing at a very fast rate, absorbing a little of the labor force. A comparison of tables on India with those of the United Kingdom proves this contention (see Table 6.2).

Though not remarkable, the declining birthrate in the urban centers, with the absence of an increasing demand for labor or capitalist transformation of the economy, in recent times has been caused by a combination of factors. First, in the urban centers, a limited number of economic activities based on highly sophisticated technology borrowed from overseas creates effects limiting the birthrate (such as the need for higher education and skill, employment opportunities for women, consumerism, etc.) in a small proportion of the high-income urban population. Second, we should note that a vast proportion of the urban population in the cities of India lives in poor areas on a low income and in slums, on labor-intensive activities as disguised unemployed. For these latter groups of people, which are expanding in number through migration from the rural areas as well as high natural growth, the government has had to introduce a forced family-planning policy through both incentives (e.g., offering a bonus, salary raises, promotions, lump sum monetary payments, loans on with favorable terms, etc.) and punishments (e.g., failure to adopt a family-planning target would cost a person his promotion, loss of raises, and loss of other financial benefits).

On the other hand, in the United Kingdom, the pattern of changes in the demand, first, for quantity labor and, then, quality labor created spontaneously and simultaneously a social and economic environment that was conducive to the rise and expansion of family planning. This is the demographic effect of the capitalist transformation of an economy, which includes technological and economic structural changes. In India, this environment was not created because of faulty technological change that resulted in stagnating structural change.

If we study the sectoral distribution of the labor force as an indicator of economic structural change and the capitalist transformation of the economy over the period of 1901–1951 (Tables 6.1 & 6.6) as against the growth in manufacturing (Table 5.11) and compare them with developments in Britain (Tables 6.4 and 6.5), it appears that the kind of economic growth and technological change that has been taking place in India cannot have the desired demographic effects that the development of an economy brings about. In this sense, we should point out that it is imperative for the demographic transition model to include the factors of technological change and the capitalist transformation of an economy to make it meaningful. Most analyses of the model have ignored this aspect.

The Demographic Effects—A Summary

The basic point about demographic effects is that with the onset of the capitalist transformation of an economy, population growth tends to decline as a result of an increasing demand for labor in productive activities. The main point concerns the spontaneous decline of population growth resulting from relatively high economic growth and a sustained demand for labor in excess of its supply. This became evident in the United Kingdom after the late nineteenth century. Children, who were hitherto regarded as assets, began to be perceived as a burden which had profound demographic effects, notably, a declining birthrate. This change in attitude was reinforced by the need for sending children to schools to acquire skills which were in great demand, as skilled jobs in the meantime became competitive. When technology was simple and at the extensive phase, the supply of quantity labor was adequate and job markets obviously were not competitive. With the technological change from the extensive to the intensive phase, however, the need for skills in a job market becoming increasingly competitive made parents conscious of family size. This was the period when the financial responsibility for the education of children was borne by parents. When technological change demanded quality labor, the supply of quantity labor automatically declined in the process. Family planning, the technique of which was already in the market, began to receive a spontaneous response. With the increased demand for labor, time became the most important factor of production. Technological change helps by reducing the need for time per unit of labor and output. Moreover, by definition, technological change at this stage requires quality labor and not quantity labor, which, in turn, creates the condition for a spontaneous response to family planning. (Technological change at the initial stage needed more labor to bring about improvements in the existing prototechnology, which was organized in large-scale units at the manufactory stage.)

Second, a sustained demand for labor indicates a relatively high rate of growth and an increasing possibility of jobs for women, both with and without skills. Thus, the opportunity cost of rearing a larger family became prohibitive. Higher education or vocational training led to delays in marriage and reluctance to have larger families.

Third, when the economy reaches the mass consumption stage (as defined by Rostow 1960), the choice between consumer durables and the number of children one will have results in a falling birthrate in capitalist system, where consumption demand at the mass consumption stage is greatly influenced by consumerism and income distribution effects. Under these circumstances, people become conscious of the need for family planning, which gradually becomes a built-in condition of such a society. High economic growth caused by the rapid expansion of foreign trade, the need for constant technological change to be competitive in the local and international markets, and, later, growing consumerism result in a falling birthrate and an increasing supply of human capital of a higher level. People become receptive to family planning, whose techniques also undergo improvement all the time with technological change. In other words, a shortage of factor labor requires skilled and more productive labor to substitute quantity labor with quality labor, and technological change with economic growth is mainly stimulated by the rapid expansion of foreign trade that technological change makes possible. In Marxian terms, stored capital embodied in human capital becomes the main factor of production in the developed, or postindustrial, economies. According to World Development Reports (1985) these economies are characterized by a very low population growth because of a falling birthrate (to almost 12 per 1,000 per annum, on average, and with an average death rate of about 14 per 1,000). However, the rapid technological change and the increasing sophistication of skills are proving more than enough to meet the requirements of labor as a factor of production in these economies, where the growing unemployment of human capital has become a disturbing trend in recent times. Technological change from the extensive through the intensive and then to the mature intensive phase of the postindustrial stage of capitalism in the developed economies is reflected in their economic structural changes (see Table 6.2).

The Population Question

According to a recent UN report on world population, India (Population BOMB 1991) will face a serious population and a consequent resource crisis by the end of this decade. It seems that India is keen on borrowing technology, education, capital, and so-called modern products from the West because it is easier to borrow them than to think about and learn from the history of these labor-short economies. When an economy creates a sustained productive demand for labor in excess of its supply, population growth (i.e., the birthrate), spontaneously tends to decline entirely, for economic reasons. Family planning then becomes a built-in condition of such development. To create an effective demand for labor is a function of technological change. Imported technology today undoubtedly brings about tremendous growth in output and in its diversification, but it creates little demand for labor.

Population growth in this kind of technological change is stimulated, or at least remains high, because of the effects of imported medical technology, on the one hand, and on the other, the lack of demand effects of such imported labor-dispensing technology. Surplus labor, therefore, has to depend on labor-intensive technology, which either stimulates the birthrate or makes people indifferent about family size. The dictum is that the larger the family, the higher the total income of the family in such labor-surplus economies. It is not generally taught that population growth and the nature of technological change are functionally related. When population growth results from increased economic demand for labor, it stimulates the fertility rate and thereby induces further economic growth, which in turn creates a further demand for labor. When an economy has reached this condition (e.g., England in the nineteenth century, which exemplified this condition), the demand for labor was so high that child labor prevailed for a long time, and even attending school was discouraged.

This is the first stage. Science is used in production to make more productive use of the existing labor force; in other words, the process of substituting quality labor for quantity labor (i.e., human resources with human capital) emerges in an economy. This results in an automatic decline in the birthrate, for entirely economic reasons (England provides an example in which the birthrate began to decline starting in the late nineteenth century). This development indicates the first criterion of the beginning of the process of capitalist transformation of a society.

The sustained and effective demand for labor is reflected in the economic structural change indicated by the dynamic sectoral distribution of the labor force away from agriculture to the secondary and, later, tertiary sectors. All capitalist countries have had to pass through these changes and are still undergoing this process. This indicates the second basic criterion of the capitalist transformation of a society. India, on the other hand, borrows technology from these countries and has a stagnant economic structure heavily biased toward agriculture (absorbing nearly 70 percent of the labor force for the last century), indicating that the capitalist transformation is confined to labor (i.e., 12 to 15 percent of the economy) as indicated by distribution of labor force engaged in industrial and service sectors (World Development Report 1987). This type of capitalist transformation lacks the essential quality of capitalist dynamism, meaning that when capitalism emerges in a society, it gradually and rapidly transforms the entire precapitalist economy into a dynamic capitalist one. In the case of introduced capitalism, the transformation process remains confined to a limited area.

Thus, by following a policy of importing technology and pushing family planning, even if an economy becomes successful in reducing population growth and

TABLE 6.3 Population of Undivided India (in Millions)

Year	Population	% growth from previous year	Year	Population	% growth from previous year
1872	255		1921	306	+ 0.99
1881	257	+ 0.78	1931	338	+ 10.46
1891	282	+ 9.73	1941	389	+ 15.09
1901	285	+ 1.T06	1951	437	+ 12.34
1911	303	+ 6.32	1961	534	+ 22.20

Source: D. P. Bhattacharyya (1969). Socio Economic Trends in India in (Ed.) M. Chaudhury Trends of Socio-Economic Change in India 1871–1961 (Simla: Indian Institute of Advanced Studies), 29.
Note: "The main reason for the growth of population by an acceleration since 1931 was the check to the so-called positive checks, eradication of malaria, weakening impact of epidemics, resulting in a stationary birth rate and a declining death rate. But qualitatively the growth has regressiveness in its blood. An economic growth implies a constant transfer of surplus population from village to urban centres of non-agricultural actives [*sic*], a constant shift from primary to secondary and tertiary sectors. But this process never started. On the contrary, after three plans, the main problem of unemployment is one of a swelling backlog gaining momentum like a snow ball in course of its movement over time towards an avalanche" (Bhattacharyya, 1969, 29).

TABLE 6.4 Broad Occupational Distribution of the Labor Force: United Kingdom

	Primary		Secondary		Service Sector				Other	
Year	Agriculture, Fishing, and Forestry	Mining	Construction	Manufacture, Elec., and Gas	Transport and Communications	Commerce and Finance	Profession and Entertainment	Government Services	Private Domestic Services	Short Services
1841	23.1	3.1	5.8	36.6	3.0	5.7	2.9	1.1	19.1	—
1881	12.3	4.1	6.7	39.9	5.9	9.2	3.8	1.9	16.6	—
1901	8.7	5.9	8.0	32.5	9.8	11.0	4.4	2.5	14.3	2.0
1911	7.8	6.9	5.2	34.6	8.0	—	18.7	4.2	9.0	5.6
1921	6.7	7.3	4.1	38.7	8.1	13.2	3.7	6.4	7.0	4.5
1951	4.5	3.9	6.3	39.5	7.8	14.2	7.0	8.0	2.3	6.8

Source: C. Clark (1957), 515.

Note: This table indicates the pattern of a broad occupational distribution of the labor force in a developed economy.

raising per capita output it will not be able to get rid of its population problem, underdeveloped economic structure, and poverty. The rapidly increasing sophistication of the industrial sector provides sufficient testimony to this.

The purported danger of worldwide resource depletion in the near future was disputed by many economists on the grounds that the history of natural resource use shows that the increasing scarcity of particular resources fosters the discovery and the development of alternative resources (which are not only equal in quality but often superior to those replaced). This is simply because every subsequent stage of the need for newer resources requires increasingly higher levels of human capital, technology, organization, and infrastructure. The physical quantity of resources is not known at any point in time because resources are only sought and found when they are needed and when societies are ready for them.

Energy consumption up to the nineteenth century was characterized by man's use of renewable energy resources, primarily through the food he consumed, and later through the utilization of beasts of burden, wind, and running water. Increasingly, population growth and its pressure on existing resources led to a more productive use of these fuels at the initial stage of the Industrial Revolution and, subsequently, to relatively more productive fossil fuels—first coal and then petroleum. In turning to the future, it seems unlikely that the nonrenewable fossil fuels will predominate in man's energy use far into the twenty-first century. Hopefully, human capital, technology, and infrastructure will also evolve so as to be ready to use effectively renewable sources based on backstop technology. (Backstop technology refers to technology developed for resources that are unlimited in supply [in super abundance]. Solar Wind and tidal power are examples. Since the resource is unlimited in supply, it is 'free', meaning that it cannot command rent.) Energy use patterns have always been conditioned by the level of economic development (i.e., by the level of the economic infrastructure and factor endowments). India has a vast but idle human resource pool due to the underdeveloped economic structure (i.e., an unutilized natural resource). The resource scarcity that it faces today is an artificial one caused by a dependence on imported technology with very little local human resource content.

CONCLUSION

Patterns of population growth depend on the growth of demand for labor in productive activities, which in turn depends on the nature of the source of technological change, whether indigenous or introduced, and on the phase of the change (i.e., extensive or intensive). The demographic transition model has ignored this aspect. Another more important implication of this study is that whether imported technology, when it has reached its mature intensive phase, can bring about the capitalist transformation of the economic, leading to full-fledged and integrated development.

In analyses by both bourgeois and Marxist economists, the capitalist transfor-

Figure 6.3 The Demographic Transition Model Reinterpreted

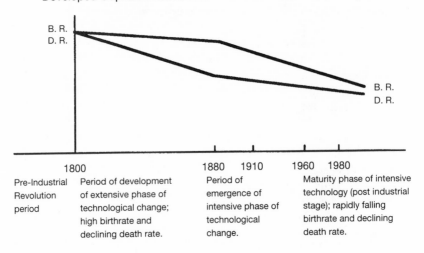

Developed Capitalist Economies: The Case of the United Kingdom

1800	1880 1910	1960 1980	
Pre-Industrial Revolution period	Period of development of extensive phase of technological change; high birthrate and declining death rate.	Period of emergence of intensive phase of technological change.	Maturity phase of intensive technology (post industrial stage); rapidly falling birthrate and declining death rate.

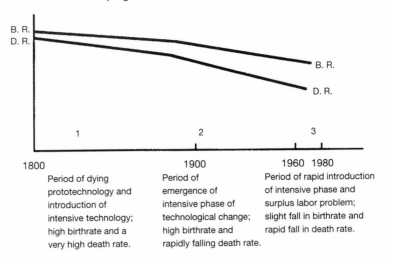

Developing Economies: The Case of India

1800	1900	1960 1980
Period of dying prototechnology and introduction of intensive technology; high birthrate and a very high death rate.	Period of emergence of intensive phase of technological change; high birthrate and rapidly falling death rate.	Period of rapid introduction of intensive phase and surplus labor problem; slight fall in birthrate and rapid fall in death rate.

B. R. = Birthrate, D. R. = Death rate

mation of an economy is an essential condition of economic development. According to the former, it is ultimate, and according to the latter, it is a precondition for ultimate development (i.e., socialism followed by communism). The collapse of the socialist system based on technology borrowed from the capitalist system has thrown a flood of light on this issue (Maitra 1992c).

Finally, I would like to refer to a valuable work of Clem Tisdell (1990, 64–72), which has an excellent summary of pessimistic and optimistic views, as well as predictions about economic growth and natural resource availability. I agree with his conclusion on this aspect: "Few, if any, grounds exist for being complacently optimistic that technological progress will extricate us without fail from the predicament that we may face due to continuing economic growth and careless and profligate use of non-renewable resources to satisfy high levels of mass consumption" (Tisdell 1990, 68).

This is the ultimate solution to the resource problem, and it depends on how we would change our present consumption and production patterns. Tisdell's conclusion is worth noting here: "In the choice of a suitable development path, we cannot be safely guided by individualist self-interest alone but must pay attention to relationships between human being and between humans and nature" (Tisdell 1990, 162 & 163). This view can be translated into Marx's concept of industrialization defined as the "humanisation of nature and naturalisation of human being" (Marx, *Capital* Vol. 3 1975, 298). This, however, raises a vital question regarding the nature of the economic system and its aim of production.

7

THE DEVELOPMENT OF EDUCATION, TECHNOLOGICAL CHANGE, AND CAPITALIST TRANSFORMATION

CAPITALIST TRANSFORMATION AND THE DEVELOPMENT OF EDUCATION

Capitalist transformation of an economy induces dynamic changes in technology which, in turn, need a constant development of education as input as well as output. That is, the development of technology raises the level of education, which pushes further technological improvement. Improvements in education of the workforce causes growth in productivity, and thereby capital accumulation, which acts as a catalyst to the capitalist transformation of an economy. This will happen in countries where education developed with the process of capital accumulation and capitalist transformation of the entire economy. Britain after the Industrial Revolution is the first case of such development. We have examined here the case where a paradoxical relationship has emerged as a result of technology transfer, which has failed to bring about capitalist transformation and the development of its economy. India has achieved, in recent time, tremendous growth in capital accumulation, but without inducing capitalist transformation as it did in Britain.

In this chapter I have made an attempt to study the relationship between education and capitalist transformation induced by technological change and economic development, using India as a case study. This relationship in the case of India reveals the following paradoxes:

1. India is considered as 1 of the 10 most industrialized nations of the world (Patel 1965, 20), yet 60 percent of its population is unable to read and write and 70 percent depends on primary activities. Political and social life is dominated by religious fanaticism and communalism, even after 40 years of independence, democracy, and modern industrial growth, which may be considered part of the paradox.
2. India is considered to possess the third largest pool of developed technological skill and education, paradoxically with only 36 to 39 percent literacy rate.
3. Many Third World countries enjoy a much higher rate of literacy (over 70 percent, which is much higher than in the West and Japan at the comparable period of their industrial growth), while in terms of industrial growth they are lagging far behind India. India, with its poor literacy rate, has much higher industrial growth today than the United Kingdom had and a much higher rate of literacy at the comparable period of industrial growth. Moreover, the United Kingdom then had much larger proportion of the labor force in industry, with a much lower proportion of capital formation (5 to 6 percent) of national income than in India today (15 to 20 percent) (Bairoch 1977, 174).

A study of such relationships is to be based on a historical analysis of two phases of industrial and technological change vis-à-vis economic growth and structural change. These two phases are known in the economic history of the Industrial Revolution as the extensive and intensive phases. The Industrial Revolution is unquestionably the source of development of modern technology, education, and industry in all latecomer countries, including the Third World.

This chapter will examine how far development in education, technological change, capitalist transformation, and industrial growth in India reflect the fulfillment of these two phases, and it intends to provide explanations of these paradoxes and suggest policy implications. The paradoxes need to be explained by analyzing the following aspects of the relationship between technological change and educational development. Although technological change and development of education are interrelated via capitalist transformation, in the case of India, such a relationship has evolved without a transformation of the economy such as in Britain.

First, there are two sources of technological change, indigenous as is the case of the Industrial Revolution in the United Kingdom or as a result of technology transfer. If change is introduced (as a result of technology transfer) from overseas, its effects differ depending on whether the technology of the lending country is (a) at its late extensive and early intensive phase (e.g., the case of technology transfer to France from the United Kingdom, (b) at its midintensive phase (e.g., the case of technology transfer from the West to Japan in the late nineteenth and early twentieth centuries, the period usually known as the one in which Japan's industrial growth began), or (c) at the mature phase of the intensive growth of the lending country or countries to latecomers of the twentieth century (e.g., the case of India and other Third World countries). Each of these phases has serious implications for the development of education. This also explains why in all latecomer countries, education preceded economic development (i.e., education, which is also borrowed, acts as a cause of growth, while in the case of the Industrial Revolution, education and its growth were an effect of the indigenous process of development).

Second, this relationship could also be studied using structural change in terms of the sectoral distribution of the labor force and national income that took place at the two phases of the lending country and of the borrowing one (e.g., India). The analysis of the economic structural changes in this sense will show the differences in effectiveness of the development of education vis-à-vis economic and technological development in these two sets of countries (i.e., lender and borrower).

The spread of literacy and gradual increase in the level of schooling are functionally related to the structural change and economic growth of a developing economy. If we look at early nineteenth-century Britain, we see a literacy rate of around 30 percent (Bowman and Anderson 1963, 252). This was the period of extensive growth. With the advancement of the economy resulting from a tremendous growth of manufacturing using manual labor in large-scale organizations, this phase reached its saturation point, with the demand for labor exceeding its supply. In this period, entrepreneurs did not want children locked up in school, thereby drying up the supply of labor.

E. G. West wrote: "The ruling class argued that with the new methods of specialisation, industry could not spare a single hour for the needs of the man who served it. In such a situation education had no place" (West 1975, 23). At that level of technology (i.e., prototechnology), increased manual labor was the only factor in production that would be used more effectively in large scale organizations. By using labor as capital, the productivity of labor increased as a result of organizational change (large-scale organization based on an extended division of labor) and the rate of capital formation also increased, creating a demand for labor. From around the 1860s, science began to be used in production (Boulding 1983, 3) which resulted in the rise of the intensive phase, accompanied by mass literacy through schools and higher education.

While the priority in schooling in the later period was to install discipline rather than provide skills that could have been of use in industry, it is possible that this priority was most beneficial in promoting industrialization in the nineteenth century. At the extensive phase of the large-scale organization of production based on the division of labor, surely to learn discipline and to work together was the key factor.

The development of education in the case of the country of the Industrial Revolution (i.e., where technological change evolved from its traditional phase using human resources as the only input) is expected to lag behind economic growth at its initial stage. At the initial stages of the growth of agriculture and manufacturing to their extensive phase acted as the principal one. This is reflected in the structural change whereby the labor force dependence moved from agriculture to industry. With economic growth and increasing capital accumulation, primary school education began to grow during the early part of the extensive phase of technological change. This is also reflected in the sectoral distribution of the labor force, with a larger proportion engaged in manufacturing, an expanding tertiary sector, and a primary sector shrinking in terms of its share of the total labor force. With the intensive growth phase, emerging from about the 1860s, this trend continued until the 1950s through 1960s, when the labor force that was dependent on agriculture dropped to less than 5 percent and the tertiary sector absorbed the largest share, of over 65 percent. This is the period known as the postindustrial stage of the economy, when human capital becomes the most important factor of production. According to Kuznets, the most important capital of an industrially advanced nation is not physical capital, but its human capital—its scientific and technical knowledge resulting from improved education and training. It might even be possible for technological progress to increase output rapidly without any addition to the stock of capital goods. The growth of applied scientific knowledge must account in a large part for unusually rapid rates of economic growth in recent centuries (Kuznets 1953, 17).

N. Rosenberg, in a study, made the same point: "It became increasingly obvious that economic growth could not be adequately understood in terms of the use of more and more physical input but rather its need to be understood in terms of learning to use inputs more productively" (N. Rosenberg 1976, 26). Obviously, this process of structural change has been accompanied by the evolution of education to meet the changing requirement of the factor labor, from manual labor through literacy and school education to higher education. In the case of India, such a relationship has not emerged; neither can it do so. Here, modern industrialization has been a result of technology transfer from industrialized nations that are in their intensive phase. Therefore, the relationship between the structural change and educational development has not gone hand-in-hand with economic development. The imported industrialization of yesteryear took a much longer time to produce structural change in their economies (e.g., Soviet Russia and Japan) than in nineteenth-century cases (e.g., France or Germany). In the former USSR, which was the third most industrialized nation in the world, the primary sector bore the burden of 18 percent of the labor force in the mid-1980s, compared to 2 percent in the United States and the United Kingdom and 7 to 8 percent in Japan (in the 1950s, over 45 percent of the Japanese labor force was in agriculture). I should discuss here briefly the terms *extensive growth* and *intensive growth* and their relationships with the growth of education and economic development. Later, I will discuss structural change in an economy and explain how the growth of education is related to this process of change in the sectoral distribution of the labor force (i.e., economic structural change) and the two phases of technological change. Before, taking up these two aspects, I would like to note the nature of educational change associated with industrial development in the nineteenth century.

The issue of a relationship between education and development has been a matter of controversy since the beginning of the Industrial Revolution. Mao Ze-dong, while building new China out of ashes of its past feudalism, held the following view on the role of education in economic development: "It is often not a matter of first learning and then doing, but of doing and then learning, for doing is itself learning" (Mao 1988, 30). Interestingly, if one takes a look at the initial period of the first and only case of the industrial revolution in the world, one gets the full support to Mao Ze-dong's views. The cases of India and all Third World countries show that education has become a matter of first learning and then doing, as they have their blueprints of development, technology, and education already before them, made available from the developed economies.

According to scholars, early agriculture or artisan workers owed little to literate men. Neither the invention of the horse collar nor improved sail rigging profited from the reading of books (Van Bath 1963, 25). Bowman and Anderson wrote that "there is a belief among economic historians that . . . the initial Industrial Revolution was carried out by an English population in which few, besides clergy and merchants, were literate" (Bowman and Anderson 1973, 247–49). Religious studies for law and order among new conglomerations in urban areas and knowledge in reading, writing, and arithmetic (the 3R's) among merchant classes were indispensable conditions for the new economic activities. Owners of merchant capital, the initiators of the modern capitalist market economy, needed their workers to have a knowledge of the 3R's for their investment. According to economic historians, a broad distribution of literacy and schooling underlay the emergence of the modern European economy of nineteenth-century latecomers to industrialization.

Even the classical economists supported education, not for its economic advantage but for its part in reducing crimes. Bowman and Anderson raised an important point when they observed: "There are educational effects of economic growth which acquire form in the varied patterns of human learning. Unfortunately, education has less often been seen or analysed as effect than as cause" (Bowman and Anderson 1973, 247). However, they did not attempt to explain the reasons. If we look at the educational development of the present-day Third World, including India, we will find the reasons for regarding education as a cause or a vital condition of economic development. The approaches to economic development of these countries are based on the policy of capital and technology transfer from the developed world, and therefore, the spread of literacy and raising the level of education are regarded as the essential conditions for the effective use of those inputs. However, the effects of such development result in some paradoxes. On the other hand, to regard education growth as effects is justified when we consider the case of the Industrial Revolution—the case of the industrial technology that has evolved indigenously from its traditional prototechnology phase. That is why many educationists and economic historians posed an interesting point, as mentioned by E. G. West:

> Most discussions on the economic history of British education usually reach a consensus that the spread of industrialisation in early 19th century Britain was accompanied by educational stagnation if not deterioration. In other words, the Industrial Revolution exposed not the effectiveness of education but the serious lack of it. Paradoxically, the same writers who adduce little connection between industrial growth and education in the early nineteenth century Britain stress its importance in the later years of the century in France, Germany, America and later Japan which overtook Britain. On this reasoning, therefore, Britain enjoyed a rapid growth despite the lack of education and slow growth because of lack of it later. (West 1975, 3)

The countries mentioned by West are all latecomers in the nineteenth-century industrialization initiated by the pioneer Britain. Latecomers imported industrialization from Britain and, therefore, had to plan their development using British experiences in education and technological change, which were available ready-made, having been developed in the United Kingdom through the process of experimentation and trial and error; hence, the difference.

The education that evolved with indigenous technological change and resulted in structural change in the British economy can also be seen from a comparative study of the sectoral distribution of the labor force that took place in these economies. C. A. Knowels mentioned in his study, "the early machine makers were men in quite a small way, and had been as a rule apprenticed to blacksmiths, carpenters, or millwrights" (1930, 74). Hobsbawm (1969)'s study about the necessary conditions for the rise of the Industrial Revolution has already been mentioned. He has rightly stressed the conditions suitable for extensive growth (i.e., the Industrial Revolution begins) by using existing resources (labour, skill, and capital) more productively, and thus paves the way for intensive growth. The technological problems of the early Industrial Revolution were fairly simple. They required merely a sufficiency of workers (which population growth by then had begun to supply) with ordinary familiarity with simple mechanical devices (prototechnology at later stages helped in this matter) and the working of metals, practical experience, and initiative (see Chapter 1; see also Hobsbawm 1969, 39).

The tendency of factors to use steam is especially noticeable after 1815. The employment of steam as power meant that the machinery became larger and more powerful and the machines were no longer suitable to be operated by young children (Knowels 1930, 93). Mechanical production provided more, and not less, employment, steadier work, and better pay. There developments had implications for the development of education and in terms of population growth (see Chapter 6), as well as for economic structural change. Up to the 1850s (usually known as the end of the period of extensive growth in England), the literacy rate was 60 percent and the proportion of pupils to school-age population was 1 to 7 in England, while the sectoral distribution of labor force statistics showed that 26 percent of the labor force were in agriculture with another 40 percent in the industrial sector (including transport and communication) and the remaining in the service sector (Table 6.2). Thus, the development of education followed the evolution of the extensive into intensive phase of industrial and technological growth in the United Kingdom.

We showed earlier, and will discuss in the final section, how the development of education followed the evolution of the extensive into the intensive phase of industrial and technological growth in the United Kingdom. The paradox is that in England in the mid-1850s, with higher literacy rates of over 70 percent, capital formation as a proportion to GDP in the nineteenth century was only 5 percent, while in India today, it is close to 20 percent, yet with even less than half the literacy rate (36–39 percent) of England in 1860–1870 (Patel 1988). The literacy rates and sectoral distribution of the labor force of both countries at a comparable period: Tables 6.1 & 6.4 also confirm this paradoxical trend. Growth in higher education in India, compared to the United Kingdom or France at the comparative period, again proves this.

Third World countries including India are trying to develop higher education at a very rapid rate so that they can use technology borrowed from the West, which has attained an all-time high level of sophistication with very low manual labor content. This has produced two effects:

1. More money is spent on the establishment of university and other higher learning institutions at the cost of primary education. Most rapid strides have been made in higher education. The number of universities has increased remarkably in recent times (Patel 1988, 19).
2. The use of sophisticated technology absorbs very little local labor, manual or processed, and therefore, vast numbers of workers are left behind in primary activities or labor-intensive, small-scale industries, living at subsistence level.

According to economists, a literacy rate of around 40 percent is a necessary base for sustained economic growth. This view is not supported by cases like India, although in terms of industrial production and capital formation, India is in a much better position than the United Kingdom, France, or Japan at their comparable stage of development, or many other Third World countries today with much higher literacy rates. We may distinguish three patterns of the relationships between educational growth and economic growth since the Industrial Revolution.

1. First, education follow economic development, as in the case of the Industrial Revolution, which in the due course of its progress improved education. Simultaneous growth in education, the economy, and technology characterized the process in the United Kingdom. This is the case where technological development has taken place indigenously from its traditional base (i.e., prototechnology). Here, economic development was accompanied by dynamic structural changes. (See Tables 6.4; see also Maitra 1986, ch. 2.)

2. Second is the case of the latecomers to industrialization of the nineteenth century (e.g., France and Germany), where development was based on borrowed technology from the United Kingdom. They demonstrate the role of education as the cause of economic growth for obvious reasons. In these cases, economic growth was accompanied by economic structural change, but at a much slower rate than in the United Kingdom. In the latter economies, education was planned and used more efficiently to suit the technology imported. However, the basic difference with latecomers to industrialization of the mid-twentieth century like India is that the technology that latecomers of the nineteenth century borrowed from the United Kingdom was at the end of its extensive phase and the early part of the intensive phase (i.e., the technological level was still labor absorbing), on one hand, and on the other, the level of traditional technology of the borrowing countries was more or less at the same level of that of the pioneer country, which had evolved into the intensive phase via the extensive phase. This implies the gradual absorption of labor from agriculture into industry and the service sector.

There is also another important factor to be noted: the rate of growth of population in nineteenth-century France and Germany was around 0.6 percent compared to India's 2.8 to 3 percent in the 1950s and 1960s, the comparable period of economic development. These latecomer countries, needless to say, had to face dualistic structure initially (i.e., an economic structure consisted of two sectors—modern and traditional), but were able to achieve an integrated development within a decade or so. However, Japan also had to face a much longer period of dualism because the technology, when transferred to Japan from the West, was passing through its early intensive phase (Maitra 1986, 16–27). One way of recognizing this phase is that the labor-intensive energy source of coal was still the dominating one in the energy and technology fields. In the more mature intensive phase, oil became the major energy source and then nuclear energy. Later, backstop fuel can be expected to dominate the scene.

3. In the case of India, or the Third World, for that matter, we find an "education miracle" or "education explosion" in the midst of economic stagnation (just the opposite of what happened in the countries of the Industrial Revolution). I prefer to use the term *education explosion* as it is comparable to the other much

used term in development economics (i.e., *population explosion* in the Third World, as distinct from the *population take-off* as the main factor in the emergence of the Industrial Revolution in the nineteenth century). Population in the explosion means population growth unaccompanied by productivity growth, whereas *population take-off* indicates population growth resulting from economic growth, as happened in nineteenth-century Europe. In the same sense, if we look at the miraculous education growth and the stagnating structural change (i.e., lack of economic development), we would choose the term *education explosion* in India as opposed to *education take-off.* Tables (7.2 and 7.3) showing growth of higher education in India with stagnating economic structure, as opposed to the case of Europe in the nineteenth century, will prove these points. Education in economic development and technological change today takes the form of development of skills in a four-step training system (i.e., literacy, primary education, secondary education, and higher education).

Many development economists consider that India and many other developing countries have achieved an education miracle, and thereby, one of the important requirements of their "own" technological development (Patel 1965, 20–24). However, they did not feel the need to enquire whether these economies could really develop their own technology with over 70 percent of their labor force engaged in the primary sector and disguised unemployed in the urban sector as well. They do not question whether these economies can afford to keep over 70 percent of the labor force in agriculture while they develop their own high-level technology. The entire process of technological change that has been introduced in these economies is a product of importation, and hence they are forced to keep a large proportion of the labor force in underdeveloped agriculture, petty service activities, and artisans and cottage industries. In India, out of the 9 percent of the labor force engaged in manufacturing activities, 3 percent work in small-scale industries and the remaining 6 percent to large-scale industries. In the 1950s and 1960s, Indian occupied the 10th position among the most industrialized nations of the world with a literacy rate of 10 to 15 percent of the total population when many less industrialized countries had much higher literacy rates (Patel 1988). However, after 25 to 30 years, India's literacy rate has gone up to 36 percent with an industrial growth rate of 6 to 8 percent per annum, while India's position on the ladder of the most industrialized nations has gone down to the 19th position. On the other hand, there are many countries in the Third World that have achieved a tremendous growth in literacy rates (in some cases, such as Ceylon and the Philippines, over 80 percent), but do not rival India in diversification and rate of industrial growth. In terms of structural change, these latter countries show less dependence on agriculture but more disguised unemployed workers in tertiary activities living in slums in urban centers of these countries. In Latin America, for example, nearly 40 percent of the urban population lives in slums. Another feature of importance to note is that India's dependence on imported capital and intermediate goods has declined to 11 percent of total imports and has been increasingly engaged in exporting India's technology, known as the so-called Third World technology, to several Third World countries. That is, a country with a 36 to 38 percent literate population and 70 percent of total population depending on agriculture has become an exporter of sophisticated technology in these days of high-level technology! To understand the implications of such paradoxical development, we have to examine the extensive and intensive growth phases of industrialization.

There are two stages of industrial growth, which may also be looked at from the point of view of the difference in the composition of capital in the two periods. As Hicks pointed out, the essential difference between modern factory industry and handicraft industry resides in the forms of capital. In prefactory industry, the principal form of capital was working or circulating capital, mainly in payments for labor and raw materials. In this sense, the distinction between artisan and trade is not economically important (Hicks 1969, 41). When these workshops and putting-out systems were gradually replaced by large-scale organization based on the further extension of the division of labor (known as the manufactory system), circulating capital still formed the major part of capital. This is the economic structure in which capital circulates as presented in Smith-Ricardian theories of economic growth. This happens at the extensive phase of industrial growth. In the first period of the Industrial Revolution, capital accumulation takes place without technical progress; this is the period of manufacture proper based on the division of labor and is called *extensive growth*, meaning the expansion of the economy by using labor more productively through an increased division of manual labor in an enlarged organization and by amassing more plants and more workers to produce more of the same output in the same way. This period of manufacture proper based on the division of labor is followed by the period of modern industry based on machinery, when the demand for labor exceeded its supply. This latter period called, the *intensive growth* period, is the result of improved techniques of production and entails more output and a higher ratio of capital to labor in investment. In Marx's works, this process is also known as the increasing organic composition of capital.

Deane observed while writing about the growing population at the time of the rise of the Industrial Revolution, that there was no doubt that as more people abandoned the kind of domestic industry that was a subsidiary activity of agriculturists and went into full-time manufacturing in the factory and workshop, the effective input of labor per member of the labor force rose (Deane 1965, 136–37).

The complex process of economic change known as the Industrial Revolution was a process that called for a massive increase in the input of labor, especially at the initial stage of technological change, and itself provided part of the occasion for that increase. The factories gave full-time gainful employment, not only to men but also to women and children, groups that had rarely enjoyed more than seasonal or part-time work for pay in the domestic industry era.

One point to note here is that even by 1850, the typical employer was not a large-scale capitalist and the typical factory operative was not yet a typical employee. This development evolved with the intensive growth stage of the Industrial Revolution in the second half of the nineteenth century. However, toward the end of the nineteenth century, the labor supply began to expand less rapidly and also became less homogeneous with the growth of precision trades requiring not only a literate workforce but also one equipped with school education and training in discipline and punctuality. School education was expected to impart these attributes.

The extensive phase in Marx's terms may be defined as follows: it evolved from individual craft work (household industries using family labor and prototechnology) with little division of labor to a phase of simple cooperation involving several workers working together in one place. They were organized gradually into large scale production using an intensified division of labor. Marx called this stage "manufactories" or "manufacture" (i.e., manually operated factories). At this stage, the collective of workers was still limited physically and numerically. As the rapid space of economic growth created an increased demand for labor, the use of science in the process of production became increasingly essential to entrepreneurs. The next phase thus involved the use of mechanical power (i.e., machine-made, steam-powered machinery, which Marx characterized as "machinofacture," by contrast with manufactory).

Machinofacture marked the beginning of a transition of the capitalist mode of production from extensive phase (large-scale production based on intensified division of labor, which increased population growth in the United Kingdom made possible) to the mature phase of intensive growth based on modern science. Instead of using more labor, this new practice of using the current supply of labor more intensively by developing the workforce through education evolved. This happens in the intensive phase. It was only with the technical basis of machinofacture for the production of further machines that capitalism created for itself a "fitting technical foundation" (Teich 1973, 241).

M. Teich (1973, 245) pointed out: "Some economists point to the necessity of differentiating between the extensive and intensive stages of growth in the development of capitalism." According to Teich, "extensive growth took place in the course of the Industrial Revolution with gradual emergence of numerous branches of industry." Thus, a relatively well-developed material, organizational, and technical basis for the industrialized capitalist society was set up during the nineteenth century in order to use growing human resources more productively. Obviously, at that level of technology and education, a large quantity of manual laborers with literacy played the dominant role.

Teich explained the term *intensive phase* saying that at the turn of the nineteenth and early twentieth centuries, tendencies appeared in several countries of Europe and the United States indicating a transition from extensive to intensive phase. The effects of science in production resulted in modern technology which needed changes in organization of production and marketing (from pure competition to monopoly and monopolistic completion and oligopoly and thus from small-scale to large-scale and international-scale), were becoming relatively greater-when compared to expenditures on production which was now growing in depth (Teich 1973, 246).

Mendels concluded that "the earlier industrialising countries (Britain, France, etc.) have begun their industrialisation through labour using industrial techniques" (1972, 214). The whole extensive growth phase and the early part of the intensive growth phase of the Industrial Revolution was labor-absorbing, as revealed in the pattern of sectoral distribution of the labor force of the period. Hobsbawm called this intensive growth phase the second phase (1840–1895) of industrial growth when there was a remarkable improvement in employment all round and a large scale transfer of labor from worse to better paid jobs. This phase is characterized by the rise of capital goods, which provided a comparable stimulus to the employment of skilled labor in the vast expansion of engineering and the building of machines, ships, and so on (Hobsbawm 1969, 117–18).

The wage fund limits the production in this system to one year and this fund is left from the previous period's net output. Obviously, under this system, an increase in the supply of labor will, in the course of time, result in the operation of the law of diminishing returns, as was pointed out in the economic theories of the time. However, Karl Marx, who was perhaps the first of the contemporary economists, pointed out that changes in the organic composition of capital together with technological change would obviate this tendency. We should note here that education and its growth became an important factor in technological change from the late nineteenth century onward (Maitra 1986, 49). The passing of Education Act in England in 1902 dealing with the introduction in science and technology at the level of higher education was effects of economic and technological change.

Economic Structural Change and Education

Dynamic structural change in an economy is a result of technological development from an extensive to intensive phase. It is not difficult to see that educational growth of literacy through school levels to higher education is functionally related to this process of structural and technological change.

A brief discussion of structural change in an economy is necessary to understand the paradoxical relations that exist today between educational growth and economic structure in India and other Third World countries. Structural change in the process of economic growth involves the transfer of resources from lower to higher productivity sectors and is marked by the decline of agriculture followed in succession by the expansion of industry and services both in terms of employment and output (see Tables 6.4, 6.5). Structural change is ultimately reflected in the importance of services in the rapidly growing free enterprise economy and the high correlation between services and income. If we look at the present-day developed economies of the West, it is evident that the service sector has become the largest sector in terms of employment, and the basic source of technology and information. The key factors in the dynamics of productive sectors are not agriculture and manufacturing. The latter sectors are together using only a little over one-third of the labor force in these economies, and the source of productivity in these economies is today the service sector (Maitra 1988c, 819–20).

Fisher, Clark, and Kuznets (Fisher 1939; Clark 1940; Kuznets 1957) are pioneers in the analysis of the relationship between economic growth and structural change. Colin Clark wrote in 1940: "Studying economic progress in relation to the economic structure of different countries, we find a very firmly established generalisation that a high level of real income per head is always associated with a high proportion of the working population engaged in tertiary industries" (6–7). He further wrote: "From Sir William Petty's day to the present time, the transfer of working population from primary production to secondary and tertiary has been continuing and perhaps will continue for as many centuries more" (176). This dynamic movement has been accounted for by these authors as the most important concomitant of economic progress. Kuznets in his elaborate study in 1957, "Industrial Distribution of National Production and Labour Force," analyzed this trend in structural change since the 1870s and with his findings showed the ever-increasing importance of the service sector for output and employment. In the World Bank *Development Report* of 1980, we find that service sector employment in the developed countries on average exceeded over 60 percent of total labor force and its contribution to national output was around 59 percent.

In all developed countries of the world, the rate of growth of services since 1945 has been faster than that of total employment, indicating the emergence of postindustrial economies. Postindustrial economies are characterized by the fact that the service sector of the economy exceeds the manufacturing and agriculture sectors—a phenomenon classical economists did not believe could happen, largely reflecting their misperception of the nature and importance of technology, which has provided both capital and labor-saving devices to the manufacturing industries. As a consequence, manufacturing, like agriculture before it, has become enormously efficient and productive requiring a much smaller input of labor (see Table 3.2; see also Stonier 1980, 7).

The "knowledge" industry has become the most rapidly growing industry in postindustrial society and consequently, information sector employment has expanded rapidly, at the cost of employment in direct production which is highly technological. As a result, the latest employment statistics of Great Britain indicate that 62 to 64 percent of the working population can now be classified as information operatives (Stonier 1980, 18), while the largest proportion of workers in this category is located in the service sector of the economy. An important and growing percentage of workers in manufacturing industries are, in fact, information operatives. Indeed, without the growth of this type of worker, the decline of manufacturing would have been more pronounced.

We will come back to this aspect of the relationship between technology and structural change in a society in the following section. If we compare this account of structural changes that have taken place in industrialized countries with the Third World situation, we get a completely different picture, with 70 to 75 percent of the workforce engaged in peasant subsistence agriculture and the rest in the nonindustrial sector. This was the condition for over 100 years, since the introduction of Western industrial capital in these countries up until the 1950s. Since the 1950s, in spite of further injection of increasing doses of highly productive capital, skills, and technology in the industrial, agricultural, and service sectors, the situation has not improved. In India, structural change in terms of the employment of labor has remained stagnant, with 70 to 75 percent of the labor force in peasant agriculture, 9 to 10 percent in secondary industries, and the rest in service sectors. In some developing countries, although the proportion of labor force engaged in agriculture has declined (to around 40 percent), the proportion of urban unemployment and disguised unemployment has gone up (World Development Report 1987). However, at the same time, industrial and overall economic growth rates have increased spectacularly because of the rapid growth of modern energy and capital-intensive industries and of the labor resource. The supply of skills is an essential condition for the successful operation of the above modern activities, which are mainly based on borrowed technology, and there has been a miraculous growth of higher education in these economies.

Dynamic structural change is essentially a function of productivity growth of the factor labor which, in turn, means a productivity increase of other factors. Hence, the importance today of developing human capital in labor-short developed economies. However, productivity growth of labor has been a long, drawn-out process of technological change, which has passed through two stages since the Industrial Revolution. Population growth patterns and the rate of economic growth creating a demand for labor were the most important influences behind these two phases.

Structural change therefore, is a result of technological change that brings about a productivity increase in factors of production, particularly labor. However, technological change can bring about structural change only when it evolves indigenously through a more productive utilization of human resources via an extensive phase of development. The stagnating economic structure of India is evident, with over 70 to 75 percent of the labor force eking out a living from subsistence peasant economy, despite the rapid introduction of modern, highly sophisticated technology from industrialized countries. It is one of the proofs of the contention that a technology, to be effective in bringing about increased productivity of human resources and thereby lead to structural changes and growth of human capital, must evolve indigenously through a more productive utilization of human resources. In this process, where structural changes have taken place in different countries, for example, in developed economies, a mutual transfer of technology among these countries does not create any gap between these nations.

This draws our attention to the stages of technological change—first the extensive growth stage, and later, the intensive growth stage. I have explained why later industrializers, like France and Germany in the nineteenth century, were able to achieve an integrated development in a decade and a half, even though their industrialization was based on imported technology, capital, and skill from the United Kingdom, and why Japan took a much longer time to eliminate dualism (nearly 70 to 75 years after the introduction of modern technology, capital, education, and skill from the West). Developing countries, while trying to industrialize with large importation of highly productive capital, sophisticated technology, wholesale transfer of education, etc., are facing the gap of dualism within the economy and the gap between themselves and rich nations is ever widening.

Education and Development (a Brief Summary, Conclusions, and Policy Implications)

Primary education in England, up to eighteenth century, was limited to the clergy and the aristocracy. Up to the last quarter of the nineteenth century, the general education of the masses of the people was to remain mostly the concern of the Church in England—the main objective was not to impart any skill but to teach pupils obedience, punctuality, honesty, discipline, and the 3Rs so that they could read the Bible and follow religious instructions, instructions at workplaces, leave messages, and keeping simple accounts. Industrial growth at that extensive phase did not even need that, as when the firms began to face labor shortages they agitated against keeping children in school. Only about 3 percent of the total population of England and Wales attended primary schools in 1834. However, by 1840, 4 to 5 percent of the population was attending primary school.

We should note here that from the 1850s onwards, the intensive growth process began to emerge and science began to be used in production. This was also reflected in the sectoral distribution of labor force with the proportion of labor force dependent on agriculture declining and that of the manufacturing sector rising. Obviously, at that stage of technology, the increasing intensity of production required more labor. With the emergence and spread of the intensive phase, enrollment in primary education jumped from 1.2 million in 1870 to 4 million by 1881 and to 6 million by 1900 (some 160 per 1,000 of population). This rapid expansion was also helped by the introduction of universal compulsory education in 1870. To compare this with the Third World, we notice the ratio for the Third World, including India, was 49 students per 1,000 of population in 1950, which rose to 137 in 1981. Between 1840 and the 1880s, the population of Europe rose by 33 percent and by nearly 60 percent in the United Kingdom, but the number of children attending school rose by 145 percent. The annual growth rate in the

United Kingdom was a modest 2 percent compared to the Third World's 5.6 percent between 1950 and 1981. The population growth rate in this period in the Third World was, however, over 3 percent per annum (see Table 7.2).

Since the late nineteenth and early twentieth century, secondary education in the United Kingdom has begun to emerge to meet the needs of the intensive phase of industrial development. The Bruce Commission was appointed in England in 1894, and the act dealing with secondary education was passed in 1902. The number of students enrolled in secondary schools also more than doubled, increasing from 2.9 per 1000 population in 1904 to 5.5 in 1914, or about the same proportion as in the Third World as a whole in 1950 (Patel 1988).

Japan began its rapid industrial growth with imported technology from the West when the Western countries were passing through the intensive phase of industrial growth. Thus, we see that the enrollment in secondary schools as late as 1885 was only 20,000 students, which increased rapidly to 100,000 by 1900 and around 10 million by 1960, or 100-fold in 60 years (1964, 29).

The expansion of enrollment in the third level of education was mostly a mid-20th century phenomenon in Japan (see Table 7.1). The proportion in Japan rose to 7 per thousand in 1960, or about the same as in the Third World. The rapid rise in the case of the Third World is indicated by the fact that Japan took 60 years to reach this level, while the Third World took only 30 years but, paradoxically, with a much larger proportion of illiteracy.

The case of Japan shows that despite a high rate of literacy of over 40 percent at the initial stage of modernization since the 1880s, which ultimately reached a mature stage of human capital by the 1960s, changes in economic structure in Japan have not been as dynamic as it has been in case of the United Kingdom, France, or Germany. For a detailed study, see P. Maitra (1980, 1986). Later cases (i.e., France and Germany) are those of borrowed technology at phases of intensive growth and that of Japan in the later phase of intensive growth.

In Third World countries, the rate of growth of secondary education was even higher, at 9 percent between 1950 and 1981. Needless to say, this is the period when the intensive phase of technology reached its high point in the developed world. One indicator of this intensity is the replacement of coal, a labor-intensive source of energy, by oil, followed by nuclear energy—a highly capital- and knowledge-intensive source.

In the meantime, higher education began to expand with, 2 per 1,000 population in Western Europe in 1900 and to 4 per 1,000 in the 1950s. The comparable level in the Third World as a whole was 0.6 in 1950, which rises to over 5 per 1,000 population if China is excluded. Tables 7.2 and 7.3 show the miraculous growth in secondary and higher education in India and in other Third World countries. However, when we examine them with the stagnating economic structure in all these economies and compare them with the development of education and structural change, the paradox in the relationship between education, technological change, and economic development reveals itself.

Some economists suggest that the education gap between developed economies and the Third World is narrowing and that the current rapid rate of transition in this respect would provide the most powerful instrument for attaining the economic transition (Patel 1965). However, the more sophisticated education becomes, the less labor an economy needs. This is true of both physical technology and social technology. This means that a decreasing proportion of people will be employed, with an increasing number of unemployed. This is already happening in the First World economies. Therefore, in my belief, education and economic development policy should stop competing over whether to resort to more productive education and technology or use more productively the existing education and technology so that available resources, human and natural, are fully utilized.

Table 6.1 shows that India's economic structure in terms of labor force has remained unquestionably underdeveloped, with 70 percent of the labor force contributing only 37 percent of GDP, while trade structure shows over the same period a remarkable dynamic change, with increasing exports of manufactures and decreasing imports of intermediate and capital goods. If we compare this with the United Kingdom and some latecomers in the nineteenth century, the basic difference becomes apparent.

Tables 7.2, 7.3 & 7.4 show the rapid growth in higher education, yet over 60 percent of the population is regarded as illiterate. This paradox looks even more startling when we place this data against the rapid growth and diversification of output and stagnant labor force distribution in India and Great Britain, or even in France in the nineteenth century. There is another side to this coin. That is, India, with such a small percentage of literate population, still has to put up with increasing unemployment rates among more highly educated people (i.e., despite the rapid growth and diversification of industries, India cannot absorb her tiny proportion of human capital; see Table 7.4). Side by side with this, we notice the total pool in early the 1980s, involving over 60 percent of the whole population, showing an increase from 42 percent in 1960–1961. With this, India's stagnant structural change and the rapid growth in higher education (see Tables 7.2, 7.3, 7.4 & &.6) should also be noted. Table 7.2 shows the rapid growth in higher education, yet over 60 percent of the population are regarded as illiterate.

POLICY IMPLICATIONS

The rapid spread of higher education and growth of human capital in both the developed and developing countries relative to the growth in absorptive capacity is creating a serious problem of unemployment and underemployment of human capital in the former countries, and of both human capital and the vast human and national resources of the later countries. This problem stems from the following fact: today's developed capitalist economies, which are increasingly competitive in the international market, are engaged in producing sophisticated technology, which requires inputs of higher education of human capital and superior natural resources (e.g., moving, from coal to oil and, lately, to nuclear power). These kinds of technology and resources required an expanding market for their products beyond their own borders.

Third World countries are borrowing this technology and are concentrating on producing ever-increasing levels of human capital while neglecting their vast human resources. Imported technology creates fewer employment opportunities in the Third World than in the developed economies. As a consequence, there is a severe limitation of the possibility of creating sufficient markets for the high-tech products of the developed capitalist economies. This means a lack of sufficient employment opportunities in the developed economies and, in turn, it stimulates further sophistication of technology in the developed economies in order to achieve efficiency in the midst of growing unemployment.

Thus a kind of vicious circle of unemployment and technological growth begins to operate. A major manpower problem facing America in the next three decades will be underemployment, accompanied by the underutilization of skills, training, education, and other human resources. About 80 percent of all college graduates were underemployed in 1978, and about 35 percent of all workers reported that their potential was not being realized on the job (O'Toole 1978, 126). With recent changes in government policy towards privatization and the dismantling of social welfare arrangements, in these developed economies education is becoming expensive, affordable only by upper income groups. The possibility of rapid growth of sophisticated human capital is thus market controlled. The less-educated human capital is expected to find employment in small-scale service activities which usually thrive in this situation. (Harman 1986; the cases of the United Kingdom and the United States are examples in recent times.) In India, under the circumstances, vast human resources and a considerable proportion of low-level human capital will remain underemployed, and only a lucky few individuals will find opportunities at home and abroad.

Education and human capital should develop in such a way that the existing available resources are fully and productively employed. An approach to further

TABLE 7.1 Japan: Numbers of Students in Universities and Institutes of Higher Learning

Year	No. of students
1885	10,000
1900	20,000
1960	600,000

Source: Japan, (1964), 29, Table 4.

TABLE 7.2 Educational Advancement in the Developed Countries and the Third World, 1950 and 1981

Areas and enrollment levels	Increases (in millions)				Share in world totals (Percentages)		
	1950	1981	1950–81	Index (1950 = 100)	Annual growth	1950	1981
Developed Countries*							
Level I	112	120	8	107	0.2	57	21
Level II	31	87	56	280	3.4	76	36
Level III	5.4	30	25	555	5.7	85	62
Total	148.4	237	59	160	1.6	60	27
Third World**							
Level I	80–90	456	370	535	5.6	43	79
Level II	10	153	1,430	1430	9.0	24	64
Level III	1	18	17	1800	9.8	15	38
Total	90–100	627	530	670	6.3	40	73
World							
Level I	200	576	376	288	3.5	100	100
Level II	41	240	200	585	5.9	100	100
Level III	64	49	43	670	6.3	100	100
Total	250	865	620	346	4.1	100	100

Source: For 1950, UNCTAD; for 1981, Khadria. 1984; based on data from UNESCO, *Statistical Yearbook* (1983).
Note: Totals may not agree owing to rounding.
* Covering OECD countries, the USSR, and East European countries.

growth in technology and education that will involve use of more productive resources and technology should be adopted in order to secure full and productive employment of all available resources. I admit, this condition cannot be met in a free enterprise economic system. A kind of social guide and state control should be the prerequisite.

This problem has become acute in the case of the Third World. The use of borrowed technology—physical (i.e., capital) and social (education, skill, etc.)—from the developed labor-short economies to achieve development results in the waste of vast human resources in the form of disguised unemployment and unemployed and of natural resources (e.g., cotton, coal, natural rubber, jute, etc.).

When we examine the issues of raising the level of technology and human capital from the perspective of world development and economic interdependence, the questions that trap us are: should we concentrate on finding more productive

TABLE 7.3 Share of the Third World in Enrollment in Higher Education, 1950 and 1981

Year	Percent
1950	15
1981	38

Source: Patel (1988).

TABLE 7.4 Number of Educated Unemployed in India (in millions)

Year	School certificate matriculation	Higher secondary	Graduate and above	Total
1961	4.63	0.71	6.56	5.90
1971	12.97	6.05	3.94	22.96
1981	50.08	23.25	16.85	90.18
1982	55.60	24.40	17.69	97.67
1983	63.74	28.14	19.68	111.56
1984	71.26	30.82	21.23	123.31

Source: *Economic Times* (Calcutta), 14 August 1986.

TABLE 7.5 Changes in the Rate of Illiteracy, Selected Asian Countries

	Percentage of illiteracy among over-15s		Adult illiteracy, 1975l	10-14 age group
	1950	1960		1960
India	80.7	72.2	64	57.7
Pakistan	81.1	81.2	79	72.4
Ceylon/Sri Lanka	37.0	32.3	22	-
Indonesia	-	57.1	38	27.9
Philippines	40.0	28.1	13	27.1
Thailand	48.0	32.3	16	14.3

Source: Paul Bairoch, The Economic Development of the Third World (London, Methuen, 1977), 136.

TABLE 7.6 Percentage of the Male Working Population Occupied in the Manufacturing Industry

	About 1950	About 1960	1978	About 1970
India	8.2 (1951)	10.1 (1961)	11	10.0 (1971)
Sri Lanka	9.4 (1953)	9.2 (1964)	15	-
Pakistan	6.2 (1951)	8.4 (1961)	19	-
Indonesia	-	4.9 (1961)	11	4.7 (1965)
Philippines	5.7 (1948)	7.1 (1960)	16	7.6 (1970)
Thailand	2.9 (1954)	4.1 (1960)	8	3.7 (1970)

Source: Bairoch, 1977, 79.

natural resources and raising further the level of human capital before we have exhausted the available resources (i.e., resources, in the case of India, are relatively low-level human capital compared to the developed economies) or should we make serious efforts toward using available natural resources, human resources, and human capital and technology more productively and fully? The first alternative has advantages: more efficiency, less labor use, and less use of costly natural resources and education. Moreover, there are concomitant difficulties—or a limited market and more wastage of resources in terms of underutilization and unemployment. The second alternative—using existing resources more productively—would mean greater employment, knowledge, development among the masses, and labor productivity (see also Maitra 1988a).

8

CONCLUSION

We have traced the process of the rise and progress of industrial capitalism and the capitalist transformation it has brought about in the economies of the United Kingdom and, later, Western Europe. Capitalism was internationalized, first via trade in goods and commodity capital and, later, through the transfer of huge amounts of financial capital that had been accumulated through trade in goods in the past. Thus, the internationalization of investment used this past huge accumulation and prepared the world economy for the present phase of the globalization of production and technology. Western capitalism, through these phases, has developed into an unprecedented productive force today.

Capitalist transformation in the United Kingdom has brought about a dynamic trend in the demographic transition to support and stimulate capitalist development and the processing of human resources into human capital by stages, which has in turn stimulated and supported the globalization process.

However, the globalization of capitalism gradually has led to the penetration of capitalism from the United Kingdom and Western Europe into India and the rest of the world economy. In the latter countries, however, as the cast study of India (Chapter 5 of this book) reveals the introduced capitalism has failed to bring about the capitalist transformation of the economy and, therefore, failed to produce favorable demographic transition effects and the transformation of human resources into human capital. It has brought about growth in the capitalist sector, but without capitalist transformation effects.

Introduced capitalist growth does not need such transformation, and therefore, modern science–based production in a limited sector of the economy coexists with the feudal mind. Land reform policy, though, has changed the feudal structure but maintained and expanded the peasant economy, with increasing numbers of peasants turned into landless laborers. Introduced industrial capitalism does not need land reforms to create conditions for the supply of cheaper labor, as it did in the United Kingdom and other Western countries. However, land reform policy, which was introduced long after the introduction of industrial capitalism as a result of political demand, has made possible unlimited supplies of surplus and cheap labor. In an unbridled, free market economy, this surplus labor tries to eke out its living in self-employed, low-income activities, with its feudal social consciousness left intact and with the hope of a better tomorrow.

The free market system fosters this type of social consciousness and, thus, chokes the forces of class antagonism and class struggle, ensuring a longer life for World capitalism. In the nineteenth and the first half of the twentieth centuries, capitalism in the West developed a strong industrial society, with the vast majority of workers engaged in an organized, large-scale capitalist sector. This led to the development of a strong and organized class consciousness among workers and to class struggle, which was helped by the growth of working-class revolutionary parties and democratic trade union movements. However, in a postindustrial society, with the vast masses of cheap labor engaged in millions of small units of self-employment or petty trading and with business activities providing only income for family labor in a market system, the exploiters are seldom visible and, hence, there is little chance of class confrontation. "It will be alright, mate" (New Zealand's favorite phrase, which is suitable for a small economy) is a mentality that pervades the entire social mind. The basic difference in this respect with the Third World countries is that the social consciousness of a developed capitalist economy has been divested of its feudal social mind through the process of capitalist transformation, whereas in India, the introduced capitalism has progressed for over 150 years without having to bring about this transformation of the economy and the social mind. Growing religious fanaticism, communal troubles, and casteism, with, on the other hand, an increasing domination of religious fundamentalist parties over the political and legislative institutions of the country, are ample proofs of one of the largest capitalist countries of the world.

This raised another interesting question concerning the collapse of the Soviet Communist system after 70 years of its operation. Two controversial issues are involved:

1. Whether the Soviet system was imposed from the above too soon, before the economy and society underwent the capitalist transformation, which Lenin began but could not complete (see Maitra 1992c).
2. Whether the collapse of the Soviet Communist system which was built on borrowed technology from the capitalist West, was inevitable as the tech-

nology was not suitable to embody the ideals of communism (see Maitra 1992c).

But that is another story.

The key to the process of globalization of production under capitalism is an unrestricted market open to all countries, which needs a rapid rate of growth of productivity and diversity of production at a reduced cost of production via rapid technological change in production, managerial, and organizational factors. In a market capitalist system, this has meant a reduction in both the quantity and quality labor contents (proportion of labor used or labor inputs), which is increasingly proving a stumbling block to the operation of the system. This is a built-in problem of the capitalist system. A second built-in problem is increasingly becoming evident, that is, the requirement of an increased supply of money capital to meet the capitalism's role of globalization of production phase.

The globalization of production phase of capitalism, together with its highly productive technology, today has reached every corner of the earth and penetrated every society (small and large, developed and undeveloped, feudal and tribal) and thus made possible an unlimited supply of resources and productivity. Simultaneously, the economic restructuring policies advocated by the International Monetary Fund, World Bank, and World Trade Organization have created unlimited scope for investment of this unlimited supply. Maintaining an increased supply of resources and a congenial environment requires a supply of money capital to invest to generate higher rate of capital accumulation.

We know that capitalist production is a result of the combination of money capital with physical or real capital (produced by labor), but the release of money capital via restructuring has not been sufficient to meet the demand for investment, as most capitalist countries still suffer from budget deficits or insufficient budget surpluses, high income tax rates, high minimum wage-rate policies (not determined by market forces), the continuation of some social welfare programs, and the existence of many state owned enterprises (SOES) which tie up money capital, mainly for consumption purposes. Thus, the increased demand and scope for investment are not matched by a sufficient supply of money capital, which results in a rise in interest rates and inflation, which is already evident. A rising rate of investment creates a demand for money capital. If its supply is short, this pushes up the rate of interest and gradually fuels inflation.

However, capitalism at its present phase of globalization of production, in which it is pushing free market forces to the extreme, is ensuring for itself a much longer life than many thought before. This may be explained as follows: the entire process shows how unfathomable are capitalism's ways of surviving, exploiting, and prospering. Rapid technological change has been making the organized capitalist sector increasingly shed labor and therefore, workers' organized power is thereby being eroded. On the other hand, the present phase of the globalization of capitalism is creating petty, low-income, self-employment jobs opportunities scattered all over the world, which serve only to permit the survival of poor people and to act as a perennial reservoir of cheap labor. However, this environment of an increasing concentration of sophisticated products and lifestyles, accompanied by the incomes and wealth of the free market system, is providing ample opportunities for self-employment in millions of small units of redistributive-type (mainly unproductive) activities, creating a hope among these workers that there may be a better tomorrow. This acts as a force against the development of revolutionary organization and social consciousness among these poor people, which would encourage them to fight against capitalism. This would keep the people stuck to these low-paid and part-time jobs and running after the mirage of a better tomorrow. Marx wrote:

> The lower middle class, the small manufacturer, the shop keeper, the artisan, the peasant, all these fight against the bourgeoisie, to save from extinction their existence as fractions of the middle class. They are therefore not revolutionary, but conservative. Nay, more, they are reactionary, for they try to roll back the wheel of history. If by chance they are revolutionary, they are so only in view of their impending transfer into the proletariat, they defend not their present but their future interests, they deserve their own stand point to place themselves at that of the proletariat (1932, 70).

As a proportion of the total workforce, they constituted a tiny segment in those days, while organized factory workers formed the largest one and, thus, supplied the strength and motivation behind class conflict. In the future, we are going to see just the reverse trend, with service becoming the largest sector.

References

Adams, B. *The Law of Civilisation and Decay.*

Agahia, F., and C. Bina. (1989). The Global Origins of Iran's Land Reform. Middle Eastern Association, Dec. 28–30, Atlanta, GA.

Aitkin, C. F. (1985). *Description of the Country from Thirty to Forty Miles round Manchester.*

Albriton, Robert. (1991). *A Japanese Approach to Stages of Economic Development.* London: Macmillan.

Aluwalia, I. (1983). *Industrial Performance in India: An Analysis of Declaration in Growth 1956–57 to 1979–80.*

Amin, S. (1974). *Accumulation on a World Scale—A Critique of the Theory of the Undeveloped.* 2 vols. New York: Monthly Review Press.

Anstey, V. (1952). *Economic Development of India.* London: Longman.

Armengaud, A. (1973). "Population in Europe 1700–1914." In C. M. Cipolla (ed.), *The Industrial Revolution.* London: The Fontana Economic History of Europe.

Bacon, R. W., and W. R. Eltis. (1978). *Britain's Economic Problems.* 2d ed. London: Macmillan.

Bagchi, A. (1976). De-Industrialization in India. *Journal of Development Studies* 12, no. 2: 132–50.

Bairoch, P. (1976). *The Economic Development of the Third World.* London: Methuen.

Bank of England. (1992). *Quarterly Bulletin.* August.

Baran, P. (1957). *The Political Economy of Growth.* New York: Monthly Review Press.

Bardhan, P. (1984). *The Political Economy of Development in India.* Calcutta: Oxford University Press.

Baumol, W. J. (1967). The Macro Economics of Unbalanced Growth. *American Economic Review* 57:415–26.

Beaver, S. E. (1975). *Demographic Transition Theory Reinterpreted.* Lexington, MA: Lexington Books.

Bernier, F. (1826). Travels in the Moghul Empire, 1656–68. London, Vol. 1, p. 281.

Bettelheim, C. (1959). New Delhi: Asia Publishing House.

Bhatt, V. V. (1982). Development Problems, Strategy and Technology Choice: Sarvodaya and Socialist Approaches in India. *Economic Development and Cultural Change* 85–89.

Bhattacharyya, B. (1969). *The Evolution of Political Philosophy of Ghandi.* Calcutta: Calcutta Book House.

Bhattacharyya, D. (1976). *India's Five Year Plan, 1976.* Calcutta: Progressive Publisher.

Bhattacharyya, D. P. (1969). Socio-Economic Trends in India. In Indian Institute of Advanced Studies (ed.), *Trends of Socio-Economic Change in India 1871–61.* Simla.

Bina, C., and B. Yaghmaian. (1988). Post-War Global Accumulation and the Transnationalization of Capital. *Review of Radical Political Economy* 22, 1:78–97.

Blackaby, F. (ed.). (1978). *Deindustrialisation.* London: Heineman Education Books.

Blackhouse, E., and J. O. P. Bland. (1914). *Annals and Memories of the Court of Peking.*

Bloomstrom, M., I. Kravis, and R. Lipsey. (1988). *Multinational Exports from Developing Countries.* National Bureau of Economic Research working paper no. 2493. London: Cambridge University Press.

Boserup, E. (1965). *The Conditions of Agricultural Growth.* Chicago: Aldine Publishing.

Boserup, E. (1981). *Population and Technology.* Oxford: Oxford University Press.

Boulding, K. E. (1983). Technology in the Evolutionary Process. In S. MacDonald et al. (eds.), *The Trouble with Technology.* London: Francis Pinter.

Bowman, M. J., and C. A. Anderson. (1963). Concerning the Role of Education in Development. In Geertz, C. (ed.), *Old Societies and New States,* 247–279. New York: Free Press.

Bowman, M. J., and C. A. Anderson. (1973). Human Capital and Economic Modernisation. In 4th International Economic History Congress, *Historical Perspectives.* London: Mourton.

Brenner, R. (1976). Agrarian Class Structure and Economic Development in Pre-Industrial Europe. *Past and Present* 70:68.

Cairncross, A. K. (1953). Home and Foreign Investment 1870–1913. Cambridge: Cambridge University Press.

Caldwell, J. C. (1976). Toward a Restatement of Demographic Transition Theory. *Population and Development Review* 2, 3–4):321–26.

Cantwell, J. (1989). *Technological Innovation and Multinational Corporations.* Oxford: Blackwell.

Chambers, J. D. (1953). Enclosures and Labour Supply in the Industrial Revolution. *Economic History Review* 5:48–53.

Chambers, J. D. (1972). *Population, Economy and Society.* London: Oxford University Press.

Chandler, A. (1977). *The Visible Hand.* Cambridge, MA: Harvard University Press.

Chaudhri, Ashm. (1985). *Private Economic Power in India.* New Delhi: Peoples Publishing House.

Chossudovsky, M. (1991). Global Poverty and the New World Economic Order. *Economic and Political Weekly*, 2 November, 25–28.

Cipolla, C. M. (ed.). (1973). *The Industrial Revolution.* Vol. 2. London: HarperCollins Publishers Limited.

Clark, C. (1957). *The Condition of Economic Progress.* London: Macmillan.

Cline, W. R. (1976). *International Monetary Reforms and the Developing Countries.* Washington, DC: Brooklyn Institute of International Economies.

Coale, A. J. (1973). "The Demographic Transition Reconsidered." In *International Population Conference.* Liege, Belgium: International Union for the Scientific Study of Population.

Collins, E. J. T. (1969). Labour Supply and Demand. In E. L. Jones and S. J. Woolf (eds.), *Agrarian Change and Economic Development.* London: Methuen.

Cowgill, D. O. (1962). Transition Theory as General Population Theory. *Social Forces* 41:270–79.

Cromwell, J. H. R., and H. E. Czerwankky. (1947). In Defence of Capitalism. Cited in M. Dobb, *Studies in the Development of Capitalism.* London: Routledge and Kegan Paul, 5.

Cunningham, W. (1916). *The Progress of Capitalism in England.* London: Cambridge University Press.

Dahlaman, C. D. (1980). *The Open Field System and Beyond.* London: Cambridge University Press.

Dandekar, V. M. (1978). Nature of the Class Conflict in the Indian Society. *Artha Vignan*, 20, 2:25–30.

Das, H. G. (1959). *Norris Embassy to Aurangzeb (1699–1702).* Condensed and edited by S. C. Sarkar, Calcutta: Firma KLM.

Dasgupta, B. (1982). *Migration and Development.* Reports and Papers in the Social Sciences no. 52. Paris: UNESCO.

Datta, S. M. (1992). Economic Transition—A Business Response. *Economic and Political Weekly*, May 9, 10–18.

Davis, K. (1951). *The Population of India and Pakistan.* Princeton, NJ: University Press.

Deane, P. (1965). *The First Industrial Revolution.* London: Cambridge University Press.

Defoe, D. (1926). *Tour Through the Whole Island of Great Britain.* Vols. 2 and 3. In J. A. Hobson (ed.), *The Evolution of Modern Capitalism.* London: Walter Scott.

Desai, A. V. (1972). *Population and Standard of Living in Akbar's time.* Indian Economic and Social History Review, 43–62.

Dharmapal, U. (1971). *Indian Science and Technology in the 18th Century.* New Delhi: Impex.

Dobb, M. (ed.). (1947). *Studies in the Development of Capitalism.* London: Routledge and Kegan Paul.

Dunning, J. H. (1991). International Direct Investment Patterns in the 1990s. In G. Jones and H. J. Shroter, eds., 1993.

Dutt, R. C. (1971). *Economic History of British India under Early British Rule.* London: Routledge and Kegan Paul.

Economist. (1990). September, 115.

Economist. (1993). 26 December–5 January, 133.

Ehrlich, P. E., and A. H. Ehrlich. (1970). *Population, Resources and Environment.* San Francisco: W. H. Freeman and Company.

Engles, F. (1955). *Anti Duhring.* London: Lawrence and Wishart.

Fei, J., and G. Ranis. (1963). A Theory of Economic Development. *American Economic Review* (June):448–60.

Fei, J., and G. Ranis. (1964). *The Development of the Labour Surplus Economy.* Homewood, IL:

Fisher, A. G. B. (1939). Production, Primary, Secondary and Tertiary, *Economic Record*, March.

Froebel, F., J. Heinrichs, and O. Keys. (1980). *The New International Division of Labour.* London: Cambridge University Press.

Galbraith, J. K. (1992). *The Culture of Contentment.* London.

Gemmel, N. (1986). *Structural Change and Economic Development.* London: Macmillan.

Glynn, A. (1989). The Macro-anatomy of the Thatcher Years. In F. Green (ed.), *Restructuring of the U.K. Economy.* London: Penguin.

Glynn, A., and R. Sutcliffe. (1972). *British Capitalism, Workers and the Profit Squeeze.* London: Penguin.

Gold, C. S. (1971). *Population, Modernisation and Social Structure.* Boston: Little, Brown and Co.

Gould, J. (1973). *Economic Growth in History.* London: Methuen.

Government of India. (1950). *Census of India's Foreign Liabilities and Assets as of June 1948.* Bombay.

Government of India. (1981). Census of Population. New Delhi.

Government of India. (1985a). *Central Statistical Organisation National Accounts, New Delhi Statistics.*

Government of India. (1985b). *Economic Surveys.* New Delhi: C.S.O.

Government of India. (1985c). *7th Five Year Plan.* New Delhi.

Government of India. Department of Company Affairs (Delhi). (1969). *Company News and Notes.* January.

Government of India. Planning Commission. (1956). *Second Five Year Plan.* New Delhi.

Government of India. Planning Commission. (1960–1979). *Economic Weekly.*

Government of Japan. (1964). Ministry of Education, 29.

Goyale, S. K. (1979). *Monopoly Capital and Public Policy.* New Delhi.

Griffiths, Sir P. (1952). *The British Impact on India.* London: MacDonald.

Gruevich, P. (1977). In R. Peet (ed.), *An Introduction to Marxist Theories of Underdevelopment.* Canberra: Australian National University.

Habakkuk, J. (1937). English Landownership. *Economic History Review* 10, no. 1:17.

Habbakkuk, J. (1962). Historical Experience. In Morgan and G. E. Betz (eds.), *Economic Development.* Belmont, CA: Wadsworth, 1–5.

Habib, I. (1963). *Agrarian System of Mughal India.* Bombay: Asia Publishing House.

Hamilton, E. (1929). Industrial Evolution. *Economica*, November, 339.

Hamilton, H. (1947). English Brass and Copper Industries to 1800. In M. Dobb *Studies in the Development of Capitalism.* London: Routledge and Kegan Paul.

Harman, C. (1993). Where Is Capitalism Going? Pt. 1. *International Socialism* (Spring):10–57.

Harman, C. (1994). Where Is Capitalism Going? Pt. 2. *International Socialism* 60 (Autumn):77–136.

Harrison, B., and B. Bluestone. (1988). *The Great U-Turn: Corporate Restructuring and the Polarizing of America.* New York: Basic Books.

Hartwell, R. M. (1973). *Service Revolution* in C. M. Cipolla (ed.), *The Industrial Revolution* (Fontane, 73).

Hazari, R. K. (1968). *Foreign Collaboration.* Bombay: Asia Publishing.

Heckscher, E. F. (1949). *The Effect of Foreign Trade on the Distribution of Income.* In H. S. Ellis and A. L. Metzler (eds.), *Readings in the Theory of International Trade* (American Economic Association).

Helleiner, G. K. (1980). *International Economic Disorder.* London: Macmillan.

Henderson, W. O. (1954). *Britain and Industrialisation in Europe, 1750–1870.* Liverpool: Liverpool University Press.

Hicks, J. R. (1969). *A Theory of Economic History.* Oxford: Oxford University Press.

Hilbroner, R. (1991). *New York Review of Books.* 24 October.

Hilton, R. (1979). Towns in English Feudal Society. *Review*, 3, no. 1:18–19.

Hobsbawm, E. (ed.). (1964). *Pre-Capitalist Economic Formation.* New York: International Publishers.

Hobsbawm, E. (1969). *Industry and Empire.* London: Pelican, Hammonsworth.

Hobson, J. (1926). *The Evolution of Modern Capitalism.* London: Walter Scott Publishing. ast ed., 1894.

Hohenberg, P. (1972). Changes in Rural France in the Period of Industrialisation. *Journal of Economic History*, 32, no. 1:224–225.

Hoslitz, B. (1970). *Capital Formation and Economic Growth.* National Bureau Committee for Economic Research.

Hudson, P. (1992). *The Industrial Revolution.* London: Edward Arnold.

Hughes, J. (1970). *Industrialisation and Economic History.* New York: McGraw Hill.

Hussbaum, F. L. (1947). *History of Economic Institutions of Europe.* cited in Dobb, (1947).

Itoh, M. (1992). The Japanese Model of Post-Fordism. In M. Stoper and A. Scott (eds.), *Pathways to Industrialisation.* London: Routledge, Jonathan Cape.

Japan. Ministry of Education. (1964). *Education in Asia: A Graphic Presentation.* Tokyo.

Jia, Liqun. (1992). Self-Reliance and Economic Balance in China. Unpublished Ph.D. thesis, Dunedin, N.Z.:Otago University.

Johnson, A. H. (1909). *Disappearance of the Small Land Owner.* Oxford: Clarendon Press.

Jones, E. (ed.). (1967). *Agriculture and Economic Growth in England, 1760–1815.* London: Macmillan.

Jones, E. L., and Woolf, S. F. (eds.). (1969). *The Historical Role of Agrarian Change in Economic Development.* London: Methuen.

Kabra, B. R. (1962). Final Population Tables, 1901–61. *Census of India,* no. 1, 325–30.

Kenwood, A. G., and A. L. Longheed. (1971). *The Growth of the International Economy 1820–1900.* London: George Allen and Unwin.

Kethineni, V. (1991). Political Economy of State Intervention on Health Care. *Economic and Political Weekly,* 19 October, 24–30.

Keynes, J. M. (1936). *The General Theory of Employment, Interest and Money.* London: Macmillan.

Khadria, B. (1984). Generation and Efficient Utilization of Skills for the Technolog-ical Transformation of Developing Countries. Unpublished ms. October. Based on data from United Nations Educational, Scientific and Cultural Organization. (1983).

Knowels, L. C. A. (1930). *The Industrial and Commercial Revolution in the 19th Century.* London: Routledge and Kegan Paul.

Kuznets, S. (1953). *Economic Change.* New York: Norton.

Kuznets, S. (1957). "Industrial Distribution of National Products and Labour Force." *Economic Development and Cultural Change,* July, 84–91.

Kuznets, S. (1964). *Economic Growth and the Contribution of Agriculture.* In Eicher, C. K., and Witt, L. W. (eds.), *Agriculture in Economic Development.* New York: McGraw-Hill.

Kuznets, S. (1966). *Modern Economic Growth.* New Haven, CT: Yale University Press.

Lal Bahedur, Sastry. (1961). Address in Parliament. *The Hindu,* January.

Lamb, H. (1955). In S. Kuznets, W. Moore, and J. J. Spengler (eds.), *Economic Growth: Brazil, India and Japan.* North Dakota: Duke University Press.

Landes, D. (1965). *The State and Economic Enterprise in Japan.* Princeton, NJ: Princeton University Press.

Landes, D. (1969). *The Prometheus Unbound.* London: Cambridge University Press.

Lewis, A. (1954). Economic Development with Unlimited Supplies of Labour. *Manchester School,* 22:139–91.

Lilley, G. (1976). Technological Progress and the Industrial Revolution. In C. Cipolla (ed.), *The Industrial Revolution.* London: Collins/Fontana Books, 190–92.

Linder, B. (1967). *Trade and Trade Policy for Development.* New York: Praeger.

Lipson, E. (1931). *Economic History of England.* Edinburgh: A. and C. Black.

McCallock, J. R. (ed.). (1863). *An Enquiry into the Nature and Causes of the Wealth of Nations*. Book 4. Edinburgh: Adam and Charles Black.

McIntyre, R. (1990). The Political Economy and Class Analysis of International Capital Flows. *Review of Radical Political Economics*, 22, no. 1:135–152.

Maddison, A. (1971). *Class Structure and Economic Growth: India and Pakistan since the Moghals*. London: George Allen and Unwin.

Maddison, A. (1991). *Dynamic Forces in Capitalist Development*. London: Oxford University Press.

Magdoff, H., and P. Sweizy. (1987). *Stagnation and Financial Explosion*. New York: Monthly Review Press.

Mahalanobis, P. C. (1953). Source Observation on the Growth of National Income Sankhya *Indian Statistical Institute* (Calcutta) 12, no. 4: 71–72.

Mahalanobis, P. C. (1961). National Income, Investment and Development—Talks on Planning. *Indian Statistical Institute* (Calcutta).

Mahalanobis Committee. (1984). Report, *Economic and Political Weekly* (Bombay), 3 November, 30.

Maitra, P. (1956). 19th Century Charter Acts and Economic Transition in India. *Calcutta Review*, November, 34–55.

Maitra, P. (1977). *Underdevelopment Revisited*. Calcutta: Firma KLM.

Maitra, P. (1980). *The Mainspring of Economic Development*. London: Croom Helm. New York: St. Martins Press.

Maitra, P. (1986). *Population, Technology and Development*. Gower, U.K.: Aldershot.

Maitra, P. (1988a). Energy Resources, Technological Change and Intergrated World Development [Paper presented to the Asia and Pacific Energy Economists Conference, Taiwan, November]. In *Proceedings*, The Asia and Pacific Energy Economists Conference, International Association for Energy Economies, 197–215.

Maitra, P. (1988b). Population Growth, Technological Change and Economic Development. In C. Tisdell and P. Maitra (eds.), *Technological Change, Development and Environment*. London: Routledge.

Maitra, P. (1988c). Technological Change, Economic Interdependence and World Development. In S. H. W. Singer, N. Hatts and R. Tandon (eds.), *Technology Transfer by Multinationals*. New Delhi: Ashish Publishing House, 819–820.

Maitra, P. (1990). Education, Technological Change and Structural Change. In G. Tortella (ed.), *Education and Economic Development since the Industrial Revolution*. Universidad International Menendez Pelayo, Valencia: Spain, 185–209.

Maitra, P. (1991a). *Indian Economic Development—Population Growth, Technological Change and Development*. New Delhi: Ashish Publishing.

Maitra, P. (1991b). *Indian Economic Development, Population Growth and Technological Change*. New Delhi: A.H.P.

Maitra, P. (1991c). National Party Employment Policy. *National Business Review*, 3 December, 5.

Maitra, P. (1992a). The Demographic Effects of Technological Change and Capitalist Transformation—UK and India. *Arthavijnana*, 34, no. 2:125–54.

Maitra, P. (1992b). On the Horns of a Dilemma—Capitalism Seeks a Way Out. *Otago Daily Times*, January, 17.

Maitra, P. (1992c). Technological Change in the USSR and Return to a Market Economy. *International Journal of Social Economics*, 19, 1.

Maitra, P. (1993). Internationalisation of Production and Capitalism's Dilemma. *International Journal of Social Economics*, 20, no. 9:21–43.

Malthus, T. (1952/1798). *An First Essay on Population*. London: J. M. Dent, Vol. 2, Book 3, 25.

Malthus, T. R. (1953). *An Essay on Population, 1797*. Vol. 1. London: J. M. Dent.

Malyarov, O. V. (1992). The Colonial Socio-economic Structure. In F. Farimelli (ed.) (Italian National Research Council, Rome), *Capitalist Form of Production*. New Delhi: Monar, Manohar, 2–3.

Mandel, E. (1968). *Marxist Economic Theory*. New York: Monthly Review Press.

Mantoux, P. (1928). *The Industrial Revolution in the Eighteenth Century*. London: Cape.

Mao, Ze-dong. (1988). Quoted in the *Economist*, November 25, 30.

Marx, K. (1861). *Capital*, Vol. 1. Chicago, 563–569.

Marx, K. (1932). *The Communist Manifesto, 1848, and Other Writings*. Edited by Max Eastman. New York: Modern Library.

Marx, K. (1953). *The Future Results of British Rule in India* in Marx and Engels on Colonialism. Moscow: Progress, 390.

Marx, K. (1959). *Capital*. Vol. 1. Moscow: Foreign Language Publishing House.

Marx, K. (1961). *Capital*. Vol. 1. Chicago.

Marx, K. (1964a). The German Ideology. Part 1. In K. Marx (1964), London, Lawrence and Wishert.

Marx, K. (1964b). Grundrisse. Translated in H. Marcause, *One Dimensional Man*. London: Routledge and Kegan Paul.

Marx, K. (1964c). *Precapitalist Economic Transformation*. London: Lawrence and Wishart.

Marx, K. (1967). *Capital*. Vol. 3. New York: International Publishers.

Marx, K. (1968). *On Colonialism and Modernisation*. Edited by S. Avineri. New York: Doubleday.

Marx, K. (1970). *Capital*. Vol. 1. London: Lawrence and Wishart.

Marx, K. (1975). Letter to N. F. Dainelson, April 10, 1879. In *Selected Correspondence*. Moscow: Progress Publications.

Marx, K. (1976). *The Poverty of Philosophy*. Moscow: Progress Publishers.

Marx, K. (1977). *Capital*. Vol. 1. New York: Vintage Books.

Marx, K. (1978a). *Capital*. Vol. 1. Moscow: Progress Publishers.

Marx, K. (1978b). Proletariat and Middle Class in Marx. Translated by M. Nicolaus In D. Macquire (ed.), *Marx, Social Change and Capitalism*. London: Quarter Books.

Mathias, J. A. (1969). *The First Industrial Revolution*. London: Methuen and Company.

Mayer, K. (1969). Developments in the Study of Population. In K. C. W. Kammeyer (ed.), *Population Studies: Selected Essays and Research*. Chicago, 15–35.

Mendels, F. (1972). Proto-Industrialisation. *Journal of Economic History*, 32, no. 4.

Merrington, J. (1975). Town and Country in the Transition to Capitalism. *New Left Review*, 93:79–92.

Mitchell, B. R., and P. Deane. (1971). *Abstract of British Historical Statistics*. Cambridge: Cambridge University Press.

Moosvi, S. (1987). *The Economy of the Mughal Empire c. 1595*. New Delhi: Oxford University Press.

Moreland, W. H. (1929a). *The Agrarian System of Moslem India*. London: Cambridge Heffer and Sons, Ltd.

Moreland, W. H., and P. Geyl. (1925). *Jahangir's India*. Cambridge: Heffer.

Moseley, F. (1991). *The Falling Rate of Profit in the Post-War U.S. Economy*. London.

Moulder, F. V. (1979). *Japan, China and the Modern World Economy*. Cambridge: Cambridge University Press.

Mukherjee, R. K. (1958). *The Rise and Fall of the East India Company*. Berlin: Deutscher Verlag Der Wissenschaftan.

Murthy, M. R. (1988). *Joint Sector Enterprises in India*. New Delhi: Corporate Studies Group.

Myrdal, G. (1968). *Asian Drama*. Vol. 2. London: Hammondsworth.

Myrdal, G. (1971). *The Challenge of World Poverty*. London: Penguin Books.

Neeson, J. (1984). The Opponents of Enclosures in Eighteenth Century Northamptonshire. *Past and Present*, 105.

Nehru, J. L. (1945). *Glimpses of World History*. London: Lindsay Drummond, 417.

New York Times. (1993). September 2, 3.

New York Times. (1993). September 3, 3.

Notestein, F. W. (1945). Population: The Long View. In T. W. Schultz (ed.), *Food for the World*. Chicago: University of Chicago Press.

Notestein, F. W. (1948). Summary of the Demographic Background of Problems of Underdeveloped Areas. *Mill Bank Memorial Fund Quarterly*, 26:249–55.

Notestein, F. W. (1950). The Population of the World in the Year 2000. *Journal of the American Statistical Association*, 45:335–45.

Notestein, F. W. (1953). Economic Problems of Population Change. In *Proceedings of the 8th International Conference of Agricultural Economists*. London: Oxford University Press, 13–31.

O'Brien, P. K., and C. Keyder. (1978). *Economic Growth in Britain and France, 1780–1914*. London: George Allen and Unwin.

Office of Economic Cooperation and Development (OECD). (1963). *Manpower Statistics, 1950–62*. Paris: OECD.

Office of Economic Cooperation and Development (OECD). (1966). *Manpower Problems in the Service Sector*. Supplement to the Report. Paris: OECD, 20.

Office of Economic Cooperation and Development (OECD). (1988). *Gaps in Technology*. Paris: OECD.

Ohkawa, K. (ed.). (1956). *The Growth Rate of the Japanese Economy since 1878*. Tokyo: Kinokuniya.

Ohkawa, K. (1965). Agriculture and Turning Points. *The Developing Economies*, 3, no. 4 (December):471–85.

Ohliu, B. (1967). *Interregional and International Trade*, revised ed. Boston: Harvard University Press.

Otago Daily Times Dunedin, N.Z. [Reuter's Report]. (1992). May, 26.

O'Toole, J. (1978). *Energy and Social Change.* Cambridge, MA: MIT Press.

Patel, S. J. (1965). Educational Distance between Nations. *Indian Economic Journal*, 13, no. 1 (July–September):20–24.

Patel, S. J. (1988). An Education Miracle. *The Third World Development International* (Institute of Development Economics, Zagreb) 1, no. 1, 1–25.

Patnaik, P. (1972). Imperialism and the Growth of Indian Capitalism. In R. Owen and R. Sutcliffe (eds.), *Studies in the Theory of Capitalism.* London: Longman.

Patrick, P. (1972). In H. R. Ghosal (ed.), *Industrial Production in Bengal in the Early Nineteenth Century.* Calcutta: Oxford University Press.

Peet, R. (ed.). (1980). *An Introduction to Marxist Theories of Underdevelopment.* Canberra: Australian National University.

Postan, M. R. (1937). Chronology of Labour Services. *Transactions of the Royal Historical Society* (4th ser.) 20:192–93.

Pranab, B. (1984). *The Political Economy of Development in India.* Oxford: Blackwell.

Reserve Bank of India (Bombay). (1950). Foreign Collaboration in Indian Industry. *Reserve Bank of India Bulletin.*

Reserve Bank of India (Bombay). (1968). *Foreign Collaboration in Indian Industry.* Survey Report.

Ricardo, D. (1951). *Works and Correspondence of David Ricardo.* Vol. 4. Edited by P. Strata and M. Dobb.

Richardson, G. B. (1975). A. Smith on Competition and Increasing Returns. In A. S. Skinner and T. Wilson (eds.), *Essays on Adam Smith.* London: Oxford University Press.

Root, F. R. (1984). *International Trade and Investment.* Chicago: Southwestern Publishing Company.

Rosenberg, N. (1976). *Perspectives on Technology.* Cambridge: Cambridge University Press.

Rostow, W. W. (1960). The Stages of Economic Growth. London: Cambridge University Press.

Rudra, A. (1975). *Indian Plan Models.* Calcutta: Allied Publishers.

Samuelson, P. A. (1941). Protection and Real Wages. *Review of Economic Studies*, 9 (November).

Samuelson, P. A. (1978). *Technology and Underdevelopment.* London: Macmillan.

Satin, M. S. (1969). An Emperial Test of the Descriptive Validity of the Theory of Transition on a Fifty-three Nation Sample. *Sociological Quarterly*, 10, no. 2.

Sen, A. (1981). *Poverty and Famile.* Oxford: Clarendon Press.

Sen, A. (1983a). *Commodities and Capabilities.* Amsterdam: North-Holland.

Sen, A. (1983b). Development: Which Way Now? *Economic Journal*, 93 (December).

Sen, A. (1983c). Goods and People [Plenary session paper]. International Economic Association Seventh Congress, Madrid.

Sengupta, J. K., and A. Sengupta. (1961). *India's Economic Growth*. Calcutta: Post-Graduate Book Market.

Shipman, M. D. (1971). *Education and Industrialisation*. London: Faber and Faber.

Simon, M. (1968). The Pattern of New British Portfolio Investment. In A. R. Hall (ed.), *The Export of Capital from Britain 1870–1914*. London: Metheun and Company.

Sinai, M. (1990). *Global Power Structure, Technology and World Economy*. London: Pinter Publishing.

Sinha, N. C. (1950). *Indo-British Economy One Hundred Years Ago*. Calcutta: Firma KLM.

Skinner, A. S., and T. Wilson. (eds.). (1975). *Essays in Honour of Adam Smith*. Oxford: Clarendon Press.

Smith, A. (1976). *An Enquiry into the Nature and Cause of the Wealth of Nations*. Book 4. Edinburgh: Adam and Charles Black. 1st ed., 1863.

Snell, K. D. M. (1985). *Annals.*

Sombart, W. Der Moderne Capitalisms, 1928.

Stonier, T. (1980). Natural History of Humanity. *International Journal of Social Economics*, 7, no. 1:7.

Storper, M., and A. Scott (eds.). (1992). *Pathways to Industrialisation and Regional Development*. London: Routledge.

Sweezy, P., M. Dobb, and H. K. Takahshi. (1976). *The Transition from Feudalism to Capitalism*. London: New Left Books.

Teich, M. (1973). Science and Technology in the 20th Century. *4th International Economic History Congress 1968*. London: Morton, 245.

Thirwall, A. P. (1982). De-industrialisation in the U.K. *Lloyds Bank Review*, 144:22–27.

Thompson, W. S. (1929). Population. *American Journal of Sociology*, 34:959–75.

Thornton, P., and V. Wheelock (1980). Technology and Employment. *International Journal of Social Economics*, 7, no. 1:25.

Tisdell, C. (1990). *Natural Resources, Growth and Development*. New York: Praeger.

Tisdell, C. (1990). *Natural Resources, Growth and Development: Economies, Ecology and Resource—Scarcity*. New York: Praeger.

Tisdell, C., and P. Maitra (1988). *Technological Change, Development and the Environment*. London: Routledge.

Turner, M. (1986). English Open Fields and Enclosures. *Journal of Economic History*, 46:669–692.

United Nations. Department of Commerce. (1989). *Survey of Current Business.*

United Nations. World Economic Survey. (1986). *World Economic Outlook, Revised Projections*. October.

United Nations Development Program. (1992). *Human Development Report 1992*. New York: Oxford University Press.

Ure, A. (1926). *History of Cotton Manufacture.* Vol. 1.

Ure, A. U.S. Industrial Capital in the 1970s and 1980s. *Review of Radical Political Economies*, no. 1:135–154.

Van Bath, S. (1963). *Agrarian History of Western Europe, 500–1880.* London: Arnold.

van de Walle, E., and J. Knodel. (1967). Demographic Transition and Fertility Decline: The European Case. Contributed papers, Sydney Conference, International Union for the Scientific Study of Population, 21–25 August, 47–55.

Weber, Max. (1961). *General Economic History.* New York: Collier Books.

Weber, Max. (1985). *The Protestant Ethic and the Spirit of Capitalism.* London: Unwin Paperbacks.

Weeks, J. (1955). Epochs of Capitalism and the Progressiveness of Capital's Expansion. *Science and Society*, 49, no. 4:414–34.

West, E. G. (1975). *Education and the Industrial Revolution.* London: Bratsford.

Wilson, C. H. (1947). *Anglo-Dutch Commerce and Finance in the Eighteenth Century.*

Woodruff, W. (1966). *Impact of Western Man.* London.

World Bank. (1985). *World Bank Development Report.*

World Bank. (1987). *World Bank Development Report.*

World Bank. (1992a). *Trends in Developing Economics.* New York: Oxford University Press.

Wrigley, E. (1988). *Continuity, Chance and Change: The Character of the Industrial Revolution in England.* Cambridge: Cambridge University Press.

Wrigley, E. A. (1969). *Population and History.* London: Weidenfeld and Nicholson.

Wrigley, E. A., and R. Schofield (1981). *The Population History of England, 1541–1871.* London: Arnold.

Index

Africa, 3
Age of Reason, 24
Albriton, R., 103
America, 57
Anderson, C. A., 203, 205
Anstey, V., 139
Armengaud, A., 190
Artisans, 16, 18
Asia, 2, 3
Asiatic societies, 131–133
Australia, 2,

Backstop fuels, 78
Bairoch, P., 202
Baran, P., 139
Baumol, W. J., 80
Beaver, S. E., 184
Belgium, 58
Bettelheim, C., 161
Bhattacharyya, D., 161
Bina, C., 94, 97–98, 100, 101, 112
Blomstrom, M., 118
Boserup, E., 21
Boulding, K. E., 177, 187, 203
Bowman, M. J., 203, 205
Brenner, R., 35, 37, 136

Britain (U.K.), 1, 3, 19, 69–72, 75, 79–81,
    100, 103, 137, 148, 177, 189, 190,
    202, 204, 207

Caldwell, J. C., 184
Canada, 2
Cantwell, J., 101–107, 117, 119
Capitalism, 1, 2, 3, 10, 12, 17, 35, 36, 37,
    50–52, 53
Capitalist transformation, 2, 25, 39, 63,
    71, 73, 75, 79, 82, 83, 100, 175–199,
    223
Casteism, 3
Ceylon, 209
China, 60, 64, 216
Clark, Colin, 66, 68, 70,71, 73, 74, 178,
    196
Classical political economy, 1, 13, 46, 67
Coale, A. J., 184
Collins, E. J. T., 56, 70
Commodity labor, 18, 63
Communalism, 3
Competition, 29
Consumerism, 4
Cowgill, D. O., 184
Cunningham, W., 52

Dadrie, K., 123
Dahlaman, L. D., 26
Dandekar, V. M., 182
Das, H. G., 137
Dasgupta, B., 181
Datta, S. M., 171
Deane, P., 188, 189
Defoe, D., 15, 17
Demographic effects, 18, 65, 98, 187
Demographic transition, 83, 177
Desai, A. V., 134–136
Diminishing returns, 6, 8, 78
Division of labor, 35
Dobb, M., 9, 10, 14, 18, 23, 30, 33, 35,
    44, 45, 47–48, 49, 53, 54, 56, 132,
    136
Dunkel's draft, 117, 122
Dutt, R., 145

East India Company, 12, 13, 23
Economic structural change, 41, 61–71,
    83, 212
Economic planning, 89, 94, 96, 123, 151
Economic Weekly, 162
Education and capitalist transformation,
    201–221
Education and development, 215–222
Education take-off, 209
European Economic Community (EEC),
    116
Egypt, 24
Ehrlich, A. H., 24
Ehrlich, P. E., 24
Enclosure, land reforms, 9, 35, 36, 37, 40,
    48, 75, 100
England, 15, 17, 58
Export-substituting industrialization, 93,
    99, 165
Extensive phase, 42, 63–64, 67

Fei and Ranis models, 75–76, 180
Feudal bondage (feudal economy), 1, 2, 3,
    7, 9, 34, 35, 36, 52, 75
Fisher, A. G. B., 66, 68, 70, 73
Ford, Henry, 105, 106
Fordism, 102

France, 23, 27, 38, 58, 106, 149, 147, 179,
    208
Frober, F., 69

Galbraith, J. K., 126–130
Gemmel, N., 78–80
Germany, 23, 27, 38, 58, 147, 149, 179,
    208
Glynn, A., and unemployment, 124, 126
Gold, C. S., 184
Government of India, 153, 154, 156, 161,
    182
Goyale, S. K., 154
Green Revolution, 75, 76
Gregory, King, 58
Gruevitch, P., 38

Habakkuk, J., 55
Habib, I., 133–140
Harman, C., 124, 126, 127, 128, 170,
    218
Hartwell, R. M., 74
Heckser-Ohlin Theory, 91, 102
Heinrichs, J., 69
Henderson, W. O., 1, 2, 23, 85, 177
Hicks, J. R., 42–43, 189, 210
Hilbroner, R., 126
Hilton, R., 36
Hobsbawm, E., 6, 132, 177, 188, 212
Hobson, J., 14, 15, 16–17, 132
Hohenberg, P., 12
Holland (Netherlands), 9, 23, 27, 38, 44,
    57, 147
Household industry, 14
Hudson, P., 9, 26
Hughes, J., 56
Human capital, 39, 79, 83
Hundis, 137

Import-substituting industrialization (ISI),
    75, 88, 89, 91, 93, 94, 99–113, 123,
    162, 165
Industrial capitalism, 1, 4, 12, 19, 20, 31,
    36, 39, 45, 46, 47–50, 58, 85, 143,
    150, 173
Industrial houses, 167
Industrial revolution, 6, 10, 27, 34, 38, 39,

42, 43, 82, 136, 180, 185, 187, 188, 201

International division of labor theory of trade, 9, 89

International Monetary Fund (IMF), 122, 161, 169, 171

International trade, foreign trade, 10, 11, 31, 44

Internationalization of capitalist production, 3, 69, 80, 96, 97, 99, 102, 108, 115, 117, 123–130, 153, 160, 165

Internationalization of goods and commodity capital, 3, 109–114, 159

Internationalization of investment, 91, 96, 99, 108, 111, 153, 158

Internationalization or globalization of capitalism, 85, 88, 89, 95

Ireland, 56

Italy, 106

Itoh, M., 104–105

Japan, 2, 19, 59, 81, 108, 116, 163–164, 204, 207, 218

Japanese Model of Post-Fordism, 104

Jia, L., 64

Jones, E., 70, 140, 141

Keynesian schools, 1, 6, 13, 72, 88, 105, 111, 124, 127, 158–162

Keys, O., 69

Knodel, J., 184

Knowels, C. A., 206

Kravis, I., 118

Kuznets, S., 21, 57, 66, 67, 68, 70, 73–74, 178, 204

Lamb, H., 144, 146

Landes, D., 12, 188

Latin America, 3

Lewis A., and the Lewis model, 28, 44, 47, 70, 74, 75

Lilley, G., 6

Linder, B., 91

Lipsey, R., 118

Lipson, E., 52

Maddison, A., 3, 4, 5, 6, 7, 8, 140, 142

Magdoff, H., 115

Mahalanobis planning model, 123, 156–163, 164–165

Maitra, P., 1, 2, 12, 13, 23, 38, 42, 62, 75, 82, 85, 144, 146, 147, 165, 168, 183, 186, 187, 208, 216

Malthus, T., 6, 8, 43

Malyarov, O. V., 147, 148, 150, 152, 153

Mandel, E., 14, 18, 20, 22, 23, 58–65, 132, 145, 189

Mantoux, P., 7, 55

Manufactory, 14, 32, 41

Mao Ze-dong, 205

Marx, K., 1, 7, 12, 13–14, 23, 24, 28, 32, 36, 40, 41, 44, 47, 49, 53, 65–68, 100, 118, 131, 132, 143–145, 148–150

Marxists, 2, 3, 4, 5, 13, 32, 34, 72, 97, 100, 101, 144, 148

Mass consumption, 102–105

Mayer, K., 184

McIntrye, R., 116

Merchant capital, commercial capitalism, 8, 9, 19, 22, 33, 36, 37, 41, 48

Middle East, 26

Money capital, 22, 40, 44

Moosvi, S., 135

Moreland, W. H., 140–141

Moseley, F., 126

Moulder, F., 132

Mughal Period, 131, 134, 140

Multinational corporations (MNCs), 94, 104, 106, 110, 111, 113, 115, 116–119, 122

Murthy, M. R., 153

Myrdal, G., 181

Neo-classicists, 6, 72, 75

New Zealand, 2

Non-Marxist, 2, 3, 4, 32, 48, 147

Notestein, F. W., 177, 183–184, 185

Organization of Economic Cooperation and Development (OECD), 67, 119–120, 126

Ohkawa, K., 76

Patel, S. J., 202, 207, 217
Patnaik, P., 151
Patrick, P., 150
Peasants, 22
Physiocrats, 29
Postindustrial, 67–69, 70, 72
Preindustrial labor shortage, 53–60
Primitive accumulation, 20, 44, 45, 46, 47–50, 98, 101
Private U.S. investment abroad, 98
Productive forces, 30, 31
Protoindustrialization, 9
Prototechnology, 8, 11, 19
Pull factor, 71
Push factor, 71

Religious fundamentalism, 3
Ricardo, D., 6, 7, 8, 10, 11, 12, 30, 31, 43, 118
Rosenberg, N., 204
Rostow, W. W., 193

Sastry, L. B., 173
Satin, M. S., 184
Savings and investment, 169
Schumpeter, J., 6, 11
Scotts, A., 92, 93
Sector "U," 161
Sectoral distribution of Labor force, 61–66, 74, 196
Self-employment, 3, 74, 79, 115, 128–129
Simon, Matthew, 86
Sinai, M., 120
Smith, A., 6, 7, 9, 10, 11, 12, 29, 30, 31, 35, 43, 45, 46, 118
Snell, K. D. M., 26
Social consciousness, 24
Socialism, 6
Sombart, W., 50, 59
South Pacific Island economies, 3
Soviet Russia, 204
Spain, 57, 58
State welfarism, 4, 88, 96, 102, 124

Stonier, T., 213
Storper, M., 92, 93
Surplus agricultural product, 21, 98
Surplus labor, 20, 44, 47, 66–68
Sutcliffe, R., 124
Sweezy, P., 33, 34, 35, 115, 136

Takahashi, H. K., 33, 35, 136
Technological change, 8, 9, 11, 31, 70–71, 73, 80, 95, 106, 175, 182, 184, 185, 193
Teich, M., 211
Third World, 1, 11, 20, 26, 28, 41, 46, 57, 65, 69–71, 81, 82, 85, 91, 98, 101, 106, 113, 115, 128, 162, 202
Thirlwall, A., 177
Thompson, W. S., 177, 183–184, 185
Thornton, P., 69, 70
Tisdell, C., 199
Todaro, M., 177

United Nations Conference on Trade and Development (UNCTAD), 122–123
United States, 2, 74, 80, 100, 102, 106, 116, 204
Unorganized sector, 181–182
Uruguay Round Table, 117, 118, 122

Van Bath, S., 134, 205
Van de Walle, E., 184

Wealth of Nations, 6
Weber, M., 50
West, E. G., 203, 206
Western Europe, 1, 2, 19, 57, 58
Wheelock, V., 69, 70
Wilson, C. H., 45
Woods, R., 191
Woolf, S. J., 70, 140, 141
World Bank, 110, 161, 171, 191
Wrigley, E., 25–26, 35, 186

Yaghmaian, B., 94, 97–98, 100, 101, 112

About the Author

PRIYATOSH MAITRA, formerly of the Indian Statistical Institute, Calcutta, and East African Institute of Economic and Social Research, is presently an Associate Professor with the University of Otago, New Zealand. He specializes in research in the effects of population, technology, growth patterns, and import substitution on economic development.

ISBN 0-275-95159-6

90000>

EAN

9 780275 951597

HARDCOVER BAR CODE